FINDING THE HISTORICAL CHRIST

AFTER JESUS, VOLUME 3

FINDING THE HISTORICAL CHRIST

Paul Barnett

William B. Eerdmans Publishing Company
Grand Rapids, Michigan / Cambridge, U.K.

Published 2009 by
Wm. B. Eerdmans Publishing Co.
2140 Oak Industrial Drive N.E., Grand Rapids, Michigan 49505 /
P.O. Box 163, Cambridge CB3 9PU U.K.

Printed in the United States of America

15 14 13 12 11 10 09   7 6 5 4 3 2 1

Library of Congress Cataloging-in-Publication Data

Barnett, Paul (Paul William)
    Finding the historical Christ / Paul Barnett.
        p.   cm. — (After Jesus; v. 3)
    Includes bibliographical references.
    ISBN 978-0-8028-4890-1 (pbk.: alk. paper)
    1. Jesus Christ — Historicity.   I. Title.   II. Series.

    BT303.2.B278   2008
    232.9′08 — dc22

                                    2008036153

www.eerdmans.com

For David and Leanne, Peter and Jane, Sarah and Tim
for love and friendship

CONTENTS

PREFACE

The third in the series *After Jesus* logically follows the first, *The Birth of Christianity: The First Twenty Years* (A.D. 33-55), and the second, *Paul: Missionary of Jesus* (A.D. 34-64). *Finding the Historical Christ* depends almost entirely on the gospels written (I think) between the years 60 and 80. So there is a chronological sequence.

Studies of second-century gospel manuscripts and the early Christian writings give us high confidence that the text of the gospels is largely recoverable and was in circulation and use well before the end of the first century. Furthermore, the raw evidence from the hostile early sources Josephus, Tacitus, and Pliny confirms the New Testament's accounts of the origin, spread, and belief structure of the new faith. As a body of literature, the gospels and most of the New Testament are effectively "sealed off" by second-century authorities, whether Christian or hostile. In this students of Christian origins are indeed fortunate.

The major problem historians face is that the texts upon which we rely for Jesus of Nazareth were written at a time when he was regarded as a heavenly, divine figure. The book of Acts is important in explaining how the historical Jesus came to be worshiped as Lord and Christ. Its answer, and the answer of the gospels, is captured in the single idea, Jesus was *the Christ*. According to the gospels and Acts, it was because the prepaschal, preresurrection Jesus believed himself to be, and was said to be, *the Christ* that he came to be worshiped postresurrection.

But many (most?) historians of early Christianity balk at this explanation. In essence they hold that the preresurrection Jesus was a lesser figure (a prophet, rabbi, or social reformer) and that the early Christians mistakenly or willfully came to regard him as a deified figure, worthy of worship.

On historical grounds I will argue that the early Christians were neither mistaken nor willful, but that the preresurrection Jesus believed he was the "One who was to come," and that his disciples also came to hold that conviction.

Those who write about Jesus are often influenced by the dominant culture of the moment. Romantic views of Jesus were popular in the era of Romanticism in the latter part of the nineteenth century. In the first part of the twentieth century existentialist, ahistorical views of Jesus became prominent in an era when existentialism was the intellectual fashion. Postwar Holocaust guilt with its sympathy for Jewish people produced a distinctively Jewish Jesus. Late-twentieth-century postmodernism has produced dozens of idiosyncratic Jesuses, including a Galilean social reformer of liberal-left idealism. While my survey could sound like criticism, it is not. Each of these passing currents of thought has found an aspect of Jesus hitherto unnoticed.

Clearly, though, this slim volume will not attempt to engage the huge volume of texts devoted to the historical Jesus.[1]

The challenge to the Jesus student, then, is twofold: to find the *historical* figure the early Christians later worshiped, and to do so as objectively as possible. The latter aspect is especially hard because no one can isolate himself or herself from the culture without or persona within.

I engage in this project as one who belongs to the "household of faith," though my approach aims to be historical rather than theological.

---

1. For surveys of leading contributions to historical Jesus studies, see, e.g., B. Chilton and C. A. Evans, eds., *Studying the Historical Jesus: Evaluations of the State of Current Research* (Leiden: Brill, 1994); M. A. Powell, *Jesus as a Figure of History: How Modern Historians View the Man from Galilee* (Louisville: Westminster John Knox, 1998); D. L. Bock, *Studying the Historical Jesus: A Guide to Sources and Methods* (Grand Rapids: Eerdmans, 2002); J. Willitts, "Presuppositions and Procedures in the Study of the 'Historical Jesus'; or, Why I Decided Not to Be a 'Historical Jesus Scholar,'" *JSHJ* 3, no. 1 (2005): 61-108. Anthologies with quoted sections from major contributors include, e.g., G. W. Dawes, *The Historical Jesus Quest: A Foundational Anthology* (Leiden: Deo, 1999); C. A. Evans, ed., *The Historical Jesus*, 4 vols. (London: Routledge, 2004); J. D. G. Dunn and S. McKnight, *The Historical Jesus in Recent Research*, Sources for Biblical and Theological Study 10 (Winona Lake, Ind.: Eisenbrauns, 2005). For a topical approach with bibliographies, see G. Theissen and A. Merz, *The Historical Jesus: A Comprehensive Guide* (London: SCM, 1998).

My personal objectives are to take a common sense, chronologically aware approach to texts, hopefully based on rigorous analysis.

I dedicate this book in thanks to my children and their spouses who have become my children.

ABBREVIATIONS

ABD	*Anchor Bible Dictionary*
ABRL	Anchor Bible Reference Library
AH	*Against Heresies* (Irenaeus)
Annals	*Annals of Imperial Rome* (Tacitus)
ANRW	*Aufstieg und Niedergang der römischen Welt*
Ant	*Jewish Antiquities* (Josephus)
b.	Babylonian Talmud
BAR	*Biblical Archaeology Review*
BBR	*Bulletin for Biblical Research*
BETL	Bibliotheca ephemeridum theologicarum lovaniensium
Bib	*Biblica*
Birth of Christianity	P. Barnett, *Birth of Christianity,* vol. 1 of *After Jesus* (Grand Rapids, Eerdmans, 2005)
BJRL	*Bulletin of the John Rylands Library*
BRev	*Biblical Review*
BTB	*Biblical Theology Bulletin*
CBQ	*Catholic Biblical Quarterly*
Did	*Didache*
ET	English translation
ExpT	*Expository Times*
HE	*History of the Church* (Eusebius)
HeyJ	*Heythrop Journal*
HTR	*Harvard Theological Review*
ICC	International Critical Commentary

JBL	*Journal of Biblical Literature*
JQR	*Jewish Quarterly Review*
JR	*Journal of Religion*
JSHJ	*Journal for the Study of the Historical Jesus*
JSJ	*Journal for the Study of Judaism in the Persian, Hellenistic, and Roman Periods*
JSNT	*Journal for the Study of the New Testament*
JSNTSS	Journal for the Study of the New Testament Supplement Series (Sheffield)
JSOT	*Journal for the Study of the Old Testament*
JTS	*Journal of Theological Studies*
LCL	Loeb Classical Library
Life	*Life* (Josephus)
m.	Mishnah
New Docs	*New Documents Illustrating Early Christianity* (Macquarie University)
NIGTC	New International Greek Testament Commentary
NovT	*Novum Testamentum*
NTS	*New Testament Studies*
𝔭	papyrus
Paul	P. Barnett, *Paul: Missionary of Jesus,* vol. 2 of *After Jesus* (Grand Rapids: Eerdmans, 2007)
P.Oxy.	Oxyrhynchus Papyri
RTR	*Reformed Theological Review* (Melbourne)
SJT	*Scottish Journal of Theology*
SNTSMS	Society for New Testament Studies Monograph Series
StudBib	Studia Biblica
TynBul	*Tyndale Bulletin*
VC	*Vigiliae christianae*
War	*Jewish War* (Josephus)
WUNT	Wissenschaftliche Untersuchungen zum Neuen Testament
y.	Jerusalem Talmud

ONE

The Postresurrection Church and the Preresurrection Christ

The question . . . has always pivoted around a fixed centre . . . the conviction of inalienable ties between Christian faith and the Jesus of ancient Palestine.

B. F. Meyer[1]

The title of this book is deliberate. It is reacting against the dichotomy between "the Jesus of history" and the "Christ of faith" that implies that Jesus became the Christ in the light of the disciples' "resurrection experience," prior to which he was (merely) the *historical* Jesus. Of course there was a "historical Jesus," but he was also the "historical Christ," as we shall argue in what follows. The resurrection confirms the messiahship of which he was conscious beforehand and which his disciples had come to recognize. Jesus of Nazareth came to Jerusalem as "the Christ" at the beginning of Passover in A.D. 33; there the Romans crucified him as "the king of the Jews."

Issues

For two centuries NT scholarship has been dominated by the quest for the real Jesus, the Jesus as he was. Obstacles against finding this person are formidable.

1. B. F. Meyer, *The Aims of Jesus* (London: SCM, 1979), 95.

1

Of primary concern is the relationship between postresurrection Christianity and the preresurrection Jesus. The biographies of the historical figure were not written contemporaneously with him but retrospectively. True, the distance was not great. Only thirty years (or so) separated Mark from the preresurrection Jesus. But by the time Mark wrote the disciples *worshiped* this Jesus as the ascended Lord and Christ (e.g., "When you come together, each one has a hymn . . ." — 1 Cor 14:26; cf. Eph 5:19; Col 3:16).[2] In other words, the gospels-biographies were written in the postresurrection era when the followers of Christ were meeting regularly to sing hymns to him as a heavenly figure, according to the images of church life reflected in the letters of Paul and in the Apocalypse.

So the question is, how could biographies written after the resurrection convey a true historical account of the preresurrection man now being *worshiped?* Surely the accounts were so colored by the writers' current Holy Spirit experience of him as the heavenly *Kyrios* that an authentic biography of the historical person *back then and there* would have been impossible.

The "history of religions" school that concentrated on the cultic Christ set against a background of Greco-Oriental mystery religions regarded access to the historical Jesus as problematic. Comparing studies of miracles in the Jewish and Greco-Roman worlds, their leaders concluded that the miracles of Jesus in the gospels had their origins in their mythical environments. Rudolf Bultmann, however, made a virtue of the perceived absence of reliable historical knowledge about Jesus, famously declaring, "we can know almost nothing concerning the life and personality of Jesus."[3] His existentialist definition of "faith" embraced a Christ as the object of worship whose historical roots were minimal because, as he saw it, they were helpfully inaccessible to historical inquiry. Bultmann made much of the paucity of Paul's references to the historical Jesus, based in part on his misreading of 2 Corinthians 5:16 ("even though we once knew Christ according to the flesh [*kata sarka*], we know him thus no longer").[4]

Perhaps, though, the problem is overstated. There is a parallel with the emperor cult associated with the Flavian dynasty (A.D. 69-96). We re-

2. See various titles by L. Hurtado, including "Homage to the Historical Jesus and Early Christian Devotion," *JSHJ* 1, no. 2 (2003): 131-36; *How on Earth Did Jesus Become a God? Historical Questions about Earliest Devotion to Jesus* (Grand Rapids: Eerdmans, 2005).

3. R. Bultmann, *Jesus and the Word* (London: Fontana, 1958), 14.

4. See Barnett, *Paul*, chapter 2.

call that on his deathbed Vespasian joked that he was "becoming a god" (Suetonius, *Vespasian* 24). The morbid humor, however, does not alter the serious underlying theology; Suetonius's title for this life is *Vespasian, Afterwards Deified*. Accordingly, Vespasian was divinized after he died and became the object of a cult. Did his divination present a barrier to sober reflections about his mundane "life" beforehand? We have only to read Suetonius's quite detailed *Life of Vespasian* to recognize a nongodlike, all-too-human *man*. Divination and a cult represented no obstacle to Suetonius's useful retrospective biography of the Vespasian who was "afterwards deified."

The latter part of the twentieth century witnessed the so-called "third quest" for the historical Jesus, who was emphatically a Jew. Unlike earlier doubts about finding anything much about Jesus of Nazareth, the third questers were confident of discovering significantly greater detail about him. For example, in 1985 E. P. Sanders wrote: "We can know pretty well what Jesus was out to accomplish . . . we can know a lot about what he said, and those two things make sense in the world of first century Judaism."[5] Sanders's last comment is critical. Through the archaeologist's spade; through discovery and scholarship in the Dead Sea Scrolls; through deeper study of the OT Pseudepigrapha, Josephus, Mishnah, and Talmud, we now know more than we did about first-century Judaism, and therefore potentially more about Jesus.[6]

This new confidence, however, did not necessarily issue in a confirmation of Jesus as the Christ of the gospels, but has often identified him as *someone else*. For some, Jesus was a prophet, whether an "eschatological charismatic" prophet (E. P. Sanders) or a "popular prophet" like John the Baptist or Theudas (R. A. Horsley and J. S. Hanson).[7] For others, Jesus was a devout rabbi, whether as charismatic miracle worker (G. Vermes)[8] or as reformist Hasid (M. Wilcox).[9] These are only some of the many Jesuses

5. E. P. Sanders, *Jesus and Judaism* (London: SCM, 1984), 2.

6. W. R. Telford, "Major Trends and Interpretive Issues in the Study of Jesus," in *Studying the Historical Jesus: Evaluations of the State of Current Research*, ed. B. Chilton and C. A. Evans (Leiden: Brill, 1994), 33-74, at 47-49.

7. R. A. Horsley and J. S. Hanson, *Bandits, Prophets, and Messiahs* (Minneapolis: Winston, 1985), 257.

8. G. Vermes, *Jesus the Jew* (London: Collins, 1973); Vermes, *The Religion of Jesus the Jew* (London: SCM, 1993).

9. M. Wilcox, "Jesus in the Light of His Jewish Environment," *ANRW* 2 (1982): 131-95.

who have been rediscovered in our era. Paul Johnson observed that "Using the same texts and scholarly apparatus, dozens, perhaps hundreds of Jesuses can be constructed."[10] In short, the greater knowledge of Jesus' world and the claim to a greater knowledge of Jesus did not identify him in terms that would be recognized from the gospels.[11] Accordingly, whether from the earlier Bultmannian viewpoint or that of (many of) the third questers, we have been left with the heavenly Christ of the apostolic era as reflected in the letters and the Apocalypse who has no meaningful connection with the preresurrection Jesus. In these and other reconstructions the historical Jesus is someone else, a *lesser, different* figure. He is not the Christ.

Another issue has been the rising interest in the gospels as narratives, that is to say, as primarily *literary* works. This is a welcome recognition since these texts are more subtle and sophisticated in their artistry than was previously understood. Writing in 1987, W. Lane noted "new and creative approaches" (to the Gospel of Mark) characterized by "narrative criticism and structural exegesis" as a "viable alternative to the historical-critical paradigms."[12] Similarly, D. Harrington noted the "growing scholarly tendency in the late 1960s and early 1970s to attribute more and more literary creativity to the Evangelist and to do away with the idea of pre-Markan traditions wherever possible."[13] This development continued and merged into the postmodern interest in "structural exegesis" and "reader response criticism," which has produced an avalanche of publications from every conceivable viewpoint and sectional interest. P. G. Bolt observed that "Whereas historical criticism looked through the text, as if it were a window to the history (or theology) behind the text, narrative criticism sought to look at the text 'as a mirror on whose surface we find a self-contained world.'"[14]

While recognizing the literary qualities of the gospels offers considerable value, there is the accompanying danger of ignoring or rejecting the

10. Quoted in Telford, "Major Trends," 46.

11. An exception is J. H. Charlesworth, *Jesus within Judaism* (London: SPCK, 1988), who identified Jesus as the Son of God.

12. W. L. Lane, "The Present State of Markan Studies," in *The Gospels Today: A Guide to Some Recent Developments,* ed. J. H. Skilton (Philadelphia: Skilton House, 1990), 69-72.

13. D. Harrington, "A Book of Maps on Mark (1975-1984)," *BTB* 15 (1985): 13.

14. P. G. Bolt, "Mark's Gospel," in *The Face of New Testament Studies,* ed. S. McKnight and G. R. Osborne (Leicester: Apollos, 2004), 397.

historical question. What if there is no connecting relationship between the Jesus in (say) Mark's artistry and *Jesus as he was?* Put simply, it means we have the possibility of a global story and individual stories that are no more than that, stories — in a word, *fiction.* Once again, we have not been able to reach back from the postresurrection worshiping church of the letters and the Apocalypse to the preresurrection historical Jesus.

Subjectivity

Subjectivity in history writing is not new. Indeed, subjectivity-based historiography was the norm in the era when the gospels were written. By subjectivity I mean the writer's discernible tendency to report and interpret events according to his values and prejudices with the intent that the reader (i.e., hearer) adopt the writer's values and prejudices in the interpretation of the events.

It is difficult to think of historians or biographers in the NT era whose writing was not subjectivist in character. Tacitus wrote his *Annals* and *Histories* from a senatorial perspective portraying the Julio-Claudian *principes* as those who robbed Rome of her ancient republican character. Josephus wrote his *Jewish War* as a polemic against those responsible for the fall of Jerusalem and the destruction of the temple, that is, the willful Jewish revolutionaries and false prophets who were so influential in the years leading up to the outbreak of the war. The gospels are also subjectivist writings. That is to say, their authors have a strong loyalty to their subject, Jesus, and they write intentionally to confirm their readers in or win their readers to the same loyalty. Subjectivity does not imply falsehood. One author may write with precise factuality while another is careless with details or may even falsify them in the interests of his agenda. Nor should we regard subjectivity as (necessarily) an evil. A subsidiary of subjectivity is empathy in the matter being reported. A writer ordinarily needs to have a strong interest in something to spend time and effort writing about it. It is the task of historical criticism to identify and allow for subjectivity and where possible to cross-check details. Our argument will be that the gospel writers, while clearly subjectivist in attitude, reported the incidents related to Jesus with as much detail as they knew or could remember.

Modern subjectivity, however, is another matter. In antiquity writers understood that objectivity was a desirable goal, but they seldom knew how to achieve it. By contrast, in modern times undergraduate students of history are forced to document their assertions and to justify their conclusions. It is not possible to complete a degree in history or to publish in legitimate history publications without evidence and argument that anticipates the potential falsification of that argument.

That, at least, is the theory! In reality recent decades have witnessed an astonishing expression of subjectivity by agenda-driven scholars. This is particularly true in Jesus studies. As S. McKnight has observed, "Everyone wants Jesus on his or her side — traditionalists and revisionists, fundamentalists and liberals, feminists and chauvinists, mystics and empiricists. . . . In addition, ideological causes gain in appealing to Jesus: democracy, federalism, republicanism, communism, socialism, Marxism and capitalism."[15] McKnight views this phenomenon as fulfilling Henry Cadbury's alarm (in 1937!) at the tendency to "modernize Jesus," that is, to "anachronize" him by projecting our world onto his so as to "enmesh" him in our ideological concerns.[16]

One example, among many, is the tendency to read a left-liberal reformist motive into the activities of Jesus in Galilee. On the basis of the tetrarch Antipas's rebuilding program begun circa 3 B.C. in Betharamphtha Julia (in Perea)[17] and Sepphoris[18] and his creation of Tiberias,[19] which he began circa 17, some scholars have posited a widespread "urbanization" in this tetrarchy. On this basis it has been argued that considerable social dislocation and economic suffering followed these extensive building activities and that Jesus' program was directed to this painful environment. In other words, there has been a tendency to define the activities of the historical Jesus by this reconstruction of the historical Galilee.

M. H. Jensen says S. Freyne, R. A. Horsley, and J. D. Crossan, among others, attribute Jesus' emergence to the harshness in Galilee under the policies of Herod Antipas.[20] To the contrary, Jensen argues that Antipas's cities were small and that his building work was minor in contrast with

---

15. S. McKnight, "Jesus of Nazareth," in *The Face of New Testament Studies*, 149-76, at 149-50.

16. McKnight, "Jesus of Nazareth," 150.

17. Josephus, *War* 2.168; *Ant* 18.27.

18. Josephus, *Ant* 18.27.

19. Josephus, *War* 2.168.

20. M. H. Jensen, "Herod Antipas in Galilee: Friend or Foe of the Historical Jesus?" *JSHJ* 5, no. 1 (2007): 7-32.

building activities elsewhere, for example, in Caesarea Maritima and Scythopolis. Given the thinness of the sources, he is wary of making far-reaching conclusions about the personality or program of this tetrarch, concluding that he was "a minor ruler with moderate impact . . . not a *remaker* of Galilee, but rather a modest developer."[21] These are cautionary observations for those who seek to define Jesus according to their own political views and argue their case from data that is either minimal and ambiguous or does not in fact support their proposals.

Disclosure[22]

Try as I might, I too am affected by my own subjectivity so that I will tend to select evidence and interpret it as it seems right to me. So it is important to say something about my inner universe from which I view the world. I admit to being a creedal believer and an Anglican churchman. There are other labels, but these two are sufficient to identify my subjectivity and to help a reader to understand the eyes through which I see things. Nonetheless, I have the goal of "attainable honesty"[23] based on the attempt to consider all the sources and to propose hypotheses that make the best sense of the evidence.

I must confess to at least one working presupposition. It is based on the conviction that causation in history is often discernible. For example, I hold that the *effect* of the war between Rome and the Jews of Palestine in 66-70 had identifiable *causes*. Also, there was most likely something about the preresurrection Jesus that explains the immediate worship of him in the postresurrection churches, especially since the time distance between the one and the other was so compressed. To assert either the hiatus, "no-connection" view (implied by Sanders) or the unknowable, agnostic view (implied by Bultmann) is unsustainable. Why would the postresurrection believers worship Christ unless there was something about his preresurrection life that warranted that adoration?

21. Jensen, "Herod Antipas in Galilee," 31.

22. J. Willitts, "Presuppositions and Procedures in the Study of the 'Historical Jesus'; or, Why I Decided Not to Be a 'Historical Jesus Scholar,'" *JSHJ* 3, no. 1 (2005): 61-108, reviews the presuppositions evident in the writings of E. P. Sanders, J. D. Crossan, J. P. Meier, N. T. Wright, G. Theissen, and D. C. Allison.

23. I owe the phrase to J. D. Crossan, *The Historical Jesus: The Life of a Mediterranean Jewish Peasant* (Edinburgh: T. & T. Clark, 1991), xxxiv.

Also relevant to the duty of self-disclosure is my longtime interest in Jewish-Roman relations in Palestine from the time of Pompey's arrival in Jerusalem circa 63 B.C. until the fall of Masada in about A.D. 74, based mainly on Josephus's documentation of this period. I have visited Israel and Jordan a number of times and can speak to how the text-based accounts of Jew-Roman relationships of that era and the rise of Christianity within it are readily imaginable. The now-unearthed Pool of Siloam and the charred stones beneath Temple Mount are examples, respectively, of visible witnesses to the events narrated in the gospels and Josephus.

Historical Method

Assessing the secure transmission of primary sources is the place to begin any historical inquiry, whether about the emperor Tiberius or Jesus of Nazareth. Surprisingly, few who write about the historical Jesus address this vital question. How can we conduct Jesus research unless we know that the texts on which we rely are close to or identical with what was originally written? For the study of Jesus this means investigation into the transmission history of the biographies of Jesus, that is, the gospels. We need to know whether the four canonical gospels are the only sources that are in touch with the historical Jesus, or whether the noncanonical gospels contribute anything to our store of early information. This will require us to comment on the manuscripts of the second and third centuries. Without credible historical sources we will not be able to find the historical figure who is the object of our inquiry. Of utmost importance is the verifiable observation that the four canonical gospels were in circulation by the end of the first century.

We must also consider references by the non-Christian sources, in particular Tacitus and Pliny. Through the Roman eyes of Tacitus and Pliny early in the second century, we see Christ executed in Judea by Pilate, Christians martyred in Rome under Nero and persecuted by Pliny for their worship of Christ ("as if a god") in northern Anatolia. In other words, Tacitus and Pliny confirm the general picture from the New Testament about the origin, spread, and religious practices of Christianity. Their evidence is of special value because it is both early and hostile.

The evidence from the second century is of special significance in establishing an information horizon that existed by the end of the first century. Christian sources from the second century establish that the four canonical gospels upon which we rely for information about Jesus of Nazareth were extant by around 100. The hostile sources likewise establish that Christianity originated in Judea circa 26-36, that it had spread to Rome by the 60s, and that at the turn of the century Christians were worshiping Christ as a deity. Since that worship of Christ in Bithynia circa 110 can be shown to have also characterized the meetings of disciples in Jerusalem from the time of the resurrection, we are forced to ask who, then, was this Jesus *beforehand?* That worship is an established effect, so we must ask what was its cause?

When we turn to the Christian tradition in the New Testament, we seek methodically to establish the earliest information about the preresurrection Jesus, that is, in Jerusalem. We observe a continuum between the oral gospel and the earliest written (synoptic) gospel, a continuum that is *biographical* in character and that identifies Jesus as the Christ.

More concentrated attention to that earliest gospel, especially its longer "Galilee" section, supports the assertion of the elder (quoted by Papias) that Peter was the oral source for the gospel his amanuensis Mark wrote. Petrine influence in this gospel is confirmed by the prominence of Peter at the beginning, the end, and the middle of Mark's text. Accordingly, the Gospel of Mark originated in an eyewitness-based testimony to the preresurrection Jesus, where he is identified as "the Christ."

The prologue to Luke-Acts (Luke 1:1-4) uniquely reveals the processes by which "eyewitnesses and ministers of the word" (i.e., the original disciples) handed over to Luke shorter written texts that he incorporated into his more comprehensive work. Source criticism reveals these earlier texts to have included (a version of) Mark and the sources known as Q and L. Significantly, comparison between these discrete sources reveals the preresurrection Jesus to be a messianic figure who performed miracles.

The Gospel of John, which I hold to be written independently of the synoptics, is of great significance for Jesus' relationship with the temple authorities and for his final visit to Jerusalem. Of special importance is John's perspective on the Roman attitude toward and treatment of Jesus as "king of the Jews." Granted the marked theological *tendenz* in this gospel, we nonetheless are given a credible picture of the preresurrection Jesus as a Christ figure. Thus John's is a fascinating alternative version to Mark's, one in which we are left in no doubt that Jesus was indeed the Christ the Son of God. It is difficult in the extreme to account for the high

Christology of this gospel unless it was to a significant degree true of the historical Jesus.

Paul is our (likely) earliest written witness to the historical Jesus. Paul, who is preoccupied with Jesus' death by crucifixion, frequently refers to *Christ* crucified, as if to say he *was* the Christ when crucified. Included in Paul's references are preformulated christological traditions that he quotes, strengthening the sense of Jesus' preresurrection messiahship. Paul's ethical teaching and his own conscious "imitation" of Christ assume considerable understanding of the preresurrection Christ.

Finally, it is necessary to assess the authenticity of the words of the historical Jesus. Examination of the Gospel of Mark pericope by pericope indicates the centrality of Jesus' words in every context, pointing to the likely historicity of those words in those specific settings. The unlikely alternative is that we attribute those words to Mark's artistry. It is possible, however, that the pericopes in Mark are not in precise chronological order. Furthermore, based on the assumption that the gospel writers would neither alter nor omit a word of the Lord, we suggest that Matthew and Luke "found a place" for those words in their respective gospels, though without necessarily knowing the right location for them in every case. The words of Jesus in Mark and the Q source (in particular) provided important glimpses of Jesus' ministry in Galilee.

Conclusion

I am confident it is possible to find the historical Christ and that to do so calls for nothing more than patient and careful reading of the gospels as historical documents. For that, in truth, is what they are.

TWO

Horizon One Hundred: The Gospels

On the day called Sunday . . . the memoirs of the apostles [which are called gospels] are read as long as time permits.

Justin Martyr[1]

The place to begin the quest for the historical Christ is not in the first but in the second century, since by then at least thirteen gospels were in circulation, including Gnostic gospels.[2] We need to establish which texts are the earliest and most underived versions as the basis for our inquiry. This issue has become important since some are saying that the Gnostic gospels are primary sources for our knowledge of Christ, predating the "canonical" gospels.

In other words, our first and most basic step is to identify, date, and assess the historical value of our sources for Jesus Christ. The same principle applies in any biographical study, whether for Herod, the king at the time of Christ's birth, or Tiberius, the emperor at the time of his death.

---

1. Justin Martyr, *First Apology* 66, 67.

2. In addition to Matthew, Mark, Luke, and John, there are surviving texts of the *Gospel of Thomas* (P.Oxy. 1), *Gospel of Peter* (P.Oxy. 4009), an *"Unknown Gospel"* (P.Egerton 2), Valentinus's *Gospel of Truth*. There are also patristic references to the *Gospel of the Ebionites* (Irenaeus, *AH* 1.26.2; 3.21.1), the *Gospel of the Nazoreans* (Eusebius, *HE* 4.22.8), the *Gospel of the Hebrews* (Clement, *Miscellanies* 2.9.45). H. Koester, "Apocryphal and Canonical Gospels," *HTR* 73, no. 12 (1980): 105-30, argued against distinguishing "apocryphal" from "canonical" gospels. See later discussion.

To anticipate, I will argue that our earliest and in fact our only first-century gospels are those by Matthew, Mark, Luke, and John. Furthermore, I will seek to establish that these were in circulation and use by the end of the first century, hence my chapter title: "Horizon One Hundred."

This view is of course traditional and remains widely held. Yet some scholars dispute it, contending instead that the many second-century gospels (extant or attested) call this time-honored view into question. If there are other gospels, it is asked, how can we know that the traditional four gospels are genuine sources of historical information about Jesus? I agree, however, with the majority, that the four gospels we call "canonical" are for all practical purposes the only authentic sources for our historical knowledge of Christ, and that they alone qualify as historical witnesses to him.

I will begin by inquiring into the century that follows the apostolic era, circa 80-180. I will seek to establish that the Christology evident in nongospel texts from the apostolic era (i.e., the epistles) continued to be cherished and protected throughout the century that followed. I will argue that gospel texts that support this Christology were deemed to be authentically apostolic whereas those that attempted to subvert it were rejected as inauthentic. Distinguishing the authentic and primary from the inauthentic (whether derived from the primary or underived) will depend on a brief inquiry into the decades that followed the era of the apostles.

Here, though, we face the problem of minimal documentation for the first decades of the postapostolic era; some exploit this, contending that it was a period of theological confusion with no discernible theological continuity from the era of the apostles.

Again, to anticipate, let me say there is sufficient evidence to establish that the theological trajectories of the previous era continued. Even though some dispute the historical validity of the four gospels for this purpose, it is not possible to do that with Paul's undisputed writings, whose dating is early (and nearly certain) and whose textual transmission is secure. It is demonstrable that Paul's Christology was preserved in the decades following the close of the apostolic age.

Fourfold Mission in the Apostolic Age (33-80)

We are able to divide the apostolic age into two periods, the earliest years and the era of the four missions.

After Jesus: The Earliest Years (ca. 33-50)[3]

One of the surprises in early Christian history is that only some of the twelve foundational apostles are known to have engaged in the mission for which they had been called and trained. That is to say, only Peter and John play any known part in the "witness" Christ commanded them to make (Acts 1:8). Furthermore, as we shall see, only two apostles of the original twelve wrote a gospel, and one of them (Matthew/Levi) was lost from sight once Jesus was no longer present. Mark and Luke are secondary figures and colleagues of better-known leaders Peter and Paul, respectively.

During the period from the first Easter (33)[4] until the (private) Jerusalem meeting (47),[5] there were three known sources of mission — Peter (with John), the Hellenists, and Paul. Initially, Peter (with John) gave witness to the ascended Messiah in Jerusalem, including to the temple authorities. Once Paul's persecutions ceased, Peter went outside Jerusalem and preached[6] throughout the land of Israel (Gal 2:7-9; Acts 9:31-32).

Soon after Peter's initial preaching in Jerusalem, Stephen began to preach in the Greek synagogues. Following his death and the expulsion of the Hellenists, Philip (later called the evangelist) took the message to Samaritans and to the Hellenized coastal settlements from Azotus to Caesarea (and likely farther north as well). Other Hellenist Jews, fugitives from Paul's depredations, escaped beyond the borders of the land, some inland to Damascus, others along the coast northward to Phoenicia, Cyprus, and Antioch. The displaced Hellenists appear to have concentrated their efforts in Antioch, so that soon enough it became the second significant center of the new faith, where the disciples were for the first time called *Christianoi* (Acts 11:26).

Following his dramatic Damascus "call," Saul himself began preach-

---

3. See generally Barnett, *Birth of Christianity.*

4. Although most favor A.D. 30 as the date of the first Easter, the chronology of Luke 3:1-2 points to John's ministry beginning in 28/29, which in turn suggests 29-33 as the span of Jesus' ministry. For a detailed defense for A.D. 30 as the date for the first Easter, see J. P. Meier, *A Marginal Jew: Rethinking the Historical Jesus,* vol. 1 (New York: Doubleday, 1991), 372-409. Meier, however, assumes (1) a brief period between when John and Jesus began their respective ministries, and (2) the earliest possible date for Luke 3:1-2.

5. Reported in Gal 2:1-10.

6. The verb "[P]eter *went here and there (dierchomenon)* among them all" may imply a preaching circuit.

ing to Jews, Godfearers, and Gentiles in Damascus, Arabia, Judea, and Syria-Cilicia (Gal 1:16–2:10). In his report of the meeting in Jerusalem circa 47, Paul claims that the Jerusalem "pillar" apostles James, Peter, and John recognized his God-given mission (apostolē) to the uncircumcised, which had run parallel to Peter's apostolate to the circumcised in the land of Israel throughout the same decade and a half (Gal 2:7-9). Furthermore, the Jerusalem leaders endorsed Paul's plan to "go" to the Gentiles.

In sum, to our surprise ten of the twelve original apostles appear not to have played a major part in earliest mission. "Apostles" are present at the Jerusalem Council circa 49 (Acts 15:2, 4, 6, 22, 23), but they do not reappear thereafter in the book of Acts. Most likely they were engaged in mission activity, but where they went and what they did is a matter for conjecture, based on scattered references in the patristic literature.[7] The spread of Christianity in the first decades was a function of strong-willed individual leaders like Peter, Stephen, Philip, and Paul.

The Four Mission Groups

From the late 40s a number of more or less discrete mission groups emerged. True, Luke gives the impression that the original Twelve would be witnesses "to the end of the earth" (Acts 1:8). The evidence from the NT, however, points rather to *four* overlapping (and sometimes competing?) mission groups led by Peter, James, John, and Paul[8] as the means by which the gospel message spread. Networks of mission churches were established in the eastern Mediterranean through the initiative of these four leaders and the labors of their surrogates.

7. According to Eusebius, *HE* 3.1, "The holy apostles and disciples of our Saviour were scattered throughout the whole world. Thomas . . . obtained by lot Parthia, Andrew Scythia, John Asia (and he stayed there ard died in Ephesus) but Peter seemed to have preached to the Jews of the Dispersion in Pontus and Galatia and Bithynia, Cappadocia and Asia and at the end came to Rome. . . . Paul . . . fulfilled the Gospel from Jerusalem to Illyricum and afterward was martyred in Rome under Nero." Eusebius, however, based his comments on his own reading of the New Testament, not on other sources. See further J. Foster, *After the Apostles* (London: SCM, 1951), 22-25.

8. This view broadly depends on the analysis of E. E. Ellis, *The Making of the New Testament Documents* (Leiden: Brill, 1999), 32-36, 251-66, 307-14. Ellis draws attention to the comment of Clement of Alexandria about "the true tradition of the blessed teaching in direct line from Peter, James, John and Paul, the holy apostles" (309).

What is the evidence for this bold assertion? The letters of the NT point in this direction:

1. Paul's letters to churches in Galatia, Macedonia, Achaia, and Asia are tangible evidence of congregations established through his mission.
2. James's encyclical to the "twelve tribes in the Dispersion" points to his spiritual hegemony over scattered congregations of Jewish Christians (James 1:1).
3. Peter's encyclical to Pontus, Galatia, Cappadocia, Asia, and Bithynia likewise indicates his leadership over a "brotherhood" distributed throughout (northern?) Anatolia (1 Pet 1:1).
4. John's encyclical "book of prophecy" to seven churches in Roman Asia assumes his authority over these widely scattered churches (Rev 1:4, 11; 2:1–3:22).[9]

At the same time, however, the base from which these leaders (and their assistants) wrote their mission letters was the center of their mission authority. For James this meant Jerusalem, for Peter Rome, for John Ephesus, and for Paul wherever he was at the time of writing — Antioch, Corinth, Ephesus, Philippi, or Rome.[10] We argue, therefore, that the sphere of the mission leader's authority was both (1) his geographic home base and (2) the jurisdiction represented by the region (or ethnicity for James) to which the leader's letters were directed.

What then of the gospels? These leaders (or their associates) produced mission literature for the churches in their respective apostolates.

9. Apostolic authorship of the Apocalypse historically is a moot point. Nonetheless, earliest authorities are in no doubt that the author was John Zebedee (Justin Martyr, *Dialogue with Trypho* 81.4; Irenaeus, *AH* 4.30.4; 5.26.1). Furthermore, the author's assumed unquestioned authority over these churches (Rev 1:3; 2:7, 11, 17; 3:6, 13, 22; 22:18-19) is consistent with apostolicity (and not with being a mere "prophet"). Differences in style from the fourth gospel can be partly accounted for by genre differences between a gospel-biography and a "book of prophecy" written in a quasi-apocalyptic manner. John's implied portrayal of himself as the true prophet against the "false prophet" (Rev 16:13; 20:10), and the calculatedly "prophetical" authority of the "book" (1:1-3; 22:6, 18-19), is explanation enough for the author's failure to claim apostolicity. The book's dependence on hundreds of OT echoes and its quasi-apocalyptic style point to the author as a Palestinian Jew.

10. Whether *Antioch* (for Galatians?), *Corinth* (for 1 and 2 Thessalonians, Romans), *Ephesus* (for 1 Corinthians [and Ephesians, Colossians, Philemon?]), *Philippi* (2 Corinthians?), or *Rome* (Philippians, 2 Timothy).

Initially various letters were written and brought to the constituent churches to meet current pastoral needs. Subsequently, each group compiled a gospel as a kerygmatic biography of Christ. Accordingly, one gospel and one or more letters are associated with each of the four mission leaders.[11]

Mission Leader	Mission Literature[12]
Peter	Gospel of Mark, 1 Peter, 2 Peter[13]
James	Letter of James,[14] Gospel of Matthew
John	Gospel of John, 1 John, Revelation
Paul	Paul's letters,[15] Gospel of Luke, Acts of the Apostles

The hypothesis stated above helpfully explains the dissemination of Christian belief as well as the origin and purpose of the greater part of the NT. The fourfold character of mission in the apostolic age may have been retained in the memories of the churches in the decades following, influencing the insistence on the fourfold gospel in the latter half of the second century.

11. I agree with R. Bauckham, "For Whom Were the Gospels Written?" in *The Gospel for All Christians: Rethinking the Gospel Audiences*, ed. R. Bauckham (Grand Rapids: Eerdmans, 1998), 9-48, that the gospels were not primarily written for the narrow interests of the authors' domestic faith community. However, his view of the authors' implied *indefinite* readership in each case is too broad; the mission literature inevitably is conditioned by the needs of the mission jurisdiction, both home-based and distant. Against Bauckham's arguments see, e.g., D. C. Sim, "The Gospel for All Christians? A Response to Richard Bauckham," *JSNT* 24, no. 2 (2001): 3-7; M. M. Mitchell, "Patristic Counter-evidence to the Claim That the Gospels Were Written for All Christians," *NTS* 51, no. 1 (2005): 36-79.

12. The anonymous Letter to the Hebrews, an early work, may have been written by a known associate of Paul's, perhaps Apollos or Barnabas. The above hypothesis accounts for most of the texts that will later be regarded as "canonical," leaving only Hebrews, Jude, and the two shorter anonymous letters attributed to John not accounted for.

13. By means of his assistants Mark, Silvanus, and Jude (?), respectively.

14. By an unknown amanuensis.

15. Sometimes by an amanuensis.

The Century after the Apostles (ca. 80-180)

One may break this century into two uneven periods. The first begins with the twilight of the apostolic age and ends with Justin Martyr (ca. 150). The second begins with Justin and ends with the definition of the fourfold gospel by Irenaeus and Tatian.

From the Apostles to Justin (ca. 80-150)

Once the apostles passed from the scene, their mission networks likely tended to dissolve, leaving individual congregations without any secure links between them. No longer was there a recognized leader to give the individual churches a sense of collective association. It would be years before the overarching episcopate emerged. Furthermore, although the basic two-part presbyter-deacon polity had been established by the end of the apostolic age, it was not yet secure. Clement's letter from the church in Rome (ca. 96) to the church in Corinth reveals continuing conflict within that church. Ignatius's letters to churches in the Aegean region (ca. 110) indicate his struggle to secure monarchical leadership to replace the collegiate system of local leadership, which in Ignatius's mind had failed.

One of the difficulties in these decades was the lack of independent church buildings; Christians continued to meet in houses, as they had from the beginning of the apostolic age.[16] Not until the late second century did Christians begin to have specialized church buildings.[17] Most likely the meeting took place in the (larger) house of a wealthier member, who as a sign of wealth would likely also have been literate, thereby increasing the likelihood that he was also a presbyter or the official "reader" (lector). This meant that the house owner, as host of the church meeting, had significant influence on what was believed and practiced within his home.[18] In effect, this host would have become de facto a patron of the

16. B. Blue, "Acts and the House Church," in *The Book of Acts in Its Graeco-Roman Setting,* ed. D. W. J. Gill and C. Gempf (Grand Rapids: Eerdmans, 1994), 119-222.

17. There are reports of church buildings in Arbil (east of the Tigris) before 148 and in Edessa in 180. The house-church building discovered in 1934 dates from the second century.

18. From the NT we know the names of the hosts of various house churches: Mary in Jerusalem (Acts 12:12); Lydia in Philippi (Acts 16:40); Jason in Thessalonica (Acts 17:6-7); Titius Justus/Gaius in Corinth (Acts 18:7); Phoebe in Cenchreae (Rom 16:1-2); Prisca and

congregation. Such idiosyncratic influence may have contributed to the doctrinal and organizational diversity of this period.

Furthermore, the decades between the apostolic age and the era following Justin, for which we have more information, are not well documented. Nonetheless, it is an overstatement to say with J. Hurlbut that "a curtain hangs over the church, through which we vainly try to look, and when at last it rises, about 129 A.D. . . . we find a church in many ways different from that in the days of Peter and Paul."[19] It is more precise to say that we have a limited but clear picture of what was (in the broad) occurring.

First, there is ample evidence that the mission literature from the apostolic age was being widely disseminated. Quite soon the apostolic literature began to cross over from one mission network to another. It was enough to know that a gospel or letter was "apostolic" in origin for it to be received by local congregations and their leaders. This explains why the postapostolic writers allude to or echo so much of the mission literature, as the following examples illustrate. Writing from Rome circa 96, Clement in his letter to the church in Corinth makes (free) use of Matthew, Mark, Luke, Acts, 1 Corinthians, Ephesians, Hebrews, James, Titus, 1 Peter, and 2 Peter.

The *Didache*, an early (but difficult to date) manual with Jewish flavor, makes (free) use of Matthew, Mark, Luke, 1 Corinthians, 1 Thessalonians, 2 Thessalonians, 1 Timothy, and 1 Peter. In the first decades of the second century Ignatius makes (free) use of Matthew, Luke, John,[20] Romans, 1 Corinthians, Philippians, and 1 Thessalonians. In short, at or soon after the turn of the first century the writings of the four mission groups had become the possession of the churches everywhere.

These writers seldom quote exactly, but rather make a recognizable paraphrase of an apostolic text. However, it is likely that they are adapting a written text rather than oral tradition (which would have a more "traditional feel" than these texts do). Furthermore, it is noteworthy that each of these three writers draws from texts of each of the four mission groups — Peter's, James's, John's, and Paul's[21] (although texts from John are significantly underrepresented).

Aquila in Ephesus (1 Cor 16:19); Nympha in Laodicea (Col 4:15); Philemon in Colossae (Philem 1-2); Prisca and Aquila, Asyncritus, Philologus et al. in Rome (Rom 16:3-5, 14, 15).

19. J. L. Hurlbut, *Story of the Christian Church* (Grand Rapids: Zondervan, 1967), 41.

20. Ignatius, *To the Philadelphians* 7.1 ("the Spirit . . . knoweth not whence it comes or whither it goes"), appears to echo John 3:8.

21. Because Hebrews was likely deemed a Pauline text?

Secondly, the Apocalypse (ca. 95) gives us a window through which we see the resolute leadership of John[22] in times of dire difficulty in Roman Asia, helping us understand how the apostolic faith managed to survive there. For one thing, disaffected Jews were harassing the churches in Smyrna and Philadelphia (Rev 2:9; 3:9). These Jews, likely grieved at the loss of synagogue members to the churches, appear to be exploiting their immunity from Caesar worship against the vulnerable Christian assemblies.[23] Worse still, each of the seven churches was located in a city where the emperor cult was present and aggressively active under the incumbent princeps, Domitian (81-96), as reflected in Revelation 2:12-14 and 13:1-18.[24] This was not the end of their troubles. Ephesus had been penetrated by visiting teachers, "who call themselves apostles but are not" (Rev 2:2). As well, there were internal troubles. In Pergamum and Thyatira local prophets encouraged participation in pagan cults and its accompanying sexual immorality (Rev 2:14, 20). The church in Pergamum had members who followed the teachings of the mysterious Nicolaitans, which the church in Ephesus opposed (Rev 2:6, 15).

Yet, for all these difficulties, the churches in Asia survived. The letters of Ignatius, written fifteen years after the Revelation, to Ephesus, Philadelphia, and Smyrna, are evidence of continuing congregations in those places, as well as in Magnesia and Tralles.

The Apocalypse tells us John was a determined leader, a strong leader with a sense of authority over a network of churches scattered over a wide expanse in Roman Asia. He had extensive knowledge of the churches and imposed his leadership on these churches by his encyclical "book of prophecy." As well, some of his references to "angels" likely point to church envoys who came from the churches to Patmos and who would return to

22. See earlier, n. 9.

23. References to the "synagogue of Satan" in Smyrna and Philadelphia indicate the Jews in those cities are as threatening to the believers as the Roman cultus in Pergamum where "Satan lives" and "where Satan has his throne." After the destruction of the temple in 70, the Jews were compelled to continue paying the *fiscus Judaicus*, except that it was now directed to the upkeep of Jupiter Capitolinus in Rome. Cf. C. Hemer, *The Letters to the Seven Churches of Asia in Their Local Setting* (Sheffield: JSOT Press, 1996), 8.

24. See Rev 13 where the portrayal of the beast from the sea and the beast from the earth represent respectively the cruel impact of Roman *auctoritas* and local priestly rule on the churches of Roman Asia, Ephesus in particular. Cf. S. R. F. Price, *Rituals and Power* (Cambridge: Cambridge University Press, 1984).

them with a stern message from this prophet-leader. It is reasonable to attribute the survival of the Asian churches in this period to the leadership of John.

A third indication of strength in the face of adversity and uncertainty was the intentional appointment of a succession of strong leaders (cf. 2 Tim 2:2). The churches of Jerusalem, Corinth, Rome, and Asia were sufficiently resolute and well organized to secure ongoing effective leadership. Hegesippus, a later contemporary within this early period, gives (through Eusebius) the names of the successive leaders in Jerusalem, Corinth, and Rome.[25] A Jewish Christian, Hegesippus reports that in Rome he associated with numbers of bishops and "received the *same teaching* from all."[26]

In Asia the dominant figure after John was Polycarp (born ca. 70). Polycarp was a disciple of John[27] and was appointed bishop of Smyrna by apostles. As early as circa 110 he was sufficiently prominent in Roman Asia to be sent a letter from Ignatius. According to Polycarp's disciple Irenaeus, Polycarp "always taught the things he had learned from the apostles."[28] He wrote a number of letters to churches, of which only his letter to the Philippians survives. Whereas Jerusalem and Rome found their strength through a succession of leaders, in Roman Asia that strength was significantly associated with one man, Polycarp. A measure of his greatness is seen in the "martyrology" written soon after his death around 155.[29]

A fourth indication of determination to preserve the truth of the apostolic era was the formulation of liturgical-sounding confessions or creeds.

These abound in the Apocalypse, for example: "Grace to you and peace from him who is and who was and who is to come, and from the seven spirits who are before his throne, and from Jesus Christ the faithful witness, the first-born of the dead, and the ruler of kings on earth. To him who loves us and has freed us from our sins by his blood . . . be glory and dominion for ever and ever. Amen" (Rev 1:4-6).

In a similar vein Ignatius writes:

25. Eusebius, *HE* 4.22. Also, Irenaeus, *AH* 3.3.4.

26. Eusebius, *HE* 4.22.

27. Eusebius, *HE* 5.20.

28. Irenaeus, *AH* 3.3.4; Eusebius, *HE* 3.36.

29. A genuine and contemporary account in the form of a letter from the church of Smyrna to the church of Philomelium.

Be deaf when any one speaks to you apart from Jesus Christ,
Who was of the stock of David,
Who was from Mary,
Who was truly born, ate and drank,
was truly persecuted under Pontius Pilate,
was truly crucified and died
in the sight of beings heavenly, earthly and under the earth,
Who also was truly raised from the dead,
His Father raising him.[30]

Likewise we find similar creedlike passages in Polycarp's letter, for example:

. . . believing in him
Who raised our Lord Jesus Christ from the dead,
and gave him glory and a throne at his right hand,
to whom are subjected all things in heaven and earth,
Whom every breath of wind serves,
Who will come as judge of living and dead.[31]

These texts are carefully structured, implying that they had been in church use for some time. Furthermore, they belong to the process of formulating doctrine for church use, links in the chain extending to the eventual formulation of the Apostles' and Nicene Creeds.

A fifth indicator of the regional strength of the Roman and Asian networks is their respective creation of ecclesiastical calendars for the observation of Easter, which as it happened were different in approach. To resolve the difference Polycarp came to Rome about 154,[32] another indication of his eminence in the Asian churches. Most likely, these calendrical observances were not of recent creation, either in Rome or in Asia. They indicate the influence of the synagogue and the growing sense of institutional permanence in these churches.

Finally, it appears that from earliest times Christians met on the first day of the week. It is striking that each of the four gospels reports that the

---

30. Ignatius, *To the Trallians* 9.4, quoted in J. N. D. Kelly, *Early Christian Creeds* (London: Longmans, 1963), 68.

31. Polycarp, *To the Philippians* 2, quoted in Kelly, *Early Christian Creeds*, 70.

32. Eusebius, *HE* 4.13.

women found the tomb empty on "the first day of the week" (Matt 28:1; Luke 24:1; John 20:1; cf. Mark 16:2). John's note that "eight days later" the disciples were gathered "again" seems deliberate, suggesting that from the beginning meeting on the "first day" became an established practice. This is supported by several passing references to "the first day of the week" (Acts 20:7 — "On the first day of the week . . . we were gathered together to break bread"; 1 Cor 16:2 — "On the first day of every week, each of you is to put something aside"). John's comment circa 95, "I was in the Spirit on the Lord's day" (i.e., "the day that belongs to the Lord"), suggests that the "first day of the week" meeting was by that time seen to be especially connected with the *Lord* Jesus. The practice of a weekly gathering was confirmed by Pliny, writing circa 108, who noted the testimony of the Christians of Bithynia that "they . . . met *regularly* on a *fixed day* to chant verses among themselves in honour of Christ as if to a god."[33] By Justin's time, circa 150, this practice of weekly meetings was clearly universal: "On the day called Sunday, *all who live in the cities or in the country* gather together in one place."[34]

In short, while the evidence is sparse for the decades following the era of the apostles, it is by no means absent. The absence of the apostles and mission leaders potentially left the field open for the influx of new ideas, and the Apocalypse and Ignatius's letters confirm this. Whereas Paul's mission provided for a broad regional association that made possible the "collection" from his mission churches for the saints in Judea,[35] in the following years the house-based pattern of gatherings probably meant that congregations became more isolated and potentially idiosyncratic, and thus became breeding grounds for extreme or eccentric doctrines.

However, there is ample evidence of resolute determination to preserve the apostolic deposit of truth. Both the Apocalypse and the letters of Ignatius reveal strong leaders who sternly kept the churches under strict doctrinal control. Embryonic creedal items in the Apocalypse and the letters of Ignatius and Polycarp reflect concern for purity of doctrine in the churches. Nor was church order neglected, as the Apocalypse and the letters of Clement and Ignatius show. The practice of meeting on a

33. Pliny, *Letters* 10.96 (Loeb). See below, chapter 3.
34. Justin, *First Apology* 67.
35. An example of the regional character of Paul's mission is his dispatch of Macedonian "brothers" to Corinth to shame the church members there into reviving their contributions to the collection (2 Cor 9:3).

"fixed day" appears to have been universal. The Quartodeciman dispute in the 140s indicates the development of church calendars among the Christians in Asia and Rome, while the meeting of Asian and Roman leaders over this issue points to an emerging east-west ecumenism. Not least, we must give due weight to the stability provided by a succession of leaders in Jerusalem, Corinth, and Rome and the lengthy leadership of Polycarp bishop of Smyrna for the churches of Asia, practices influenced perhaps by the succession of great teaching rabbis soon to be reflected in the Mishnah.[36]

Justin Martyr in Rome (ca. 150)

We cannot overestimate the importance of this great teacher and writer, for two reasons. To begin, the extensive details Justin gives of his theology and praxis likely reveal church practice and beliefs that had been in place in the previous decades but were not written in sources. At the same time, Justin's writings are the key to understanding the future, the rapid developments that were to occur in Irenaeus's formulations and were presupposed in Tatian's *Diatessaron*.

Around 150 Justin Martyr provides the earliest glimpse into the extent of activities typically occurring in the house-church meetings, not only in Rome but also universally. He writes, "On the day called Sunday, *all who live in the cities or in the country* gather together in one place."[37] Justin wants his reader (Emperor Antoninus Pius) to understand that he is speaking about church practices *everywhere.*

In his *First Apology* 65-67 Justin gives extensive detail about a typical church meeting.[38] After a *baptism,* "where there is water," the baptized is brought to "the place where the other Christians are assembled" and where they pray for the newly baptized. This is followed by the members' *kiss* of mutual greeting. Then the lector *reads* at length from the memoirs of the apostles or the writings of the prophets, upon which the president *"instructs and exhorts"* the people, based on these readings.[39] Next, "the presi-

36. *m. Avot* 1:1-18.
37. Justin, *First Apology* 67.
38. Justin, *First Apology* 65-67.
39. See 1 Tim 4:13 — "Until I come devote yourself to the *reading,* the *exhortation* and the *teaching.*"

dent of the brethren" leads the congregation (standing) in the prayer called *Eucharist* ("Thanksgiving"), after which the people share in the meal of bread and wine. Finally, the wealthy members are invited to make a *contribution* for the care of orphans, widows, the sick, the poor, those in prison, and foreigners.

Earlier (*First Apology* 13) Justin mentions *prayer* and *thanksgiving, invocation,* and *hymns,* and he rehearses a form of words that resembles a creed.

> Thus we are not atheists, since we worship
>> The creator of this universe. . . .
> And that with good reason honour
>> him who taught us these things
>> and was born for this purpose,
> Jesus Christ,
>> who was crucified under Pontius Pilate,
>>> the governor of Judea in the time of Tiberius Caesar,
>> having heard that he is the Son of the true God
>> and holding him in second rank,
>> and the prophetic Spirit third in order,
>>> we shall proceed to demonstrate.[40]

This is one of several creedlike statements in Justin's writings.[41] Their quasi-liturgical structure and frequent (embryonic) trinitarian references with extended Jesus sections point to both catechetical and liturgical use. These are so frequent and well rounded that they likely were formulated some time before Justin wrote.

The information in Justin's writings indicates a significant degree of fixity for the typical Sunday activities, details of the content of those activities but also the existence of "officials" — the *president,* the *reader,* and the *deacons.* The nature of Justin's apology to the emperor strongly suggests that these were not merely peculiar to the Roman church, but were universal church practices.

---

40. Kelly, *Early Christian Creeds,* 72.
41. Kelly, *Early Christian Creeds,* 70-76.

The Gnostic Challenge (ca. 140-170)

Gnostic versions of Christianity began to appear in the first part of the second century, though they had their roots in the apostolic era. The so-called Colossian heresy appears to be a version of Jewish Gnosticism (see Col 2:8-23), and Paul warns Timothy in Ephesus to avoid "what is falsely called knowledge *(gnōsis)*, for by professing it some have swerved from the faith" (1 Tim 6:20-21).

We face several difficulties regarding second-century Christian Gnosticism. One is that we are uncertain about its origins and how it came to be so powerfully influential. It is marked by a radical vertical spatial dualism found also in Platonism and Iranian and Zoroastrian thought that, by the Hellenistic era, was found in Jewish thought, including among the Qumran sectaries. It is unclear, however, how the Egyptian Christian teachers Basilides and Valentinus came to embrace their Gnostic framework.

The other problem is that Basilides and Valentinus come from that early period of Christianity in Egypt about which we have very little knowledge.

Basilides

An Alexandrian, Basilides (active ca. 140) was an influential teacher and a prolific writer. Apart from one brief passage *(Exegetica* 23),[42] Basilides' works are known only in incomplete descriptions in the hostile heresiologists, Irenaeus, Clement of Alexandria, Hippolytus, and Agrippa Castor; no original texts have come to light in the Nag Hammadi cache.

Although his critics are not altogether united in their accounts of Basilides, there is no doubt that he created an elaborate mythology to account for the emergence of the material universe. The "ungendered parent" expanded into a spiritual universe from which emanated a material universe of 365 concentrically enclosed heavens (it was calendrically based). Evil angels, ruled by the creator god of the Jews, created the lowest such heaven, the material world familiar to humans. Humans trapped in the material world seek to escape by bodiless ascent through the 365 levels to their ultimate spiritual home. Reference to 365 suggests daily ascetical

---

42. Found in Clement of Alexandria, *Stromateis* 4.12.81.

practices to purify oneself so as to be absorbed upward into the nonmaterial purity of the divine. Significantly Christ was not truly incarnate and did not suffer and die; Simon of Cyrene died for him.

Basilides' teaching, then, is a mythological restatement of the "heavenly" aspect of NT Christology, which however denies Jesus' "earthly" reality. This idea appears to have been current at the time of 1 John, which declares, "Every spirit which confesses that Jesus Christ has come in the flesh is of God, and every spirit which does not confess Jesus is not of God. This is the spirit of antichrist [that] . . . is in the world already" (1 John 4:2-3).[43] The ideas being rejected here may have influenced Basilides' more fully stated Gnostic theology.

Marcion

According to second-century heresiologists, the one who posed the greatest threat to the true church was Marcion of Sinope.[44] Although often called a Gnostic, Marcion should be regarded more as a radical Paulinist who on that account rejected the Jewish law. Accordingly he rejected the Jewish God as a mere demiurge and not the true God. Marcion came to Rome circa 144, though there is debate whether his idiosyncratic views were formulated there (under Cerdo's influence) or beforehand. In his major work, *Antitheses,* Marcion rejected the God of the OT and limited his recognition of NT writings to those that de-emphasized Christianity's Jewish roots as much as possible. Accordingly, Marcion accepted only an expurgated version of Luke's gospel[45] and of Paul's letters.[46]

43. A number of other NT texts appear to be addressing the challenge of a nonmaterial Christ (e.g., John 1:14; 20:24-29; Luke 24:40-43), mythical accounts of Christ's origin (e.g., 1 Tim 1:4; 6:20), and ascetic practices (e.g., 1 Tim 4:1-5), elements that will be soon more fully (if varyingly) expressed in the Gnostic texts.

44. Marcion's teachings are known only through those who refute him, chiefly Justin Martyr, Irenaeus, Tertullian, and Hippolytus. According to R. L. Fox, *Pagans and Christians* (New York: Knopf, 1989), 516, Marcion's views were sufficiently well known to have been used by Celsus in his attack on Christianity.

45. Marcion omitted from Luke (1) the "Jewish" chapters 1 and 2, (2) the temptation narrative in 4:3 (referring to Deuteronomy), (3) Jesus' claim — while teaching in a synagogue — that his ministry was a fulfillment of the OT (4:16-30), (4) reference to "the old is good" (5:39), and (5) reference to Jesus' family (8:19).

46. Marcion eliminated from Paul's letters (1) Abraham as an example of faith (Gal

Excommunicated from the church in Rome, Marcion established a church of his own, which spread throughout the empire. In effect, he created his own "canon" of acceptable texts (Luke and Paul) as vehicles for his theological beliefs.

Marcion's theological views and his considerable ability in establishing a powerful rival church (based on ascetic principles) imposed great pressure on those who cast him out. His wholesale rejection of the OT forced others to evaluate the place of the OT in the church's life and the relationship with Jesus' "Father" as the creator of the universe. Marcion's definition of texts acceptable to him forced the issue of "canonicity" on the leaders in the next generation.

Valentinus

Besides Marcion, other writers of the era also came under criticism. The evidence for these is found in refutations in Irenaeus, Tertullian, and Hippolytus.[47] The best known was Marcion's contemporary Valentinus, an Egyptian who came to Rome circa 135-160, where he may have aspired to become the bishop. Like Marcion, Valentinus was excommunicated. Again, like Marcion, Valentinus founded his own movement. For this he created literature, notably the *Gospel of Truth* and *The Letter to Rheginos*.[48] It appears that Valentinus moved step-by-step from a position of relative orthodoxy to outright Gnostic heresy.[49]

Irenaeus refers to the *Gospel of Truth*, though it is not clear that he attributes it to Valentinus, though modern authorities tend to do so.[50]

3:6-9), (2) the connection between the law and the gospels (Gal 3:15-25), (3) Rom 1:19-21, 3:21–4:25, and most of Rom 9–11, and everything after Rom 14:23. See further, F. F. Bruce, *The Canon of Scripture* (Glasgow: Chapter House, 1988), 140.

47. Until the discovery of the cache of documents at Nag Hammadi (upper Egypt) in 1945, the Gnostic writings were mainly known through citations in the Church Fathers.

48. See M. L. Peel, *The Epistle to Rheginos* (London: SCM, 1969), who notes the respect of the author (Valentinus?) for the scriptural authority of NT texts including the Gospels of Mark, Matthew, and John, the Acts of the Apostles, most of Paul's letters, 1 and 2 Peter, and 1 and 3 John. His use of such texts (mostly Paul's) is tendentious.

49. It is possible that the teachings attributed to him by Irenaeus were those of disciples of Valentinus's pupil, Ptolemy. See K. Grobel, *The Gospel of Truth* (London: A. & C. Black, 1960), 15-16.

50. Grobel, *The Gospel of Truth*, 26.

Valentinus likely wrote the *Gospel of Truth* between 140 and 170, antedating Irenaeus's *Against Heresies* (written ca. 180) by a period that was "not long" (3.11.9). Irenaeus writes scornfully of the *Gospel of Truth:* "[T]hose who are from Valentinus . . . boast that they possess more gospels than there really are. Indeed, they arrive at such a pitch of audacity, as to entitle their comparatively recent writing 'the Gospel of Truth,' though it agrees in nothing with the gospels of the Apostles. . . . What they have published is . . . totally unlike those that have been handed down to us from the apostles . . . these gospels are alone true and reliable, and admit neither increase or diminution[51] of the aforesaid number."[52] In effect, Marcion and Valentinus created their own gospels, written to articulate their theological understanding over against those from whom they so radically differed. For Marcion the Paulinist and anti-Semite, this meant severely editing an existing gospel, that is, Luke's gospel.

The Fourfold Gospel (ca. 150-180)

The crisis created by Marcion and the Gnostics forced the church leaders to make the fourfold gospel explicit. This likely had more or less been assumed, possibly with a degree of toleration of other texts. The rival churches established by gifted leaders like Marcion and Valentinus forced the issue of canonical definition.

Irenaeus: The Fourfold Gospel

Irenaeus, a native of Roman Asia who later became a missionary in southern Gaul, understood well that he was joined to the apostolic age through his mentor Polycarp, bishop of Smyrna.

> Polycarp . . . was not only instructed by apostles, and conversed with many who had seen Christ, but was also by apostles in Asia appointed bishop in the church in Smyrna, whom I also saw in my early youth.

51. At that time Gaius of Rome and the Alogi were repudiating the Gospel of John (cf. *AH* 3.11.9). As well, no doubt Irenaeus had in mind Marcion's single (expurgated) Gospel Luke.

52. Irenaeus, *AH* 3.11.9.

> [Polycarp] . . . always taught the things he had learned from the apostles, and which the church has handed down and which alone are true. To these things all the Asiatic churches testify, as do those who have succeeded Polycarp . . . a man who was of greater weight, and a man of more steadfast witness of truth than Valentinus and Marcion and the rest of the heretics.[53]

It is important to connect Irenaeus's conviction about the "true" apostolic gospels (as opposed to the false) with his sense of unbroken continuity with the era of the apostles, through the human link Polycarp.[54] Furthermore, note that Irenaeus measures the novelties of Valentinus and Marcion against Polycarp, who had been "instructed by the apostles."[55]

Irenaeus's two chief enemies, then, were Marcion and Valentinus, whose theological errors were expressed in their views about authoritative texts. Marcion articulated his version of Christianity by reducing the extant gospels to *one,* an emasculated Luke. Valentinus stated his revised Christianity in "*more* gospels than there really are," including a gospel he himself wrote that was a radical reinterpretation of the apostolic texts.

In his work *Against Heresies* (written ca. 180) Irenaeus famously insisted against the various Gnostic gospels that there could be only four authentic gospels. "[I]t is not possible that the gospels can be either *more* or *fewer* in number than they are."[56] It scarcely matters that Irenaeus argued by dubious means for the fourfold gospel.[57]

The point is that the Gnostics pointed either to only one gospel (Marcion) or to more than four gospels (Valentinus); for Irenaeus there could be only four authentic gospels, neither more nor fewer.

His order is unusual, symbolized by the creatures in Revelation 4:7 — lion (Mark), ox (Luke), man (Matthew), and eagle (John). This differs from the order he gave elsewhere, namely, Matthew, Mark, Luke, and John.[58] It

---

53. Irenaeus, *AH* 3.3.4.

54. Irenaeus, *AH* 1.3.6.

55. Irenaeus reports that when Polycarp met Marcion, he called him "the first-born of Satan" (*AH* 3.3.4).

56. Irenaeus, *AH* 3.11.6.

57. T. K. Abbott, "Taylor's Witness to the Four Gospels," *Classical Review* 6 (1892): 453-54, argues that Irenaeus's imagery for the one fourfold gospel derived from imagery in *Shepherd of Hermas,* an early-second-century work.

58. Irenaeus, *AH* 3.1.1.

seems likely that Irenaeus's conviction of the fourfold gospel predated this assertion by some years and, moreover, that the four gospels had by that time been collected in one codex since no single *scroll* could accommodate four gospels.[59] It comes as no surprise, then, that Irenaeus quotes from and echoes gospel texts on numerous occasions.

At the same time, Irenaeus speaks of the one gospel as *quadriform:* "For the living creatures are *quadriform,* and the gospel is *quadriform.*"[60]

Accordingly, we may state that Irenaeus held the view that the gospel existed as a single entity, a *kanōn* of four gospels.[61] A mark of Irenaeus's conviction of the "canonical" *fourfold* gospel is his account of their origin. "*Matthew* composed his gospel among the Hebrews in their language, when Peter and Paul were preaching the gospel in Rome and founding the church (there). After their death, *Mark,* the disciple of Peter, handed down to us the preaching of Peter in written form. *Luke,* the companion of Paul, set down the gospel preached by him in a book. Finally, *John* the disciple of the Lord, who also reclined on his breast, himself composed the gospel when he was living in Ephesus (in the province of Asia)."[62]

We may quibble over Irenaeus's account of the origins of the gospels, but his conviction of their delimited *fourfold* character is reinforced by his explanation of their beginnings.

As noted above, it is most likely that Irenaeus's contention that the *one* true gospel is *quadriform* — articulated in four gospels — was not a novelty, but a reassertion of an established view. Consistent with this, it is more likely than not that Irenaeus and those before him had already begun to use the codex in place of individual scrolls.[63] The location of four gospels in one codex along with the claim that the one gospel was found in four gospels was a potent assertion of the authenticity and authority of these texts as apostolic.

---

59. So T. C. Skeat, "Irenaeus and the Four-Gospel Canon," in *The Collected Biblical Writings of T. C. Skeat,* ed. J. K. Elliott (Leiden: Brill, 2004), 77.

60. Irenaeus, *AH* 3.11.8 — *euangelion tetramorphon.*

61. See M. Hengel, *The Four Gospels and the One Gospel of Jesus Christ* (London: SCM, 2000), 10-11.

62. Irenaeus, *AH* 3.1.1.

63. The dating of the emergence of the codex is not certainly known, and remains a subject of debate. Skeat, "The Origin of the Christian Codex," in *The Collected Biblical Writings of T. C. Skeat,* 79-87, conjectures that Christians began using the codex for the gospels as early as A.D. 100. See further L. Hurtado, *The Earliest Christian Artifacts* (Grand Rapids: Eerdmans, 2006), 43-89.

Superscriptions

Irenaeus's assertion of *one* gospel in *four* gospels was also anticipated in the superscriptions of the gospels, an argument neglected in recent scholarship according to M. Hengel,[64] who points out that the superscriptions are always the same: *euangelion kata Maththaion,* or *euangelion kata Markon,* or *euangelion kata Loukan,* or *euangelion kata Iōannēn.* This pattern of uniformity is not due to church synods, which do not appear until later in the second century. One likely explanation deals with the significance of the church in Rome, which even within NT times was emerging as an important center, a trend that intensified in the next century. The special role of Justin Martyr as a teacher in Rome, as well as the convergence of ambitious teachers Marcion and Valentinus on Rome, points in that direction. It is reasonable to argue that the format of the superscriptions *(euangelion kata . . .)* and the use of the one codex for four gospels arose in Rome, and were disseminated from there, influenced by the eminence of the world capital and the importance of its church.

This "one gospel through four gospels" is confirmed by the Muratorian Canon, which originated a decade or so after *Against Heresies.* The opening line of the intact text begins: "The third book of the gospel, according to Luke *(tertium euangelii librum secundum Lucan),*" implying two prior "books." Following the comments about Luke, the Canon continues, "The fourth gospel is by John, one of the disciples." The point to notice is that the gospel is a *single* entity of which there are four "books" or "gospels," each written "according to" a named evangelist. This formula is demonstrated by the earlier papyri and by references in the Church Fathers.

Hengel argues that the form of the superscriptions — the one saving message of Jesus Christ "according to" four writers — implies that (in the mind of the early church) these writings were not biographies of Jesus, but rather *four* expressions of the *one* saving message.[65]

---

64. So Hengel, *Four Gospels,* 48.
65. Hengel, *Four Gospels,* 48-49.

Tatian: One Gospel "through Four"

For Irenaeus the *one gospel that was also four* (neither more nor fewer) was his response to the claims of other (Gnostic) gospels. For Tatian, however, the principle of multiple gospels was not a solution but a problem. Even in those precritical times, many were perplexed over the verbal contradictions between these texts.[66]

A disciple of Justin in Rome, Tatian returned to his native Assyria after his master Justin's martyrdom in 165. His solution to the discrepancies between the gospels was to "unpick" them and then "restitch" them together in chronological order as one entity, which became known as the *Diatessaron (dia tessarōn = "through four").*[67] Tatian used the Gospel of John as the broad framework for his harmonized gospel, into which he inserted Matthew, Mark, and Luke.[68]

The creation of the *Diatessaron* appears strongly to support the idea of the fourfold canonical gospels. Yet doubts have been raised. Some argue that Tatian did not limit the sources for his harmonized gospel to Matthew, Mark, Luke, and John but included other material, including a fifth,

66. So B. M. Metzger, *The Canon of the New Testament: Its Origin, Development, and Significance* (Oxford: Clarendon, 1987), 116. T. Baarda, "ΔΙΑΦΟΝΙΑ — ΣΥΜΦΟΝΙΑ: Factors in the Harmonization of the Gospels, Especially in the Diatessaron of Tatian," in *Gospel Traditions in the Second Century: Origins, Recensions, Text, and Transmission,* ed. W. L. Petersen (Notre Dame, Ind.: University of Notre Dame Press, 1989), 133-49, argues that Tatian, mindful of discrepancies between the gospels, harmonized the four into one to symbolize the unity of Christianity against the disunity of the Greeks.

67. The Syrian church accepted the *Diatessaron* as its authoritative gospel into the fifth and sixth centuries and was reluctant to give up using it as its basic gospel. No copy of the *Diatessaron* has survived, apart from the fragment discovered in Dura-Europos in Syria in 1933. Its text must be reconstructed from a number of other sources. See further B. Metzger, *The Early Versions of the New Testament: Their Origin, Transmission, and Limitations* (Oxford: Clarendon, 1977), 10-25; W. L. Peterson, "Tatian's Diatessaron," in *Ancient Christian Gospels: Their History and Development,* ed. H. Koester (London: SCM; Philadelphia: Trinity, 1990); C. D. Allert, "The State of the New Testament Canon in the Second Century," *BBR* 9 (1999): 1-18; Hengel, *Four Gospels,* 24-26.

68. It is likely that Tatian's teacher, Justin, also used a harmonized gospel, though not based on the Gospel of John (so Hengel, *Four Gospels,* 25). The *Diatessaron* was translated into many languages over the centuries following — from Arabic, Persian, and Armenian, through Latin and Old Italian, to Old High German, Middle Dutch, and Middle English. It was with difficulty that bishops in the centuries following forced the churches to abandon the harmonized gospel in favor of the canonical gospels.

apocryphal gospel.[69] Others contend that it was not Tatian who called his "gospel of the mixed"[70] the *Diatessaron*.[71] If either or both of these contentions were to be upheld, Irenaeus's insistence on the one *quadriform* gospel could be regarded as idiosyncratic and sectional.

As regards the first obstacle, it appears that Tatian may have included small items from the lost *Gospel of the Ebionites* and the *Protevangelium of James*.[72] But these are quite minor additions and in no way support the suggestion that Tatian employed a fifth, apocryphal gospel.[73] It is beyond contention that for all practical purposes Tatian created his harmony from Matthew, Mark, Luke, and John.

Although the second obstacle is of less importance, there are good reasons to attribute the title the *Diatessaron* to its author, Tatian. The earliest to refer to it is Eusebius (260-340): "Tatian *composed* in some way a combination and collection of the gospels, and *gave* this the name of *The Diatessaron*."[74] A fourth-century Syriac translation (in Tatian's language) of Eusebius's text confirms *Diatessaron* as the author's title: "[T]atianus... *collected* and *mixed up* and *composed* a gospel and *called* it Diatessaron."[75] It appears, then, that both obstacles can be removed, and accordingly we are justified in attributing the title *Diatessaron* to Tatian and that it was in effect based on Matthew, Mark, Luke, and John.

Papyrus 45

Dramatic archaeological evidence for the fourfold gospel was discovered in 1931 in a Coptic graveyard in Middle Egypt where eight manuscripts stored in jars were found. Five were manuscripts of various

69. J. H. Charlesworth, "Tatian's Dependence upon Apocryphal Traditions," *HeyJ* 15 (1974): 5-6.

70. As it is called in a fourth-century Syriac version of Eusebius's account.

71. R. P. C. Hanson, *Tradition in the Early Church* (London: SCM, 1962), 230.

72. See Peterson, "Tatian's Diatessaron," 11.

73. According to Metzger, *Early Versions*, 36, "the amount of extra-canonical material that seems to have been present in Tatian's Diatessaron hardly justifies the opinion of some scholars that Tatian used extensive use of a fifth, apocryphal Gospel when he compiled his harmony."

74. Eusebius, *HE* 4.29.6.

75. W. Wright and N. McLean, eds., *The Ecclesiastical History of Eusebius in Syriac* (Cambridge: Cambridge University Press, 1904), 243.

books of the Old Testament, but three were texts of the New Testament, each a codex (early book) rather than a scroll. The first was a codex of the four gospels and the Acts (known as Papyrus 45), the second a codex of Paul's letters (known as Papyrus 46), and the third a codex of Revelation (Papyrus 47).

That $\mathfrak{p}^{45}$ was a collection of texts in a codex or "book" indicates that they had been used in church gatherings for public reading. The codex was easier to store than a scroll, and was also cheaper, since the leaves (pages) could be written on both sides. All surviving papyri of texts of the New Testament were written in codex format.

$\mathfrak{p}^{45}$ is significant because it is the earliest collection of all four gospels and is dated to the first part of the third century.

Conclusion: The Fourfold Gospel

Irenaeus and Tatian faced different problems, that is, respectively, the *number* of authentic gospels and *discrepancies* between the four true gospels. Outwardly, their responses were different. Yet Irenaeus *(euangelion tetramorphon)* and Tatian *(dia tessarōn)* both sought to defend the common conviction that Matthew, Mark, Luke, and John were the only authentic apostolic gospels.

Scriptures for the Churches

Our argument so far has been that the christological trajectory of the NT era (undeniable for Paul) can be shown to have continued in the decades following him. Furthermore, that the alternatives to this doctrine demonstrably qualified that trajectory (Marcion, by eliminating the OT) or subverted it (Basilides and Valentinus, by redefining the Creator). In short, it must be regarded as historically secure that the four gospels from the apostolic era were the benchmark from which various writers in the second century chose to depart. There is no case for granting the Gnostic gospels any significant status as sources of historical inquiry into the historical Christ. Their historical interest resides solely as commentary on the emergence of deviant forms of Christianity in the second century.

We turn now to more direct discussion of the gospel texts.

Gospel Manuscripts

Following are fragments of papyri from the second century that attest the canonical gospels.[76] They were all originally in codex form (written on the front and the back of leaves) and were all discovered in Egypt (where there is minimal humidity).

Papyrus	Other Name	Date	Content
$\mathfrak{p}^{52}$	Gr. P457	early 2nd cent.	a few verses of John 18
$\mathfrak{p}^{67}$	P.Barcelona 1	ca. 125-150	a few verses from Matt 3 and 5
$\mathfrak{p}^{64}$	P.Magdalene 17	ca. 125-150	a few verses from Matt 26
$\mathfrak{p}^{4}$	P.Paris 1120	ca. 125-150	portions of Luke 1, 2, 3, 4
$\mathfrak{p}^{75}$	Bodmer P. XIV/XV	ca. 175	portions of Luke 3, 4, 5, 6, 7, 9, 17, 22; much of John
$\mathfrak{p}^{77}$	P.Oxy. 2683	ca. 175-200	a few verses of Matt 23
$\mathfrak{p}^{103}$	P.Oxy. 4403	ca. 175-200	a few verses from Matt 13 and 14
$\mathfrak{p}^{104}$	P.Oxy. 4404	ca. 175-200	a few verses from Matt 21
$\mathfrak{p}^{90}$	P.Oxy. 3523	ca. 175-200	a portion of John 18-19
$\mathfrak{p}^{1}$		ca. 200	portions of Matt 1
$\mathfrak{p}^{66}$	Bodmer P. II	ca. 200	most of John
$\mathfrak{p}^{45}$	Chester Beatty P. I	early 3rd cent.	portions of all four gospels and Acts
$\mathfrak{p}^{95}$	PL II/31	3rd cent.	a few verses from John 5

Comments:

1. The chance survival of fragile papyri in the sands of Egypt is evidence that John, Matthew, and Luke were in circulation and use by the beginning of the second century and that all four canonical gospels were in circulation and use by the end of the second century.[77]

76. See P. W. Comfort, *The Quest for the Original Texts of the New Testament* (Grand Rapids: Baker, 1992), 31-32.

77. In defense of the distributed provenance of these texts being more widely represented than Egypt, see Comfort, *Original Texts*, 37.

These fragments were originally part of codices that were read in church meetings at the end of the apostolic age.

2. While most surviving fragments of John come from the late second century, the discovery of p^{52} dating from the beginning of the second century establishes a first-century origin of this gospel. Furthermore, the extensive parts of this gospel in p^{90}, p^{75}, p^{66}, and p^{45} support the widespread early use of this gospel.

3. Conspicuously absent is any surviving fragment of the Gospel of Mark. Yet Matthew's and Luke's reproduction of Mark in their gospels, as agreed by most scholars, establishes the prior existence of Mark.

4. The extensive use of Matthew, Luke, and John in the Bodmer texts (p^{75}, p^{66}) plausibly anticipates p^{45}, where (fragments of) the four gospels are found.

References to "Gospels"

If it is dated circa 100, the *Didache* contains the earliest references to "the gospel" as a literary genre. Of these references, three also echo texts in the Gospel of Matthew (*Did* 8.2; 15.3, 4); the other is uncertain (11.3).

The next extant reference to "gospel" is by Justin Martyr (ca. 150). Justin refers to "the memoirs composed by the [apostles], which are called gospels," which were read in church meetings and which Justin gives as the basis of the Eucharist.[78] Furthermore, Justin frequently echoes texts from each of the four gospels, for example, Matthew 1:22 (*First Apology* 33), Mark 2:17 (*Dialogue with Trypho* 8), Luke 1:32 (*First Apology* 33), and John 3:5 (*First Apology* 61). We reasonably assume, therefore, that by "gospels" Justin has in mind these and many other texts that he quotes or echoes.

Precise References to Gospel Authors

Papias, bishop of Hierapolis, writing in the first decades of the second century, explains the origins of two gospels (without using that word).[79] He

---

78. Justin, *First Apology* 66-67.
79. Reported in Eusebius, *HE* 3.39.3-16.

says Mark wrote his work based on Peter's "instruction," and in an implicit reference to Luke 1:1-3 affirms that "Mark" wrote "accurately." Papias also states that "Matthew compiled his oracles in the Hebrew language." Furthermore, by giving the name of six disciples in the order they appear in the Gospel of John, Papias appears to know that gospel also.[80] We conclude that Papias referred directly to the origins of the Gospels of Mark and Matthew and indirectly to the Gospels of Luke and John. Based on Papias's information, it is reasonable to assert that these gospels were in circulation and use by the end of the first century at the latest.

Echoes in Valentinus's Gospel of Truth

Valentinus's *Gospel of Truth* has no narrative but is a meditation in which he freely adapts passages from the NT books, in particular John's gospel and letters and Paul's letters. G. Quispel called the *Gospel of Truth* "the Charter of ancient Gnosticism."[81]

Gospel of Truth	New Testament Gospels
	Matthew
31.35	18:12-14
32.19-21	12:11
33.5	11:28
33.25	7:16
36.15	7:7
	Mark
20.10	10:45
33.5	5:39
	Luke
32.1	15:2-6
33.15	12:33
33.24	12:58
33.34	6:35

80. See R. Bauckham, *Jesus and the Eyewitnesses: The Gospels as Eyewitness Testimony* (Grand Rapids: Eerdmans, 2006), 417-20.

81. G. Quispel, "The Original Doctrine of Valentinus the Gnostic," *VC* 50 (1996): 331.

	John
18.15	14:6
19.35	10:14; 13:31
20.29	10:17f.
22.10	7:17
26.5	1:14
30.19	9:39-41
30.25	20:22; 6:38-40; 1:2
31.15	17:14
42.29	17:21f.

This survey[82] of Valentinus's texts is informative. True, any conclusions must be made with caution since his use of texts is allusive rather than precise, and moreover, it is based on a translation from a Coptic original that is corrupt and at some points emended by an ancient editor. Nonetheless, it is clear that Valentinus depended on all four gospels (as well as on many of Paul's letters, Hebrews, and Revelation). Although Irenaeus and others regard him with disdain, his meditation touching numerous NT texts is its own testimony to their currency in the first part of the second century.

Echoes in the Apostolic Fathers

As noted earlier, the *Didache* (late first century) echoes Matthew and Luke, and Clement (ca. 96) and Ignatius (ca. 110) echo (freely) texts from Matthew, Mark, Luke, and John. These texts were written in the last years of the first century and the early years of the second century. Because their echoes of NT texts are often free paraphrases, there may be some debate about specific texts. Yet overall we conclude that the apostolic fathers witness to the fact that the four gospels were in circulation by the end of the first century.

Scriptures for the Churches: Conclusion

The survival of codices of fragments of gospels, whole sections of gospels, and the fourfold gospel, together with references to "gospels," named gos-

---

82. Based on text notes in Grobel, *The Gospel of Truth*.

pel writers, and echoes of gospel texts in a continuity of writers from Clement to Justin, including the Gnostic Valentinus, is strong evidence of the currency of the four gospels in the first half of the century following the apostolic era. From the second part of that century, as already noted, Irenaeus's and Tatian's respective approaches to the fourfold gospel, together with the superscriptions and the discovery of the $\mathfrak{P}^{45}$ codex, serve emphatically to confirm this understanding. In short, the four canonical gospels were in circulation and use by the end of the first century. But are they the only contenders for this status? What of the other "gospels" mentioned earlier?

Other Gospels

We divide these into two classes. First, the Church Fathers allude to gospels for which we have little or no direct evidence, to wit: the *Gospel of the Ebionites* (Irenaeus, *AH* 1.26.2; 3.21.1), the *Gospel of the Nazoreans* (Eusebius, *HE* 4.22.8), the *Gospel of the Hebrews* (Clement, *Miscellanies* 2.9.45). In the absence of passages from these texts, we can do little more than speculate on their origin or character. These works appear to have been compiled for Jewish Christians who remained outside the Great Church (known as Ebionites and Nazoreans), and who likely continued Jewish practices (circumcision, Sabbath observance, the calendar).[83] There are hints in the Church Fathers that these gospels are adaptations of Matthew (as the most "Jewish" of the gospels).

The second category consists of surviving papyri texts like Valentinus's *Gospel of Truth*, an *"Unknown Gospel,"* the *Gospel of Peter*, and the *Gospel of Thomas*.

We are able quickly to eliminate Valentinus's *Gospel of Truth* from our considerations. As noted above, it is not a gospel since there is no narrative whatsoever. Furthermore, it is obviously derived from a pastiche of texts from the NT.

The *"Unknown Gospel"* (P.Egerton 2) is an important text since it is confidently dated to the middle of the second century.[84] It consists of sev-

---

83. See J. E. Taylor, "The Phenomenon of Early Jewish-Christianity: Reality or Scholarly Invention?" *VC* 44 (1990): 313-34.

84. H. I. Bell and T. C. Skeat, *Fragments of an Unknown Gospel and Other Early Christian Papyri* (London: British Museum, 1935).

eral short fragments of broken text. It is cast in narrative form, and can thus be called a "gospel." It has connections with the canonical gospels (including John's), and perhaps with the *Infancy Gospel of Thomas*. It is free of any explicitly heretical doctrine and lacks the exaggerations found in many second-century works (*Gospel of Peter,* for example). The major issue, of course, is whether it is a source of or a redaction of the canonical gospels.[85] The careful observation of E. C. Colwell should be noted: "The new evangelist had read the fourfold gospel more than once and uses it as a source for his own work."[86] The fragmentary remains of this work most likely attest an early attempt at creating a gospel harmony, anticipating the efforts of Justin Martyr, who created expanses of harmonized texts drawn from the canonical gospels. These, in turn, anticipated Justin's pupil Tatian's full-scale harmony, the *Diatessaron* (see later).[87]

The *Gospel of Peter* is a second-century work that is identifiably in narrative format, chiefly related to the passion and resurrection of Christ. Although some have argued that (an earlier version of) the *Gospel of Peter* was a source of the synoptic gospels,[88] the reverse is more likely.[89] Against those who identify Docetic or Gnostic elements (which are ambiguous) as reason to assign a second-century date, it is better to reach this conclusion on other grounds. Chief among these are the similarities to second-century martyrologies, the blurring of lines relating to the "Lord's" death/ascension, the great height of the resurrected Jesus, and the hagiographic character of the miracles. P. Head concludes, "The cumulative evidence for a second century date is strong and adds to the impression that the *Gospel of Peter* is a redaction of the canonical material (perhaps also influenced by oral traditions)."[90]

---

85. Bell and Skeat, *Unknown Gospel,* 26-29, believe this text may be a source for the Gospel of John. See also Koester, "Apocryphal and Canonical Gospels," who is more emphatic that it "preserves features which derive from a stage of the tradition that is older than the canonical Gospels" (120). For a contrary view see C. A. Evans, *Fabricating Jesus* (Downers Grove, Ill.: IVP, 2007), 85-92.

86. E. C. Colwell, review of *Fragments of an Unknown Gospel and Other Early Christian Papyri,* by H. I. Bell and T. C. Skeat, *JR* 16, no. 4 (1936): 478-80.

87. See further, Evans, *Fabricating Jesus,* 89.

88. So P. A. Mirecki, "Peter, Gospel of," in *ABD* 5:278-81, following Crossan and Koester.

89. P. M. Head, "On the Christology of the Gospel of Peter," *VC* 46, no. 3 (1992): 209-24.

90. Head, "Gospel of Peter," 218.

The *Gospel of Thomas* does not belong to the gospel genre since it is not a narrative but rather a series of sayings of Jesus. It is a fourth-century Coptic text that appears to have been translated from a second-century Greek version (a view supported by Greek papyri fragments P.Oxy. 654, I, 655). The *Gospel of Thomas* is not a straight translation, since in the intervening century the Coptic version seems to have assimilated to the Coptic version of the NT. Consequently we cannot confidently retrovert the Coptic version back to a second-century Greek original. In effect, we are left with the fourth-century version.

Many of the sayings bear close similarity to sayings of Jesus in the synoptic gospels. So the burning question is: Did *Thomas* depend on the gospels or was it written independently of them? The issue is complex and the scholars are divided. One complication (of many) is that *Thomas* may have borrowed from a now-lost gospel (e.g., *Gospel of the Hebrews*).

The main argument for its independence is that its order differs from that of the canonical gospels. If it is dependent, so the argument runs, why does it change the synoptics' order? Against this, however, it is pointed out that the order of the earlier Greek fragments is different from the Coptic version. Furthermore, the sequence of the Coptic *Gospel of Thomas* appears to follow an idiosyncratic structure as dictated by link words. The argument based on sequence is inconclusive.

For the dependency argument, C. Tuckett[91] has pointed to a number of passages where the *Gospel of Thomas* appears to depend on finished (i.e., redacted) versions of the synoptics, for example, 5 ("there is nothing hidden that will not be manifest . . ."), 9 (parable of the sower), 16 ("[I] have to throw divisions upon the earth . . ."), 20 (parable of the mustard seed), 55 ("Whoever does not hate father and mother . . ."). While Tuckett resists the temptation "to deduce . . . that *Gos.Thom.* is dependent on the synoptics *in toto*," he finds that the texts he has reviewed point in that direction.

A second consideration (noted by Tuckett) is that the parable of the sower in *Thomas* is a "gnosticising redaction of the synoptic parable." In other words, at this point at least *Thomas* reflects a Gnostic origin in the second century or later. Related to this, J. H. Wood has found *Thomas* to have many points of contact with other second-century texts that reveal

91. C. Tuckett, "Thomas and the Synoptics," *NovT* 30, no. 7 (1988): 132-57; Tuckett, "Synoptic Traditions in Some Nag Hammadi and Related Texts," *VC* 36 (1982): 173-90.

dependence on the canonical gospels.[92] Indeed, Wood argues for the reliance of the *Gospel of Thomas* on all four gospels, and therefore holds it to be an early witness to the fourfold gospel.

Parallels between Gospels of Matthew, Luke, and John, and the *Gospel of Thomas*

Matthew	*Thomas*	Luke	*Thomas*	John	*Thomas*
5:10	69a	11:27-28	79	1:9	24
5:14	32	12:13-14	72	1:14	28
6:2-4	6, 14	12:16-21	63	4:13-15	13
6:3	62	12:49	10	7:32-36	38
7:6	93	17:20-21	3	8:12; 9:5	77
10:16	39				
11:30	90				
13:24-30	57				
13:44	109				
13:45-46	76				
13:47-50	8				
15:13	40				
18:20	30				
23:13	39, 102				

Who is depending on whom, the above three gospels on *Thomas* or *Thomas* on the above three? For two reasons at least we conclude that *Thomas* is depending on Matthew, Luke, and John. The first is that *Thomas* does not follow the sequence of Matthew, Luke, or John (which more or less follow the same sequence) but has diverged dramatically from each. It is more likely that *Thomas* has selected sayings of Jesus from the above three according to a predetermined sequence than that the three each "scrambled" *Thomas*'s sequence. The second reason is *Thomas*'s identifiable tendency to infuse second-century Gnostic "color" into the non-Gnostic words of Jesus in Matthew, Luke, and John. Most likely the *Gospel of Thomas* is a later work based on selected parts of three extant gospels.

While some have hoped that the *Gospel of Thomas* would prove to predate the gospels and to reveal new information about Jesus, the evi-

92. J. H. Wood, "The New Testament Gospels and the Gospel of Thomas: A New Direction," *NTS* 52 (2005): 579-95.

dence points rather to the significance of this text as a window into second-century Gnostic Christianity. In any case, it is a late Coptic text whose connections with its second-century Greek antecedent remain problematic.

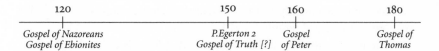

120		150	160		180
Gospel of Nazoreans		*P.Egerton 2*	*Gospel*		*Gospel of*
Gospel of Ebionites		*Gospel of Truth [?]*	*of Peter*		*Thomas*

In short, the extant gospels accessible to us — the *Gospel of the Nazoreans* and the *Gospel of the Ebionites,* the *Gospel of Truth,* the *Gospel of Peter,* the *"Unknown Gospel"* (P.Egerton 2), and the *Gospel of Thomas* — all prove to be of second-century origin. In each case their similarities with canonical gospels are best explained by their dependency on them. Whereas the *Gospel of the Nazoreans,* the *Gospel of the Ebionites,* and the *"Unknown Gospel"* generally reproduce Matthew with a markedly Jewish interest, the *Gospel of Peter* appears to be a Gnosticized version of Mark. The *Gospel of Truth* and the *Gospel of Thomas* are not cast as narratives and should not be called "gospels."[93] We are able to eliminate each of these as primary sources of information for the works of the historical Christ. It is possible that some genuine words of Jesus have survived in the *Gospel of Thomas,* though with Gnostic overtones.

Horizon One Hundred: The Canonical Gospels

We conclude that the four gospels belong to the first century and that they are the only "gospels" that qualify for this early dating. The implications of this are considerable, chiefly that the four gospels were in use in the churches within six decades of Jesus.

One of the curiosities about "historical Jesus" studies is their tendency not to notice the chronological closeness of the available sources to Jesus, the subject of their inquiry.[94]

---

93. For a generally negative assessment of the value of the apocryphal gospels, see J. H. Charlesworth and C. A. Evans, "Jesus in the Agrapha and Apocryphal Gospels," in *Studying the Historical Jesus: Evaluations of the State of Current Research,* ed. B. Chilton and C. A. Evans (Leiden: Brill, 1994), 479-533.

94. One exception is N. T. Wright, *The New Testament and the People of God* (London:

It is instructive, for example, to compare the sources for Jesus and the emperor Tiberius under whose imperium the Nazarene was executed. Both men died within a few years of each other, Jesus in 33 and Tiberius in 37. For Jesus the available sources (the twenty-seven texts of the New Testament) are both numerous and chronologically close to him, whereas for Tiberius the main literary sources (Tacitus, Suetonius, and Dio) are relatively fewer and considerably later.[95]

The main reason for the difference is that Jesus became the object of a continuing and growing movement (cult) that preserved the key texts by using them. Tacitus comments that, notwithstanding the death of "the founder of the name [Christian]," the "pernicious superstition *(superstitio)*[96] . . . broke *out once more,* not only in Judaea . . . but in the capital itself."[97] Within three decades of the execution of the "founder," the movement had not only survived but had also become numerically "vast" in Rome.

This movement, like Judaism from which it was an outgrowth, was *text* dependent. The gatherings of the movement were characterized by members *reading* texts to one another.[98] Within twenty years of Jesus' life span, the first texts (Paul's letters to his mission groups) had begun appearing. Within forty years a kerygmatic biography (Mark's) for church reading (Mark 13:14) had appeared, which was soon followed by two others (Matthew's and Luke's) based on the earlier version. The literary sources for Tiberius were written due to Roman concern to document their past, whereas the sources for Jesus, the gospels, were written to provide texts for *current* church-based instruction and worship, based on the conviction that he was a living contemporary ("Lord"). This, above all, accounts for the frequency and earliness of the texts about Jesus.

SPCK, 1992), who attempted to establish "fixed points . . . landmarks in the reconstruction of the first century or so of the Christian church" (370).

95. Tacitus, *Annals of Imperial Rome* (books 1-4), written after 115; Suetonius, *Lives of the Caesars,* written after 120; Dio Cassius's Roman history was written circa 210. Velleius Paterculus was a contemporary of Tiberius, but his *Historiae Romanae* is fragmentary in character and overly adulatory of Tiberius.

96. *Superstitio* does not mean "superstition" in the modern sense. Rather, Roman writers used it to portray a foreign cult whose core beliefs were inimical to the Roman state. See L. F. Janssen, "'Superstitio' and the Persecution of the Christians," *VC* 33 (1979): 131-59.

97. Tacitus, *Annals* 15.44.

98. See, e.g., Mark 13:14; 2 Cor 1:13; Eph 3:4; Col 4:16; 1 Thess 5:27; Rev 1:3.

Historians of Christian origins, however, seldom take the interest that might be expected in the chronological proximity of the sources to their subject. It is not sufficiently noted, as it should be, that the fourfold gospel witness to Christ was in circulation within one generation, following the first generation after Jesus. In terms of the documentation of key figures in antiquity, this is a phenomenon almost without parallel. The letters of Paul and perhaps James's letter are earlier still and begin to appear within a decade and a half of the first Easter.

Equally noteworthy is the literary ingenuity reflected in this gospel literature. Most scholars agree that the gospels, while resembling biographies of the period, are nonetheless innovative, in effect pioneering a new genre. Recent scholarship has commented on significant levels of literary sophistication evident within these texts (their engagement with the implied readers, for example).[99] Yet the literary development in the three synoptic texts occurred from first to last over a period as brief as twenty years. This is not as often noticed by students of Christian origins as it deserves to be. Scholars sometimes give the impression that gospel texts developed over several generations, rather than within just one.

99. For the Gospel of Mark see, e.g., P. G. Bolt, "Mark's Gospel," in *The Face of New Testament Studies,* ed. S. McKnight and G. R. Osborne (Grand Rapids: Baker Academic, 2004), 396-405; for the Gospel of Matthew, e.g., D. Senior, *The Gospel of Matthew* (Nashville: Abingdon, 1997); D. C. Allison, *Studies in Matthew* (Grand Rapids: Baker Academic, 2005), 135-55.

THREE

Horizon One Hundred:
The Hostile Sources

They maintained that their guilt or error had amounted only to this: they had been in the habit of meeting on an appointed day before daybreak and singing a hymn antiphonally to Christ as if a god.

Pliny[1]

The three earliest non-Christian sources for Christianity are Josephus, Pliny, and Tacitus. All three write within a few years of one another, just before the end of the first century (Josephus) or near the beginning of the second century (Pliny, Tacitus). Significantly, each is hostile to Christians.

Our concern here is chronological. We want to know what Christianity looked like within a lifetime of the lifetime of Jesus, that is, before the end of the first century. The church sources from the second century establish that the four gospels were in use by the end of the first century. That is to say, they were sufficiently close in time to Jesus of Nazareth to be credible historically.

The three major non-Christian sources are valuable from another perspective. They tell us from an equally early vantage point how Christianity began (Josephus), how it spread from Judea to Rome (Tacitus), and what Christians believed and did (Pliny). Significantly, while each is stridently antipathetic to Christians, each version confirms the raw facts found in the Christian accounts.

1. Pliny, *Epistle* 10.96.

46

Josephus

Josephus (ca. 37-100) was an aristocratic Jew from Jerusalem who for a period had belonged to the sect of the Pharisees. When the Romans invaded Israel in 66, Josephus was appointed military leader to defend Galilee. There he was captured and went over to the Roman side. After the war Josephus lived in Rome, receiving a pension from successive Flavian emperors (Vespasian, Titus, Domitian), hence his cognomen Flavius.

Through relevant sections of his four works *(Jewish War, Jewish Antiquities, Life,* and *Against Apion)* Josephus is our most extensive source for the history of Israel in the first century. Josephus provides important information about the key figures Luke places at John the Baptist's beginnings — Herod the tetrarch of Galilee, Pilate prefect of Judea, and the high priests Annas and Caiaphas (Luke 3:1-2).

Five passages in Josephus (two direct, three indirect) throw light on Christ and Christian origins. The first is his account of the death of John the Baptist. Although it does not mention Jesus, it nonetheless provides important indirect evidence about his movements in Galilee evading capture by the tetrarch Herod Antipas.

> But to some of the Jews the destruction of Herod's army seemed to be divine vengeance . . . for his treatment of John, surnamed the Baptist *(Iōannou tou epikaloumenou baptistou).* For Herod had put him to death, though he was a good man and had exhorted the Jews to lead righteous lives, to practice justice towards their fellows and piety towards God, and in so doing to join in baptism. . . . When others too joined the crowd around him, because they were alarmed to the highest degree by his sermons, Herod became alarmed. Eloquence that had so great an effect on mankind might lead to some form of sedition, for it looked as if they would be guided by John in everything that they did. Herod therefore decided that it would be much better to strike first and be rid of him before his work led to an uprising, than to wait for an upheaval, get involved in a difficult situation and see his mistake. . . . John, because of Herod's suspicions, was brought in chains to Machaerus . . . and there put to death. (*Ant* 18.116-119 LCL)

Josephus's source is evidently not from the NT since his emphasis and details are quite different. He does not mention that John was baptizing in the Jordan, that Machaerus was the place of his imprisonment and death, that John was "forerunner" to the Messiah as prophesied, or that Herod's adultery was the occasion for John's imprisonment and death. But there is no necessary contradiction between these sources. The Jordan is the most likely place for his baptisms; remote Machaerus was a suitable place for John's dungeon; and Josephus's description of John as "a good man" who "exhorted" and who preached sermons is consistent with the gospels' description of John as a prophet (e.g., Matt 11:9). Josephus knows of Herod's adultery, explaining this as the reason his Nabatean wife fled back to her father, Aretas IV, king of Arabia.[2] The gospels' portrayal of John as the messianic "forerunner" is likely historical, being broad-based, found in the synoptic sources (Q, M, and L) as well as in the underived gospels of Mark and John.

Josephus's information is important because it confirms that John was baptizing in Herod's jurisdiction (Perea — so John 10:40), and his disclosure about Herod's sense of insecurity about his incumbency as tetrarch due to John's popularity with the masses is historically credible. This helps explain Jesus' apparent wariness of the tetrarch of Galilee, based as he was in nearby Tiberias (Luke 13:31-32). It makes sense of the menacing attitude of the Herodians toward yet another charismatic figure (Mark 3:6), and it explains Jesus' reticence to appear in public within Herod's jurisdiction after the feeding of the multitude where (in John's account) the men attempted to make Jesus king (John 6:14-15; Mark 9:30). In short, Josephus's report about Herod's attitude toward John establishes a background that makes good sense of Jesus staying out of reach of his menacing power, in particular following the feeding of the multitude.

The second passage is the famous and controversial *Testimonium Flavianum*. While minorities of scholars take the extreme positions that it is totally authentic or entirely spurious, a majority hold that it is a genuine text that has been compromised by Christian interpolations.[3] Since Eusebius (writing in the early third century) quotes the text exactly[4] but Origen, writing in the middle of that century, declares that Josephus did

2. *Ant* 18.103-113.

3. For a comprehensive review of opinion, see C. A. Evans, "Jesus in Non-Christian Sources," in *Studying the Historical Jesus: Evaluations of the State of Current Research*, ed. B. Chilton and C. A. Evans (Leiden: Brill, 1994), 466-67.

4. Eusebius, *HE* 1.11.7f.; *Demonstrations* 3.5.105.

not believe Jesus was the Christ,[5] we must conclude that the insertions occurred sometime between Josephus and Origen.

> About this time there lived Jesus, a wise man [if indeed one ought to call him a man]. For he was one who wrought surprising feats and was a teacher *(didaskalos)* of such people who accept the truth gladly. He won over many Jews and many of the Greeks. [He was the Messiah *(Christos)*.] When Pilate, upon hearing him accused by men of the highest standing amongst us, had condemned him to be crucified, those who had in the first place come to love him did not give up their affection for him. [On the third day he appeared to them restored to life, for the prophets of God had prophesied these and countless other marvellous things about him.] And the tribe of Christians, so called after him, has still to this day not disappeared. *(Ant* 18.63-64 LCL)

The authenticity of words in square brackets is doubtful.[6] It is unlikely that Josephus a Jew would write "if indeed one ought to call him a man" since this calculated aside could be made only by a Christian. Likewise dubious is the assertion "on the third day he appeared to them restored to life" in fulfillment of the prophets, since this is an adaptation of 1 Corinthians 15:4. Again, Josephus is not likely to confess that Jesus "was the Christ" since (as we shall see) later in the *Antiquities* he refers to him as the "so-called Christ." These words or something like them likely appeared in the *Testimonium,* since Josephus goes on to speak of "the tribe of Christians, *so called after him.*"

Thus Josephus's original may have looked like this:

> About this time there lived Jesus, a wise man. For he was one who wrought surprising feats and was a teacher of such people who accept the truth gladly. He won over many Jews and many of the Greeks. He was the so-called Christ. When Pilate, upon hearing him accused by men of the highest standing amongst us, had condemned him to be crucified, those who had in the first place come to love him did not give up their affection for him. And the tribe of Christians, so called after him, has still to this day not disappeared.[7]

---

5. Origen, *Against Celsus* 1.47; *Commentary on Matthew* 10.17.

6. For extensive discussion see J. P. Meier, *A Marginal Jew: Rethinking the Historical Jesus* (New York: Doubleday, 1992), 56-69.

7. Support for this reconstruction has been found in the medieval Arabic work by Agapius, *Book of the Title,* which does not have "if indeed one could call him a man" nor "he

This translation, however, may be misleading since Josephus appears to take a neutral attitude to Jesus.[8] Attention has been drawn to the verb "won over" *(epēgageto),* which in its middle verb form is usually negative in Josephus's works and means "bring something upon someone, mostly something bad."[9] That is to say, Josephus's verdict on Jesus is actually negative, a point confirmed by his location of the *Testimonium* following an uprising under Pilate and prior to "another outrage" (by the priests of Isis in Rome).

According to Josephus, then, Jesus was a teacher and a wonder-worker who deceived the gullible, including the Greeks (= Gentiles). At the same time, however, Josephus does not damn Jesus in the way he does the charlatans and impostors who led the people into a series of disastrous conflicts with the Romans.[10] No loss of life occurred for those who followed Jesus, the "wise man."

Where then does the significance of the *Testimonium* lie? It is in Josephus's "men of the highest standing amongst us" *(prōtoi andrōn par' hēmin),* which cross-checking establishes as his way of referring to ruling priests and temple hierarchy.[11] Pilate, upon "hearing" from these "first men" the "accusation" against Jesus, "condemned him to be crucified." In other words, Josephus's words confirm the gospels' account of the step-by-step process that led to the crucifixion of Jesus. Jewish leaders accused him to Pilate, who tried him, found him guilty, and crucified him.

This, too, is consistent with the imperium enjoyed by the prefect who alone held the authority to execute a provincial *(ius gladii),*[12] as reported by

---

was the Christ." That version, however, does have "he appeared to them three days after his crucifixion . . . alive." See further S. Pines, *An Arabic Version of the Testimonium Flavianum and Its Implications* (Jerusalem: Israel Academy of Sciences and Humanities, 1971). Alice Whealey, "The Testimonium Flavianum in Syriac and Arabic," *NTS* 54 (2008): 573-90, argues that apart from the *textus receptus Testimonium* assertion "he was the Christ," the other problematic statements about Christ are likely authentically Josephan (588).

8. For argument supporting Josephus's neutral attitude to Jesus in the emended *Testimonium,* see R. E. Van Voorst, *Jesus Outside the New Testament* (Grand Rapids: Eerdmans, 2000), 95-101.

9. So Evans, "Jesus in Non-Christian Sources," 470-71.

10. *Ant* 20.97-99, 167-168 (*War* 2.259); *Ant* 20.168-172 (*War* 2.261-263; Acts 21:28); *Ant* 20.188; *War* 6.285-286.

11. Evans, "Jesus in Non-Christian Sources," 472-73.

12. The first governor sent to rule Judea had "full authority" *(tē epi pasin exousia —* *Ant* 18.2; *War* 2.118).

the Gospel of John (18:31). The Romans, however, did not impose capital punishment on merely religious grounds, for example, that Jesus was a "wise man . . . who wrought surprising feats and was a teacher." There must have been something "political" about Jesus that secured his capital punishment by crucifixion. The Romans had no reason to execute a *didaskalos*/rabbi who reputedly performed miracles. That "something" most likely was his claim or the claim of others that he was "the Christ." This is the reason Josephus calls him "the so-called Christ," and it explains why his followers are called *Christianoi* "after him." In short, Josephus corroborates the gospels' account that the temple authorities in Jerusalem handed over Jesus to Prefect Pilate on the treasonable charge that he was a self-appointed Christ, "a king of the Jews," and it was for this claim that he was crucified.

How did Josephus (in the emended text) know about Jesus? The key term "wise man" *(sophos anēr)* and the portrayal of him as one "who wrought surprising feats" *(paradoxōn ergōn)* find no parallel in the NT and most likely reflect Josephus's own understanding of Jesus that was current in Palestine before he left for Rome in the early 70s. As a young adult in the years before the war in 66, Josephus had ample opportunity to observe the sequence of prophets and insurgents he later blamed for the devastating defeat by the Romans. This would explain his only moderate negativity toward this "wise man" Jesus, whose influence was unfortunate but not lethal. Writing from Rome two decades later, he observes with mild surprise that "the tribe of Christians" who took their name from a "so-called Christ" has "still to this day not disappeared" (as it should have).

The third passage narrates events thirty years after the execution of "wise man" Jesus and makes brief reference to his brother James. It comes in the closing stages of Josephus's great work *Antiquities of the Jews,* which ends just before the outbreak of the war in 66. Governor Festus died in office in 62, and before the new procurator Albinus arrived the incumbent high priest Annas II seized the opportunity to remove James and "certain others."

> Ananus (Annas) thought he had a favourable opportunity because Festus was dead and Albinus was still on his way. So he convened the judges of the Sanhedrin and brought before them a man named James, the brother of Jesus who was called Christ, and certain others. He accused them of having transgressed the law and delivered them up to be stoned. Those of the inhabitants of the city who were considered the most fair-minded and who were strict in observance of the law were

offended at this. They therefore secretly sent to king Agrippa urging him, for Ananus had not even been correct in his first step. . . . King Agrippa, because of Ananus' actions, deposed him from the high priesthood. (*Ant* 20.200-201, 203 LCL)

Unlike the *Testimonium*, the authenticity of this passage is not in doubt and does not require emending. It does, however, pose some questions. Why did Ananus (who had been only recently appointed) illegally convene the Sanhedrin (in the absence of a procurator) to remove James and his companions? Who were the "strict" observers of the law who felt that James was not guilty of transgressing the law, whose appeal to Agrippa led to the dismissal of the high priest?

Ananus was son of former high priest Ananus (spelled Annas in the NT), whose son-in-law Caiaphas accused Jesus to Prefect Pilate. Annas I was patriarch of a high priestly dynasty; four of the brothers of Annas II had been high priests in earlier times. It is no exaggeration to say that Annas I, his son-in-law Caiaphas, and his five sons dominated the political life of Jerusalem from the time of Annas's appointment in A.D. 6/7. For the preceding twenty years James had been the leader of the church in Jerusalem, which by the late 50s had grown in number to "many thousands" (Acts 21:20). Even allowing for some hyperbole, the author of Luke-Acts, who was present at the time, means for us to understand that James presided over a very large community.

The most likely reason Annas II illegally and hastily eliminated James (and others) is that although they had removed Jesus, his movement had not died but had grown to become in some sense a rival. Furthermore, a mark of James's prominence is that by about 49 he presided over a meeting in Jerusalem that issued a decree to Gentile churches in Antioch and Syria-Cilicia (Acts 15:23-29) and sent instructions specifically to Jewish believers in Antioch (Gal 2:11-14). It appears that James was easily viewed as in some ways a parallel high priest, and a competitor for the hearts and minds of the people of Jerusalem. Accordingly, Annas II seized his brief opportunity and killed James and his associates.

Those "strict" ones who in turn had the Sadducee Annas II deposed must have been Pharisees. Their support for James against the charge that he transgressed the law can only mean that James and his community were known as law-observant. This is consistent with the elders' claim that their numerous members were "all zealous for the law" (Acts 21:20) and with the earlier indication that Pharisees belonged to the church in Jerusalem (Acts 15:5).

This passage provides valuable insight into Christianity in Jerusalem in the early 60s. It also assists us in understanding Jesus. First, it confirms the NT references that James was a brother of Jesus (Gal 1:19; Mark 6:3 par.) who became leader of the church in Jerusalem (Gal 2:9; Acts 15:13; 21:18). Second, by declaring that Jesus was the "so-called Christ" *(Iēsou tou legomenou Christou)*, it corrects the unemended *Testimonium* assertion that "Jesus . . . was the Christ" *(ho Christos houtos ēn)*. As noted earlier, the claim that Jesus was the Christ most likely was the basis of the accusation of the temple leaders against him to Prefect Pilate.

The fourth passage has no direct references to Jesus or to any other figure in the NT. Its interest to us resides only in Josephus's description of a Roman trial in Jerusalem. In 66 the Roman soldiers arrested a number of Jerusalem Jews who — in his absence — had mocked the procurator Florus. Florus came up to the Holy City from Caesarea bent on vengeance. "Florus lodged at the palace and on the following day had a tribunal *(bēma)* placed in front of the building and took his seat; the chief priests, the nobles, and the most eminent citizens then presented themselves before the tribunal *(bēma)*. Florus ordered them to hand over the men who had insulted him, declaring that they themselves would feel his vengeance if they failed to produce the culprits" *(War* 2.301).

Josephus's description of the events casts some light on Pilate's trial of Jesus more than thirty years earlier. Florus set up the *bēma* (Roman magistrate's bench — cf. Matt 27:19; John 19:13; cf. Acts 18:12, 16, 17; 25:6, 10, 17) in front of the palace (i.e., Herod's former palace, now the governor's praetorium = barracks). Most likely the Roman trial of Jesus by Pilate also occurred not at the Antonia but at the former palace of the king, now commandeered as the governor's HQ in Jerusalem. In this forensic setting the chief priests, the nobles, and the most eminent citizens (i.e., the leaders of the Sanhedrin) were present and played an active part, as at the trial of Jesus. Unlike the case of Jesus, however, where those leaders sought the death of Jesus, here they defended the accused. Unmoved, Florus had a number of people brought before him who were then scourged and crucified. This passage is helpful in understanding the legal processes under Roman rule and the involvement of Jewish religious authorities.

The final passage, like its predecessor, does not mention Jesus but is of indirect interest. It concerns Jesus son of Ananias who, four years before the war, began to pronounce doom on Jerusalem and the temple. Here Josephus describes this man's bizarre behavior as one of a series of supernatural portents that pointed to the inescapable destruction of the Holy City and its sanctuary. His death by a chance Roman projectile only adds to Josephus's rather superstitious presentation. "There came to the feast (Tabernacles) . . . one Jesus, son of Ananias, a rude peasant, who, standing in the temple suddenly began to cry out, 'a voice from the east, a voice from the west, a voice from the four winds; a voice against Jerusalem and the sanctuary, a voice against the bridegroom and the bride, a voice against all the people.'"

Similarities with Jesus of Nazareth are superficial.[13] Jesus of Nazareth had disciples; his final appearance in Jerusalem was between the feasts of Tabernacles and Passover; and he entered into extensive disputation with the religious leaders (John 7–12). By contrast, Jesus ben Ananias was a lone figure who did not engage in debate with the temple authorities and who kept up his mantra of doom for seven years.

But this narrative once more relates what happened when someone spoke (or acted) publicly against the temple, as Jesus of Nazareth did. Most likely the temple authorities thought his "clearing of the temple" was tantamount to a messianic claim and accordingly sought the intervention of the Romans. As with Jesus of Nazareth, the temple authorities brought this other Jesus to the Roman governor for trial and punishment. As it happened, Albinus declared him to be mad and, following a severe flogging, released him.

In summary, the value of Josephus's information is its indirect corroboration of the political context of Jesus both in Galilee and Judea, the two jurisdictions where he performed the greater part of his public ministry.

First, Josephus's account of John the Baptist establishes that he was active sometime before Jesus and that he died as a martyr at the hands of Herod Antipas, which the gospels also establish. Furthermore, Josephus's account of the tetrarch's ruthless removal of John makes likewise credible the gospels' hints of Herod's menace toward Jesus and the latter's defensive movements in response to that menace.

The *Testimonium Flavianum*, as emended, reflects Josephus's negative but not damning impression of Jesus as teacher/rabbi and wonderworker. It may reasonably be inferred that the temple authorities accused Jesus to Pilate as a pretended messiah, for which he was crucified. Josephus

---

13. Contra Evans, "Jesus in Non-Christian Sources," 476-77.

shows mild surprise that, given Jesus' execution, "the tribe of Christians" was "still" around sixty years later.

Josephus's account of Annas's illegal trial and execution of James and others confirms the NT account of the size and conservative nature of the Jerusalem church, which likely represented an alternative constituency against the high priest. It was as if the crucified false messiah lived on in his brother's leadership of the spurious messianic community in Jerusalem.

The *Testimonium,* when joined to the two incidents involving the temple authorities and the governors Florus and Albinus, provides a global account of the processes that would have been involved in the arrest, trial, and execution of Jesus. (1) Where an individual blasphemed the temple, (2) the temple leaders would bring the offender to the Roman governor, where (3) at a hearing the plaintiffs gave evidence against the accused before the governor seated on his "bench," whereupon (4) he permitted the accused or others to make a defense, after which (5) the governor passed his verdict and released or punished the offender.

In short, Josephus's information makes credible the gospels' narrative of Jesus' ministry in Galilee under Herod the tetrarch and the sequence of events after Jesus had been arrested by the Jews and handed over to Pontius Pilate, who condemned and crucified him for the crime of claiming to be the Christ, the king of the Jews.

Tacitus

Cornelius Tacitus (ca. 56-120) served as consul in Rome in 97 and proconsul of Roman Asia in 112-113. His major work, *Annals of Imperial Rome,* covers the principates of Tiberius, Gaius (Caligula), Claudius, and Nero in eighteen books, of which only books 1-4 (Tiberius) and 12-15 (Claudius and Nero) are intact.

The passage following is part of his lengthy account of the fire in 64 that raged for six days leaving only four of the fourteen districts of Rome untouched (book 15, chapters 38–45). In the weeks after the fire many came to believe that Nero had ordered the torching of the city so as to rebuild it on a grand scale. To counteract these suspicions Nero engaged in ambitious building projects and elaborate religious sacrifices to appease the gods, but to no good effect. Because the rumors about him persisted, Nero arrested, tried, and executed numerous members of the Christian sect to deflect attention away from himself.

> But neither human help, nor imperial munificence, nor all the modes of placating Heaven could stifle or dispel the belief that the fire had taken place by order.
>
> Therefore, to scotch the rumour, Nero substituted as culprits, and punished with the utmost refinements of cruelty, a class of men, loathed for their vices, whom the crowd styled Christians.
>
> Christus, the founder of the name, had undergone the death penalty in the reign of Tiberius, by sentence of the procurator Pontius Pilatus, and a pernicious superstition (*superstitio*) was checked for the moment, only to break out once more, not merely in Judea, the home of the disease, but in the capital itself, where all things horrible or shameful in the world collect and find a vogue.
>
> First, then, the confessed members of the sect were arrested; next, on their disclosures, vast numbers were convicted, not so much on the count of arson as for hatred of the human race.
>
> And derision accompanied their end; they were covered with wild beasts' skins and torn to death by dogs; or they were fastened on crosses, and when daylight failed were burned to serve as lamps by night.
>
> Nero had offered his Gardens for the spectacle, and gave an exhibition in his Circus, mingling with the crowd in the habit of a charioteer, or mounted on his car. Hence, in spite of a guilt which had earned the most exemplary punishment, there arose a sentiment of pity, due to the impression that they were being sacrificed not for the welfare of the state but the ferocity of a single man. (*Annals* 15.44 LCL)

For two reasons Tacitus digresses to explain the origin of the name Christian. Due to the similarity of pronunciation, these people were popularly known as "Chrestians,"[14] meaning "good, useful ones," which clearly

---

14. Oldest ms of *Annals* has *Chrēstianoi*; cf. Suetonius, *Claudius* 15 — "Since the Jews constantly made disturbances at the instigation of Chrestus, he expelled them from Rome." See also W. Tabbernee, "Christian Inscriptions in Phrygia," in *New Docs* 3 (Sydney: Ancient History Documentary Research Centre, Macquarie University, 1983), 128-39, where the earliest inscriptions bearing the word "Christian" occur and where the spelling has both *Christianoi* and *Chrēstianoi*.

they were not! Rather, says Tacitus (with utmost economy), "Christians" derive their name from the man named "Christ."

Furthermore, Tacitus uses the same verb, "punished" *(adficere)*, for both Nero's execution of the Christians in Rome and the execution of Christ in Judea under Tiberius. Appropriately, the punishment of "the founder of the name" was now the fate of the followers of that name.

Is this passage a Christian forgery? Whereas Josephus's *Testimonium Flavianum* has been corrupted by Christian interpolation, there is no reason to suspect this of the "Testimonium Taciteum" in *Annals* 15.44. The text throughout is stylistically seamless. Furthermore, no Christian would have described his fellows in Rome as a foreign cult *(superstitio)*[15] needing to be checked, a "disease" *(malum)* belonging to the "horrible and shameful things of the world" that gravitate to Rome, a people "hated for their vices" *(flagitia)*,[16] who have a "hatred of the human race" *(odio humani generis)* and whose terrible punishment under Nero is justified.

This passage reflects Tacitus's conservative values and his diagnosis of Rome's woes. Tacitus laments that whereas Roman practices should civilize the provinces, the reverse is happening; foreign cults have come to Rome and are corrupting the heart of the empire. The arrival in vast numbers of this *superstitio* whose founder was an executed criminal in Judea is evidence of this corruption.

Tacitus is well known for his hostility toward Jews and Judaism: "They regard the rest of mankind with all the hatred of enemies. They sit apart at meals, they sleep apart . . . they abstain from intercourse with foreign women. . . . They believe [God] to be supreme and eternal, neither capable of representation nor decay. They do not allow any statues to stand in their cities, much less in their temples. This flattery is not paid to their kings, nor this honour to our emperors."[17]

Most likely Tacitus saw a close connection between the Christians and the Jews. Because Christus was executed in Judea, he was likely a Jew, which would explain his followers' "hatred of the human race." Nonetheless, Nero did not scapegoat the Jews and Tacitus does not say the Chris-

---

15. *Superstitio* was not a "superstition" in the modern sense but a foreign cult whose core beliefs were inimical to the Roman state. See L. F. Janssen, "'Superstitio' and the Persecution of the Christians," *VC* 33 (1979): 131-59.

16. Tacitus last used *flagitia* ("shameful acts") in *Annals* 15.37 for Nero's visible sexual acts in the sham wedding with Pythagoras.

17. Tacitus, *Histories* 5.5 LCL.

tians were Jews but (we assume) regarded them as a breakaway sect from Judaism that shared its fundamental evils.

Can we be confident that Tacitus has his facts right? He was, after all, writing seventy or so years after the execution of Christus. A problem has been found with his title "procurator" for Pilate's official position in Judea. The "Pilate Stone" discovered in Caesarea Maritima in 1961 establishes that in A.D. 6-41 the governor of Judea was a "prefect" (a military commander) whereas only in A.D. 44-66 was he a "procurator" (combining a more directly fiscal role with the military role). Tacitus's imprecision, however, is not evidence of more general inaccuracy, since writers like Philo and Josephus (who are closer to the events) employ the same fluidity of reference.

What sources did Tacitus use? We are able to eliminate several possibilities. The evident hostility of the passage means that he did not depend on Christian sources, oral or written. Moreover, his precise and succinct statement does not sound like rumor or hearsay. Nor does Tacitus seem to depend on the *Acta Senatus* where Pilate may have lodged a report (his account would have been more extensive). Of the two remaining options, dependence on a now-lost earlier history or information he learned while proconsul of Asia (including from his friend Pliny), the latter is the more likely. No doubt senior Roman officials shared information among themselves, including about the origin of new sects from the east.

It is difficult to overstate the importance of Tacitus's text for the study of Christian origins. The text itself is uncorrupted, is secure from suspicion of forgery, and is demonstrably accurate. It comes from the greatest Roman historian of that era, who is, moreover, profoundly hostile to the Christians and their founder Christus.

First, Tacitus makes a point of identifying Christ as "the founder of the name" *(auctor nominis)* Christian. By Tacitus's time Christ had indeed become a "name," but it is clear from the NT that it was originally his title, *the* Christ. Furthermore, the suffix *-ianoi* refers to those who were adherents of a named leader, for example, the *hērōdianoi*/Herodians were "supporters of Herod" (i.e., Herod Antipas; cf. Mark 3:6; 12:13). By the time Tacitus wrote, he was likely unaware that the *Christ-iani* were followers of one whose *title* was *the* Christ.

Tacitus's accurate but innocent connection of "Christians" with "Christ" exactly confirms what happened in Antioch in the late 30s when the people of Antioch (or the local Roman administrators) coined the word *Christianoi* (Acts 11:26; cf. 26:28).[18] It is likely the authorities in Antioch invented the term for the followers of a leader called *the* Christ.[19] At so early a date "Christ" was not yet merely a proper name.

The earliness of the word *Christianoi* as disciples of *the* Christ in Antioch supports the contention that the title *the* Christ did not originate there in the four or five years after the crucifixion of Jesus. Rather, it suggests that the title originated in Jerusalem where the Romans crucified him because he claimed to be or (more likely) "was said to be" *the* Christ, the king of the Jews. In short, because they crucified him as "the king of the Jews" (that is, as "the Christ"), we must conclude that the title *the* Christ did not begin postcrucifixion, but precrucifixion.[20]

Second, Tacitus confirms the raw facts about the rise and spread of early Christianity we find in the Christian writers, notably Luke-Acts. Tiberius was emperor (14-37) and Pilate was his prefect in Judea (26-36). Pilate executed Christ sometime between 26 and 36. Christ's movement, however, was not stopped by his death but "broke out once more, not merely in Judea . . . but in the capital itself." Although Tacitus does not specify crucifixion as the mode of execution, it was the routine punishment for those like Christus who led a movement against Roman *imperium*.

In conclusion, Tacitus's hostility toward Christus and the *Christiani* makes him an important historical source. His connection of Christus with *Christiani* takes us back to the first usage of the word *Christianoi* in Antioch a few years after the crucifixion, which likely occurred because of the claim that Christus was *the* Christ.

Moreover, in one brief sentence Tacitus confirms the broad sweep of NT history, that Christ was executed in Judea under Pilate but that, nonetheless, the movement (an evil *superstitio*) spread from Judea to Rome.

Pliny the Younger

Pliny the Younger (ca. 61-112), formerly a consul in Rome, was sent circa the year 110 by Emperor Trajan to govern the disorganized province of

18. Perhaps Peter exhorts his readers to stand firm for the name Christian (1 Pet 4:14) on account of Nero's pogrom in Rome in the middle 60s.

19. D. G. Horrell, "The Label *Christianos:* 1 Peter 4:16 and the Formation of Christian Identity," *JBL* 126, no. 2 (2007): 361-81, argues for a later date, 39-44.

20. See below, chapter 10.

Bithynia. His correspondence with Trajan, from 110 to 112, is recorded in book 10 of his letters.

In letter 96 he reports on the rapid spread of Christianity in the province, both in rural and in urbanized areas. Temples were abandoned and the businesses of those who sold fodder for sacrificial animals had been affected.

Pliny interrogated those accused of being Christians and sentenced them to death if they insisted they were Christians, despite being asked the question three times. Those who were Roman citizens the governor dispatched to Rome for trial.

Others who were accused, however, acknowledged that they had been Christians but no longer were. Pliny subjected them to a formal forensic procedure. They were required to invoke the state gods according to Pliny's dictated statement, engage in an act of worship with incense to the emperor's image, and also "curse Christ" *(maledicerent Christo)*.

Pliny twice refers to Christ, but without further explanation. We reasonably assume that Pliny knew (but did not need to tell the emperor) that Christ had been executed in Judea some years before. Since his friend Tacitus (governor of neighboring Asia) made this clear (as noted above), we assume it was common knowledge among Roman bureaucrats.

Pliny informed the emperor about the confessions of these lapsed Christians:

> They maintained that their guilt or error had amounted only to this: they had been in the habit of meeting on an appointed day before daybreak and singing a hymn antiphonally to Christ as a god *(carmenque Christo quasi deo dicere secum invicem),* and binding themselves with an oath — not to commit any crime but to abstain from theft, robbery, and adultery, from breach of faith, and from repudiating a trust when called upon to honour it. After this ceremony, it had been their custom to disperse and reassemble to take food of a harmless kind. (*Epistle* 10.96.7)[21]

To confirm his understanding, Pliny tortured two active Christians who were "slave women, whom they call deaconesses *(ministrae)*." But, Pliny said, "I found nothing but a degenerate sort of *superstitio* carried to extravagant lengths."

---

21. Translated by M. Harris, "References to Jesus in Early Classical Authors," in *Gospel Perspectives 5*, ed. D. Wenham (Sheffield: JSOT, 1984), 345.

The authenticity of this passage is not in doubt. The style is Pliny's and the comments about Christians are so harsh ("a *superstitio*" — foreign cult[22] — that was "degenerate" and "contagious") that Christian forgery is unlikely.

Their meeting "before daybreak" is explained by the presence of slaves among them; the "appointed day" likely points to resurrection-day meetings, on "the first day of the week"; and the apologetic tone of "food of the *harmless* kind" suggests the Eucharist.

Pliny's information about Christian practices is of special importance since its source is lapsed Christians mediated to the emperor by a writer who despises Christians. Pliny, like his friend Tacitus, classifies Christianity as a *superstitio*, a foreign cult that had the potential to corrupt Roman ways.

Apart from witnessing to the rapid and extensive spread of this vile movement, Pliny's statement is important for its insight into Christians' attitude to Christ at that time. Being required to "curse Christ" is evidence that Pliny and the (lapsed) Christians regarded Christ as a historic person; people didn't curse gods. In any case, since Tacitus knew that Christus was a man executed in Judea in Tiberius's principate, his friend Pliny must also have known this.

Yet, when these Christians met they sang a hymn (or recited a poem) to this crucified *Christo quasi deo*, "to Christ *as if to* a god." Harris points out that if Pliny "had regarded Christ as a god comparable to Asclepius or Osiris, he would have written *Christo deo*, 'to the god Christ.'"[23]

In other words, Pliny's report reflects that the Christians worshiped the (crucified) Christ, as if a god. If this is correct, it approximates to the NT conviction that (by his resurrection and ascension) the man Jesus of Nazareth who had been crucified was worshiped as the exalted *Kyrios* and *Christos*.

Pliny's passage is valuable because it confirms the NT's representation of Christians worshiping or acclaiming the crucified Christ as an exalted figure. It does not matter that we do not know whether the Christians in Bithynia were singing a hymn, reciting a poem, or reciting a creed or confession. The NT abounds with creeds (e.g., 1 Cor 15:3-5, 11), hymnlike passages (e.g., Phil 2:5-11; Heb 1:1-4; Rev 1:4-6),[24] and invocations (*Maran*

---

22. See earlier, n. 15.
23. Harris, "References to Jesus," 346.
24. M. Hengel, "Christological Titles in Early Christianity," in *The Messiah*, ed.

atha — 1 Cor 16:22; cf. Rev 22:20). It is well known that the early churches "sang" to the Lord (Eph 5:19; cf. Col 3:16).

Bithynia was one of the destinations of the First Letter of Peter (1 Pet 1:1), so perhaps a kerygmatic passage from that letter became a liturgical element in the churches in that province. What is clear, however, is that by the early years of the second century these Bithynians were worshiping the crucified but now exalted man, Christ. This, in turn, confirms the witness of the NT literature that the believers in the previous decades did that too.

Conclusion: In a passage that is authentic beyond doubt, Pliny, a deeply hostile witness, reproduces the evidence of apostate Christians about their weekly practice of meeting before dawn. At their meetings the Christians together directed their words to the crucified but now exalted Christ, "as if to a god." It does not matter that we do not know whether they sang a hymn or recited a creed. The critical detail is that they worshiped the crucified Christ *as if* a god.

Josephus and Tacitus corroborate the NT witness to the human circumstances of Christ's ministry in Jerusalem; they lay out the respective roles of Jewish leaders and the Roman governor in his trial and execution. The great contribution of Pliny, a hostile outsider, is to show that sympathetic insiders spoke the truth in saying that at their meetings Christians addressed words to the crucified man Christ, as to a divine figure.

Conclusion: Josephus, Tacitus, and Pliny

Evidence from (the emended) Josephus, Tacitus, and Pliny corroborates or supports a number of matters relating to the historical Christ.

i. Josephus's account of the martyrdom of John the Baptist under tetrarch Herod Antipas gives us insight into how menacing a figure he would have been to Jesus of Nazareth and explains Jesus' defensive movements at various points.

ii. Josephus's portrayal of Jesus as "wise man," "wonder-worker," and "teacher of Jews and Greeks" likely reflects the opinion about Jesus that may have later been current in Palestine. Although Josephus is negative

---

J. Charlesworth (Minneapolis: Fortress, 1992), points out that "most of the christological hymn fragments . . . have this quasi deo as theme, often counterpointed with the cross motif" (429).

about Christ, he does not damn him the way he vilifies the false prophets and messianic figures of the 40s-60s.

iii. Josephus confirms the gospels' accounts by defining the respective roles of the chief priests and Pilate in the arrest, trial, and execution of Christ.

iv. Jesus was executed under Pilate (Josephus, Tacitus) by crucifixion (Josephus).

v. Most likely this was for the crime of claiming to be (or "was said to be") *the* Christ. For the Romans it was no crime to be a teacher/rabbi because this involved religion, not politics.

vi. The word *Christianoi* was first used in Antioch in the middle to late 30s and likely points to the perceived following not of a man named Christ but of a leader called "the Christ."

vii. By the time Tacitus wrote in the early second century, "Christ" was a proper name, not a title. Yet Tacitus closely connects the word "Christian" to its founder, "Christ." According to Tacitus, Christus was the founder of the "Christian" *superstitio* from Judea that had come in vast numbers to Rome.

viii. There were "Christians" in Antioch in the 30s (Acts 11:26), in Rome in the 60s (Tacitus), in Rome in the 90s (Josephus), and in Bithynia in 110, and at least twenty years beforehand (Pliny). Christ as a proper name or as a title gave his followers their name "Christian"; either way, the word "Christian" derives from the man "Christ." The name *Iēsous-ianoi*/"followers of Jesus" does not appear in any records, Christian or non-Christian, in the first century.

ix. Around 110 Christ was worshiped in Bithynia "as if a god" (Pliny), confirming the NT evidence that from Easter disciples worshiped (the crucified) Christ as a divine figure.

Reflection: The Hostile Sources

Evidence from second-century Christian sources and evidence from late-first-century and early-second-century hostile sources have at least one important detail in common. Both establish an important horizon or time line.

The Christian sources from the second century establish that there were four genuine gospels and that they had been written before the end of the first century, between 33 and (say) 90. In other words, the main bio-graphical information about Christ had been written by the lifetime after his lifetime.

Likewise, chronologically proximate to Christ is the evidence from the non-Christian sources. Josephus, Tacitus, and Pliny write just before or just after the turn of the century. This locates their evidence once more within the lifetime after the life span of Christ. Apart from the corruption of parts of Josephus's text, the texts of Tacitus and Pliny are not seriously doubted. It is significant that these authors are hostile to Christ and Chris-tians, especially the Romans Tacitus and Pliny. Their raw data about Christ does not contradict but rather corroborates the evidence from the New Testament. From Josephus's indirect information we imagine Christ as menaced by the ruler of Galilee who had killed the earlier prophet, John the Baptist. Josephus explicitly traces the Jewish leaders handing Christ over to Pilate for trial and execution in Judea. Pliny confirms the NT that the Christians worshiped this crucified but now exalted Christ, *as if* a god.

FOUR

The Jerusalem Biographical Tradition

Whether then it was I or they, so we preach and so you believed.

1 Corinthians 15:11

"Gospel" in the Earliest Synoptic Biography

The earliest of the three synoptic biographies[1] of Jesus identifies itself in its opening sentence as a "gospel." The anonymous author expects his gospel book to be used in two ways. First, he expects that a lector will read his gospel to an assembled group of disciples (Mark 13:14 — "let the reader/lector understand").[2] As we shall argue later, this part of Mark's gospel was likely written in the early 40s with the express purpose of being *read aloud* in a nascent Christian congregation. If this dating is correct, it means the "Jerusalem" chapters of Mark's gospel are the first written texts of the New Testament.

Equally, however, Jesus (as reported by Mark) expected the *message* of this gospel to be "proclaimed to *all* the nations"/"in *all* the world" (13:10; 14:9). That is to say, Mark (based on Jesus' mandate) expected the component stories in the text of his gospel to be proclaimed *universally*.

---

1. Majority opinion regarding synoptic relationships remains the "two-document" hypothesis, that is, Mark and Q are prior to and the basis of Matthew and Luke.

2. Likewise reflecting the church practice of reading texts in church is Rev 1:3 ("Blessed is he who *reads* aloud the words of the prophecy, and blessed are those who *hear*").

In this latter (verbal) sense the gospel's *message* and the *person* of Christ are closely related, indeed, indistinguishable. He said that to be ashamed of his "words" is as serious as being ashamed of him (8:38). Likewise, to lose one's life for "the gospel" is the same as saving one's life (8:35; 10:29-30). Mark understands that his gospel is Jesus Christ's own "gospel" (so 1:1), his very words, so that to receive them is to receive him.

In sum, the seven appearances of the word "gospel" in this earliest synoptic biography mean either the *written* biography itself or an *orally* proclaimed version of this biography. In their effects they are one and the same.

"Gospel" in 1 Corinthians 15

It is clear, however, that *summary* versions of that "biography" existed in purely oral form, predating Mark's written form. Paul cites a section of that gospel-biography (the items as of "first importance" for the current pastoral concerns in Corinth) to remind the believers in Corinth of his initial preaching that brought their church into existence circa A.D. 50.

> Now I would remind you, brethren, in what terms I preached to you the *gospel*. . . . For I delivered to you as of first importance what I also received, that Christ died for our sins in accordance with the scriptures, that he was buried, that he was raised on the third day in accordance with the scriptures, and that he appeared to Cephas, then to the twelve. Then he appeared to more than five hundred brethren at one time. . . . Then he appeared to James, then to all the apostles. (1 Cor 15:1-7)

This summarized gospel-biography picks up its latter ("Jerusalem") elements, focused on the resurrection appearances. The resurrection of the body was the presenting issue Paul addresses in this chapter ("Now if Christ is preached as raised from the dead, how can some of you say that there is no resurrection of the dead?" — 15:12). To buttress his arguments Paul reminds them that apostles (including the leaders Peter and James) proclaim exactly the same gospel as he does even though the risen Christ appeared to him in a different time and manner, "as to one untimely born" (15:8). Despite this, "whether then it was *I or they* [the Jerusalem authorities], so *we* [Paul and the Jerusalem authorities] preach and so you believed" (15:11).

In short, between the Jerusalem-based apostles and Paul there was a commonly agreed, oral, summarized gospel-biography.

Furthermore, we must note two other related aspects about this *verbal* gospel-biography. First, Paul did not formulate it but rather "received" *(parelabon)* it. Second, Paul "received" it early, in the shadow of the historical Christ, either from the apostles Peter and James in Jerusalem around the year 36, or more probably from the disciples in Damascus circa 34, who in turn had earlier received it from the Jerusalem apostles.

Here we note rabbinical overtones from the ex-Pharisee. As Paul "received" the "gospel" that was "delivered" to him, so Paul "delivered" it to the Corinthians, who also "received" it from him. The point to emphasize is that this biographical summary arose from the apostolic leaders in Jerusalem; Paul merely "delivered" to others the words that came *from them.*

The ultimate source of this commonly agreed apostolic gospel was Peter, the first apostolic leader in Jerusalem (Gal 2:7-8).

1 Corinthians 15:3-5 and Acts 10:40-41, 43

As we noted earlier,[3] the latter parts of Peter's message (the "Jerusalem" narrative) to Cornelius in Caesarea Maritima are strikingly similar to Paul's cited gospel in 1 Corinthians 15:3-5.

1 Corinthians 15:3-5	Acts 10:40-41, 43
Christ *died for our sins according to the scriptures.*	To him *all the prophets* bear witness that every one who believes in him receives *forgiveness of sins through his name.*
He was *raised* [by God] on the *third day (tē hēmera tē tritē).*	God *raised* him on the *third day (tē tritē hēmera).*
He appeared to *Cephas* . . . the Twelve . . . etc.	God gave him to be manifest . . . to *us* . . . witnesses.

---

3. Barnett, *Birth of Christianity,* 152-53.

In these two passages we see the convergence of ideas but also close verbal parallels. Both passages teach:

   i. The vicarious death of "[the] Christ."
   ii. This fulfilled the prophetic scriptures.
   iii. God raised Christ "on the third day."
   iv. He appeared alive to various witnesses.

So striking are these common ideas and words that some theory of dependence is to be inferred. The most likely explanation is that a prior Peter tradition was the basis of the tradition Paul himself "received" and "delivered" to the churches of his mission.

So we make this observation. Paul's cited verbal gospel-biography, which he stated as a reminder for specific pastoral reasons in Corinth, coincides closely with the same "Jerusalem" part of Peter's verbal gospel (which he calls "God . . . preaching the *gospel* by Jesus Christ" — Acts 10:36). Accordingly, we reasonably argue that had Paul needed to, he could have cited previous elements of Peter's summarized verbal gospel-biography, elements that began with John preaching baptism and continued with Jesus' own preaching and healing in Galilee. In other words, we propose that, had he needed to, Paul could have cited a biographical summary that broadly corresponded with Peter's earlier "Galilee" section, as in Acts 10:36-39a.

This is precisely what we find in the single biographical summary attributed to Paul in the book of Acts (13:23-31), as discussed below.

What, then, can we conclude from this evidence in 1 Corinthians 15:3-5 and Acts 10:40-41, 43? Put simply, historically speaking, soon after the first Easter the Jerusalem apostles formulated a verbal gospel-biography for preaching purposes. Quite early Paul "received" this message, which in turn he "delivered" to the churches of his Gentile mission, hence his claim that he and they proclaim the same gospel.

Subsequently *someone* expanded the original verbal gospel as a *written* gospel-biography with two purposes: it was to be read to assembled disciples, and it was to serve as the basis of a gospel preached to "all the nations"/in "all the world."

The million-dollar question is this: How can we be confident who wrote this earliest but *anonymous* synoptic gospel-biography? We defer the answer to this question for the moment.

Paul in Antioch in Pisidia (Acts 13:16-41)

Circa 47 Paul and Barnabas arrived in Antioch in Pisidia and Paul preached in the synagogue. In this, Paul's only recorded synagogue sermon, he provides extensive biographical information about John the Baptist and what happened to Jesus in Jerusalem. It is of utmost importance that we recognize that Paul identifies his summarized Jesus biography as "gospel" (Acts 13:32-33 — "we *gospel* [*euangelizometha*] you, that what God promised to our fathers he has fulfilled to us their children").

Here, though, we face an important question.[4] Whose voice do we actually hear in this sermon in the synagogue in *Colonia Antiocheia*, Paul's or Luke's?

Luke's own words from his gospel appear to a significant degree as Paul's words, as in the following table.

Acts 13		Luke
v. 24	John was before Jesus, preaching a baptism of repentance	3:3
v. 25	John denied he was the "seed of David," but one unworthy to untie his sandals	3:15-16
v. 28	The role of the "rulers" seeking Jesus' execution	23:13, 35; 24:20
	References to his "crime" (*aitia*)	23:4, 14, 22
v. 29	His burial in a tomb (*mnēmeion*)	23:55–24:9 (passim)
v. 31	His "appearance" (alive) for many days	24:34; cf. Acts 1:3

So strong are these echoes that it is difficult to avoid recognizing that to a substantial degree the words we are hearing are Luke's, drawn from his gospel and to a lesser degree from the book of Acts. Furthermore, the sermon reflects a discernible "political" bias that we find also in Luke's gospel. It portrays the Galileans in a good light, but "those who dwell in Jerusalem and their rulers" as culpable for their failure to recognize the promised "seed of David" and for their request to Pilate to execute him. Antioch of

---

4. For discussion of authenticity of speeches in Acts, see C. J. Hemer, *The Book of Acts in Its Hellenistic Setting* (Tübingen: Mohr, 1989), 415-27.

Pisidia was a *Roman* colony and its Jews were of course *Diaspora* Jews. Luke's account of Paul's speech inferentially exculpating the Roman governor but inculpating the rulers in Jerusalem might have received a good hearing in this city. This *tendenz,* too, was implicit in Luke's narrative of the Jewish and Roman trials of Jesus (Luke 22:66–23:25).

At the same time, there are three qualifications to this observation. One is the evidence of distinctive Pauline "coloring" in the speech Luke records.

Acts 13	Paul's Letters
v. 27 "The utterances of the prophets which are *read* every sabbath"	2 Cor 3:14, 15
v. 38 "through this man forgiveness of sins is proclaimed to you"	
v. 39 "and by him every one that *believes* is *freed* (*dikaioutai* 'justified')"	Rom 5:1

These items are not characteristically Lukan but notably Pauline, suggesting significant Pauline influence in the author's record of this message.

Another qualification is the seemingly gratuitous reference to John the Baptist. Given Luke's bias against Jerusalem and her rulers, we can perhaps understand his omission of the narrative of Jesus' ministry in Galilee as irrelevant to his interests. What is difficult to grasp is his otherwise gratuitous account of *John's* appearance prior to Jesus, his preaching of the baptism of repentance, and his disavowal of a messianic role. Luke is interested in recording a summarized Jesus biography and not merely in accusing the people and leaders of Jerusalem.

Most important of all, however, are elements in Acts 13:16-41 that point to the conventions of a typical synagogue homily. Elements that have been recognized are the proem text (1 Sam 13:14) chosen by the preacher to link the seder reading (Deut 4:37-38) and the haftarah reading (1 Sam 7:6-16). The preacher delivered the homily by a process called *haruzin,* the "stringing of beads." Various authorities on synagogue preaching have discerned these characteristics in Acts 13:16-41.[5] In other words, it would be consistent for this, the sermon most like a synagogue homily of all the ser-

---

5. See Hemer, *Acts,* 423-24.

mons recorded in Acts, to come from the lips of the most highly qualified synagogue teacher known to us in the NT, Paul.[6]

What, then, do we conclude from this? On one hand, Luke expresses Paul's sermon in Luke's words and reflects his viewpoints. On the other, the sermon contains distinctively Pauline motifs, notably "justified" (= "forgiven") from breaches of the law by "believing." Moreover, and of great importance, the format of the sermon conforms to conventions of a synagogue exposition, which would be consistent with Paul's abilities as a trained scribe but not with Luke as a Gentile (Col 4:11, 14).

Could Paul have delivered the essentials of this message, notwithstanding its presentation in Lukan dress and in line with Luke's anti-Jerusalem, pro-Roman, pro-Diaspora interests? In our view, this is readily imaginable. The "we" passages in Acts identify Luke as Paul's companion for many years, so that the author of Acts had firsthand access to details of Paul's ministry, including at Antioch in Pisidia.[7] It is easy enough to imagine Paul telling Luke what he said on this and other occasions. It is also likely that Paul and Luke shared similar negative attitudes toward Jerusalem and positive attitudes toward Jews of the Diaspora and to the Pax Romana. It is likewise realistic that Luke would relay the speeches of Peter and Paul in terms of his *own* strongly held worldview.

The Sermons of Peter (Acts 10:34-43) and Paul (Acts 13:16-41)

Paul's gospel-sermon at Antioch in Pisidia (Acts 13:16-41) circa 47 is much longer than Peter's sermon a decade earlier at Caesarea Maritima (Acts 10:34-43). Most likely this is due to Luke's greater access to Paul and his preaching than to Peter's ministry.

There are other differences. Unlike Peter's sermon at Caesarea, Paul asserts that Jesus is the "seed of David" (13:33) who, unlike his famous forebear, did not see corruption following death (13:34-37). As well, Peter offers no comment about the culpability of the rulers in Jerusalem for the death of Christ whereas Paul is critical of their rejection of Jesus (13:27-29a). Further, Peter expands on Jesus' ministry in Galilee, the "country of the Jews," whereas Paul makes no reference to Jesus' ministry in Galilee, though he does mention "those who came up with him from Galilee to Jerusalem"

6. See Barnett, *Paul*, chapter 3.
7. Barnett, *Birth of Christianity*, 190-93.

(13:31). Despite differences in length and content, the two summarized sermons have a common biographical thread.

Peter (Acts 10)	Paul (Acts 13)
John's preaching of baptism	John preached a baptism of repentance
	Jesus, "seed" of David
Jesus preached and healed in Galilee	
Peter a witness in Galilee and Judea	
The Jews in Jerusalem put him to death	Jerusalemites and rulers secured his death at Pilate's hands
	They buried him in a tomb
God raised him on the third day	God raised him from the dead
God made him manifest to chosen witnesses	He appeared to those who came up from Galilee for many days
These he commanded to preach to the people	These are now witnesses to the people

These sermons are different in tone and setting, yet they follow the same broad sequence, beginning with John the Baptist and ending with the death, resurrection, and appearances of the Risen One in Jerusalem.

Conclusion

We observe that the word "gospel" (as noun or verb) is used to describe the recorded summarized biographies of Jesus as given by both Peter and Paul (Acts 10:36; 13:32) and that the word "gospel" appears as the title of the earliest synoptic "gospel," in which the word also appears throughout.

When we compare Peter's and Paul's summarized gospel-biographies, we find a common biographical thread that begins with John's preaching of baptism and ends with Christ's death, resurrection, and risen appearances in Jerusalem.

As to the origin of these common Petrine-Pauline summarized biographies, we are confident that they were formulated in Jerusalem within the college of the apostles led initially by Peter. Moreover, there are good reasons to believe they were established very soon after the events surrounding Jesus in Jerusalem.

Historically, the oral summarized gospel-biography of Jesus predated the written, expansive gospel-biography. Yet, as noted above, the author of the written gospel (based on Christ's mandate) expected the verbalized version of his written text to be proclaimed throughout the world. Moreover, he expected his written text to be read within the churches.

Finally, as we set these earliest Jerusalem verbal summaries alongside the earliest synoptic gospel, we discover, as many others have, that the written text broadly follows the sequence and viewpoint of the Jerusalem oral tradition.

FIVE

Mark and Memory

Mark . . . Peter's interpreter . . . wrote accurately as many things as he remembered.

The Elder John[1]

In our attempt to find the historical Christ, the most important question is: How did the things Jesus did and the words he said come to be written? As we will argue, Mark wrote our earliest synoptic gospel, upon which Matthew and Luke each depends. But when did Mark write? I have suggested A.D. 70 as a date broadly acceptable to NT scholarship.[2] In my opinion, Mark may have written earlier, though for the sake of convenience let me stick to 70, since a few years either way do not affect my arguments. Since Jesus' earthly span ended in 33 (or 30), we are dealing with a period of forty years, at or near the end of which Mark completed his gospel.

Which resources were available to Mark, as he eventually opened his scroll and dipped his stylus in ink? Did he have an earlier written draft version, a number of shorter narratives, or was he dependent upon memorized stories that he heard?

1. Elder John, quoted in Eusebius, *HE* 3.39.15.
2. Barnett, *Birth of Christianity*, 162.

Memorized Oral Transmission

For the greater part of the twentieth century and into the twenty-first century, scholarship has argued that the source of the earliest synoptic biography of Jesus Christ is memorized oral tradition.

To anticipate, I too will argue for memorized oral tradition as the primary source for Mark's *bios Iēsou*. There are, however, several versions of the mode of memorized oral transmission that vary so considerably as to be mutually exclusive.

A prior issue has to be addressed, namely: What was *the social context* in which the traditions were memorized and transmitted? Almost certainly, the words and works of Jesus were initially formulated in the land of Israel in the first decades after Jesus. In which kind of setting do we imagine these traditions being articulated and passed on? Was it a village square where a gathered community heard storytellers describe and redescribe the exploits of Jesus? This seems unlikely since we have no reason to believe such storytelling and listening was part of Jewish culture in first-century Palestine, however much it became part of other cultures in the Middle East and Asia.

Did it, then, in some way correspond with the synagogue culture of Judea and Galilee? This is a more promising possibility due to the centrality of the synagogue culturally in that era, perhaps in ways analogous to the importance of the village parish church in Europe in the late Middle Ages. The synagogue culture was a didactic culture, with a special and unique role given to the teacher and his use of the sacred text; communal storytelling (to our knowledge) was not part of that culture. Our argument is that the churches in the land of Israel in the earliest decades would have resembled synagogue meetings, even though their members gathered in private homes rather than in dedicated religious buildings.

But let me return to the modes of memorized oral transmission.[3] Here there are four viewpoints, two of which I reject, one that is partly correct, and one that (in my opinion) deserves overwhelming support.

Kenneth Bailey, who spent many years observing Middle Eastern village life, proposed three types of oral transmission: *informal uncontrolled* tradition, *informal controlled* transmission, and *formal controlled* transmis-

---

3. See Richard Bauckham, *Jesus and the Eyewitnesses: The Gospels as Eyewitness Testimony* (Grand Rapids: Eerdmans, 2006), 240-63, for helpful discussion.

sion.[4] The first represents Bultmann's model, the third Gerhardsson's model, and the second Bailey's own model (now broadly followed by N. T. Wright and James Dunn).

The first and the second models are defective. Bultmann's (*informal uncontrolled* transmission) is untenable because it depends on sequences of successive and unrelated transmissions by anonymous persons over a very long period (longer than the actual three to four decades). So unrelated are these successive transmissions that their terminus, Mark's gospel, contains a bare minimum of authentic historical information. Bailey's model (*informal controlled* transmission) is superficially better, but suffers from the fatal problem that the *hearing community* is the guarantor of the storyteller's veracity. Why do we attribute such a guarantee to an audience?

Gerhardsson's approach (*formal controlled* transmission) more realistically identifies the setting as rabbinic and didactic, but is open to the criticism that it depends on models of transmission that postdate the NT era by some centuries; furthermore, Gerhardsson (in his earlier works) may not have allowed adequately for the place of *written* traditions. Nonetheless, Gerhardsson's approach warrants support on several counts. It recognizes the rabbinic ethos of first-century Judea and Galilee (see later) and Jesus' place in it as a teacher of parables (Mark 2:17-22; 3:23-27; 4:3-9, 21-32; 7:15; 12:1-11) and aphorisms (e.g., 2:27; 6:4; 10:14) and other teaching media employed by rabbis of that era.[5] Gerhardsson's hypothesis would explain how the disciples came to learn many of Jesus' teachings. Furthermore, the rabbinic ethos created by Jesus most likely continued into the early church and would explain the didactic character of the early church in Jerusalem (e.g., Acts 2:42; 5:21, 28) and the rabbinic character of the transmission of kerygmatic and other formulae reflected in Paul's letters (e.g., 1 Cor 11:23; 15:1-3; 1 Thess 4:1-2). In my view, however, Gerhardsson's explanation does not account for the transmission of shorter narrative units (pericopes) in

---

4. As analyzed by Bauckham, *Jesus and the Eyewitnesses,* 240-63. Bauckham's interesting suggestion, that various named persons in the gospel stories were the sources of the information we find in the gospel, is beyond confirmation. It is possible, however, that people like Jairus and Bartimaeus were like "footnotes" who could be referred to for corroboration of the gospel story, perhaps analogous to the "five hundred" (mostly) living witnesses to an appearance of the risen Christ (1 Cor 15:6).

5. See, e.g., C. L. Blomberg, *Interpreting the Parables* (Leicester: Apollos, 1990), 58-68; H. K. McArthur and R. M. Johnston, *They Also Taught in Parables: Rabbinic Parables from the First Centuries of the Christian Era* (Grand Rapids: Academie Books, 1990).

Mark 1–10 nor for the connected longer narrative(s) in Mark 11–16 (see below).

Is there, then, a fourth model that merits our broader support? Indeed, there is, though it is not at all novel, but in fact arose in the first century. In brief, it is that report of the Elder John that he heard from the original "disciples of the Lord" and subsequently passed on to Papias. The elder told Papias that Mark wrote his gospel based on what he *remembered* of Peter's teaching, which Mark had many times relayed as Peter's "interpreter." This is the transmission model for which we shall argue throughout this chapter.

Papias, Once Again

Once again[6] we refer to Papias's account of the origins of Mark's gospel.

> And the Elder [John] was saying this: On the one hand, Mark, having become Peter's interpreter *(hermeneutēs)* . . . wrote accurately *(akribōs)*, as many things as he remembered *(hosa emnēmoneusen)*, on the other hand, [he did not write] in order *(taxei)* the things said and done by the Lord. For he neither heard the Lord, nor did he follow him, but later, as I said, [he followed] Peter. [Peter] arranged his teachings as anecdotes (or according to needs — *chreias)* but not as a collection *(syntaxin)* of the Lord's teachings *(logia)*. So Mark did nothing wrong in writing some things as he remembered them *(apemnēmoneusen)*. His single intention was not to omit anything he had heard or to falsify anything in them.[7]

Papias was bishop of Hierapolis in the Lycus Valley. It is usually assumed that he wrote circa 130, though some are arguing for a date as early as 110.[8] Whatever the date, Papias depended for his information about Mark's gospel on John the Elder, who in turn depended for his information on "the disciples of the Lord." Papias himself had not heard the original disciples of the Lord but only Aristion, the Elder John, and the daugh-

---

6. See Barnett, *Birth of Christianity,* 159; also C. E. Hill, "Papias of Hierapolis," *ExpT* 17, no. 8 (2006): 309-15.

7. Eusebius, *HE* 3.39.15, quoting Irenaeus.

8. See Barnett, *Birth of Christianity,* 159.

ters of Philip the evangelist[9] (cf. Acts 21:8-9), who were his contemporaries in Hierapolis. The point is that the elder's report to Papias came from "disciples of the Lord," that is, in the first century, perhaps circa 80.

It will be helpful to set out the chain of tradition implied by Papias's comments in an earlier passage:

> The Lord
> > What the disciples of the Lord *said*
> > > [Andrew, Peter, Philip, Thomas, James, John, Matthew]
> > > > What Aristion and John the Elder *say*
> > > > > Papias

Overlapping transmission is implied. Papias heard what John the Elder *was saying* (ca. 120); John the Elder heard what the disciples of the Lord *said* (ca. 80); disciples of the Lord *heard* the Lord (ca. 29-33).

Papias's observation about Mark's gospel has both positive and negative elements. Positively, Papias is able to hear the "living and abiding" voice of the disciples of the Lord through their hearer, the elder. Papias does not have to depend on unprofitable "things out of books" but depends on the witness of the disciples of the Lord mediated through Aristion and the elder. The chain of transmission is short. Moreover, and of great importance, according to the elder, Mark's wellspring of information for this gospel was Peter, the leading disciple and apostle of the Lord.

There are some negatives. Papias must defend Mark, as signaled by his words "So Mark did nothing wrong" *(ouden hēmarten).* Which "wrongs" was Mark perceived to have committed? Mark was not himself a follower of the Lord and committed Peter's oral instruction to paper only at a later date, based on his memory. Perhaps Papias's contemporaries were also contrasting Mark with John (the fourth Evangelist), who *was* a follower of the Lord and who wrote his gospel based on *his own* direct memory of the words and deeds of the Lord.

Moreover, Mark's written words depend on Peter's teachings, which, however, were not cast in the form of a "collection *(syntaxis)* of the Lord's words." Papias is likely negatively comparing Peter's teachings with Matthew, who "compiled *(synetaxato)* the oracles" of the Lord. Papias is probably contrasting the fruits of Peter's teaching found in Mark's written text

---

9. Papias mistakenly calls him "Philip the apostle" (Eusebius, *HE* 3.39.9).

with major "collections" of teaching in the Gospel of Matthew, notably the Sermon on the Mount. In fact, Mark's gospel contains little recorded teaching compared to the other three gospels.

Furthermore, Mark did not write "in order" *(taxei)*, referring either to a dislocation of sequence in his narrative or to a lack of aesthetic form. Perhaps again, Papias is contrasting Mark with John, whose gospel could be seen as either more sequential or more polished (or both).

Perhaps, too, Papias's observation that Mark "wrote accurately," which he qualified with "as many things as he remembered," is a half-hearted defense of Mark. There may be an implied contrast with Luke's claim that he "wrote . . . accurately in sequence" *(akribōs kathexēs . . . grapsai* — Luke 1:3), based on written texts "handed over" to him by "those who from the beginning were eyewitnesses and ministers of the word."

In short, Papias is somewhat ambivalent about the testimony of the elder. True, his account of Mark's origin rested on the "living" voice of the disciples, and, yes, the source of that gospel was Peter. On the other hand, various deficiencies in Mark the man (not an eyewitness) and in his gospel (not written *taxei*) had for many relegated this gospel to an inferior status in relation to Matthew, Luke, and John. Papias is lukewarm in his defense of the elder's report.

What the ancients saw as weaknesses in Mark, however, we moderns should regard as strengths. And great strengths they are. In fact, Papias's information about Mark's gospel resolves the most pressing question of all — he tells us once and for all how "the things said and done by the Lord" came to be written to provide access to the historical Christ for all who were not his original disciples. In one stroke Papias demolishes several of the much-loved theories about the transmission of information about Christ, based on orality, as noted above. On the basis of the elder's report, we know what others merely guess.

Our clue here is the twofold reference to Mark's "memory": he "wrote accurately as many things as he *remembered*" and wrote "some things as he *remembered* them." Contrary to theories of the words and works of Christ being relayed by generations of village storytellers before being blindly recorded by the earliest synoptic author, the reality was dramatically otherwise. What the Lord said and did was taught by the preeminent eyewitness, Peter, and recorded by his "interpreter" Mark, based on Mark's recollection of words he had heard and (verbally) translated many times.

In other words, those theorists are wrong who assert that generations of faceless raconteurs were interposed between Jesus and our earliest written synoptic text. Between Christ and that written text stand only two persons, persons whose *names are known to us,* Peter the teacher and Mark his interpreter and scribe. It is not clear from Papias when Mark wrote down Peter's words, whether soon afterward, or at or after Peter's passing. In the end, "when" this was written matters less than knowing "who" wrote it. The "who" was Mark, an accomplished and well-connected leader throughout the generation following the life span of the historical Christ.

If Papias's information is correct, we would expect to find traces of Peter's influence in this gospel, and that is precisely what we do find.

Yet there is a prior issue to resolve.

Is Papias's "Mark" the Canonical Mark?

The author of the Gospel of Mark does not identify himself. So how do we know that the "Mark" Papias writes about was the author of the anonymously written gospel?

First, we reasonably assume Papias's Mark to have been the person so named in the New Testament. Who else would second-century Christians be referring to? He is known more fully as John Mark in several references in Acts, but only as Mark in Paul.

Mark was a son of Mary whose house was associated with Peter and was a center for Christian meetings in Jerusalem (Acts 12:12). He was a cousin of Barnabas (Col 4:10) who accompanied Barnabas and Paul to Cyprus as their assistant (*hypēretēs,* Acts 13:5). Due to his unexpected return to Jerusalem from Perga in Pamphylia, Paul declined to take him on his next missionary tour, and Mark went instead with Barnabas to Cyprus (Acts 13:13; 15:37-39). Later he was reconciled with Paul, who commended him for a visit to Colossae (Col 4:10; Philem 24). Paul instructed Timothy to bring Mark with him to Rome (2 Tim 4:11). Evidently Mark went to Rome ("Babylon"), where Peter called him "my son" and the sender of greetings to disciples in Pontus, Galatia, Cappadocia, Asia, and Bithynia. Evidently many in northern Anatolia knew Mark.

Mark's byname, John Mark, suggests social superiority, implying affluence and literacy[10] ("John" is Jewish and "Mark" is Greek or Roman),

---

10. Contra *New Docs,* 1:55, which suggests "Mark" was added during his missionary vocation.

and his extensive travels in Hellenized regions imply fluency in Greek. Furthermore, he had close connections with prominent leaders Peter, Barnabas, and Paul, and with important but lesser figures Aristarchus, Epaphras, Luke, and Silvanus (Col 4:10-14; Philem 23-24; 1 Pet 5:12-13). We note that Mark's missionary experience involved him in both the Pauline and Petrine missions.

Therefore, since we know of no one else in the NT by the name of Mark, we can be confident that he is the author of the gospel, which by the early second century was associated with him. It may have been tempting to early-second-century leaders to attribute this gospel to a more prominent figure, including one of the original twelve. That Mark was a "second tier" leader supports the authenticity of the superscription.

Second, the evidence from the second century identifies the second gospel as written by "Mark." Based on earlier discussion,[11] we noted the early-second-century *superscription* attached to "[The Gospel] according to Mark." Furthermore, this gospel was one of the canonical four gospels as indicated by several authorities: (i) Irenaeus's insistence on the exclusive *fourfold (quadriform)* nature of this gospel, (ii) Tatian's compilation of the *Diatessaron* ("one through *four*"), and (iii) the Muratorian Canon's reference to *four* books of the gospel. The discovery of the four gospels in *one early codex* (p^{45}) dated to the early third century confirms the fourfold gospel, to which Mark belonged. In short, a gospel by Mark was from early times identified as an authentic gospel, one of the exclusive *four*.

In brief, the author the elder identified to Papias as Mark was the John Mark of the New Testament, and he wrote the second of the four canonical gospels.

Are there aspects of Mark's gospel that support the elder's assertion of underlying Petrine influence and character?

The Lopsided Final Chapters of Mark

Mark's gospel is curiously lopsided. Martin Kähler called it (and the other gospels) "a passion narrative with an extended introduction."[12] In Kähler's

11. See chapter 2 above.
12. M. Kähler, *The So-called Historical Jesus and the Historic Biblical Christ* (Chicago: Fortress, 1964), 80.

terms, Mark's "extended introduction" narrated Jesus' ministry in *Galilee* and the north (chapters 1–10) up to his account of the "passion" in *Jerusalem* (chapters 11–16).

In length, Mark's six final chapters occupy approximately a third of the whole gospel, yet they narrate just a few days. By contrast, Mark's first ten chapters narrate several years of Jesus' ministry, though there is uncertainty over the passage of time. We are left to guess the time frame based on passing references to a winter (?) storm (4:35-41) and (a year later?) to springtime "green" grass (6:39; cf. John 6:4 — Passover) followed by his crucifixion at Passover a year later. If these details are in chronological sequence, it means that the public ministry of Jesus recorded in Mark exceeded two years, but by how much more we cannot say.

Moreover, these two parts of Mark's gospel have different textures, as many have noticed. Whereas the passages in Mark 1–10 are mostly shorter units, which may or may not be sequential, those in chapters 11–16 tend to be longer and, moreover, are organically part of a tightly connected story. It seems that chapters 11–16 (or perhaps 14–16) originated as a separate entity, most likely as a *written* text.

Those final chapters are also different from the preceding chapters in another important respect. They are relatively more precise and detailed in terms of *time, place,* and *people.* The concentration of information so confidently narrated supports the idea that these chapters were written quite early and were incorporated in the whole gospel sometime later.

Details of Time

11:11   "And he entered Jerusalem, and went into the temple . . . it was *already late.*"

11:12   *"On the following day,* when they came from Bethany . . ."

11:20   "As they passed by *in the morning,* they saw the fig tree withered."

11:27   "And they came *again* to Jerusalem. And as he was walking in the temple . . ."

14:1   "It was now *two days* before the Passover and the feast of Unleavened Bread . . ."

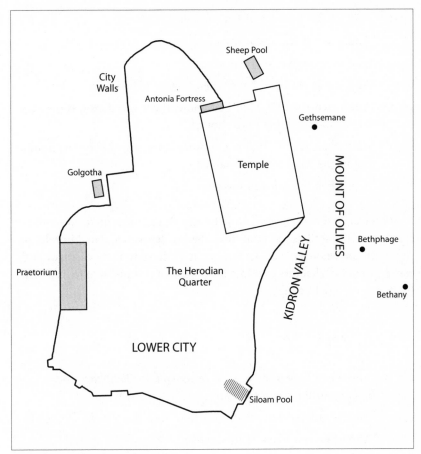

Jerusalem in the time of Jesus

14:12   "And on the *first day* of Unleavened Bread . . ."

14:17   "And when it was *evening* . . ."

15:1   "And as soon as it was *morning* . . ."

15:25   "And it was *the third hour,* when they crucified him."

15:33   "And when *the sixth hour* had come, there was darkness over the whole land until the ninth hour."

15:42   "And when *evening* had come, since it was the *day of Preparation,* that is, the day before the sabbath . . ."

16:1   "And when the *sabbath* was past . . ."

Based on these details, it is possible to plot three consecutive days initially (11:11, 12, 20) as well as the final three days of Jesus, calculated in relationship with the Passover (14:1, 12; 15:1, 42; 16:1). In only a few passages in the earlier "Galilee" chapters and to a lesser degree is it possible to establish a tight chronology like this.

Details of Place

11:1   "And when they drew near to *Jerusalem,* to *Bethphage* and *Bethany,* at the *Mount of Olives* . . ." (cf. 11:15, 27; 14:16)

11:11   "And he entered *Jerusalem,* and went into the *temple*" (cf. 14:3).

13:1   "And as he came out of the *temple* . . ."

13:3   "And as he sat on the *Mount of Olives* opposite the *temple* . . ." (cf. 14:26)

14:3   "And while he was at *Bethany* in the house of Simon the leper . . ."

14:16   "And the disciples set out and went to the city, and found it [*an upper room*] as he had told them."

14:26   "And when they had sung a hymn, they went out to the *Mount of Olives.*"

14:32   "And they went to a place which was called *Gethsemane.*"

14:54   "And Peter had followed him at a distance, right into the *courtyard of the high priest.*"

15:1   "And as soon as it was morning the chief priests, with the elders and scribes, and the whole council held a consultation; and they bound Jesus and led him away and delivered him to Pilate."

15:16   "And the soldiers led him away inside the *palace* (that is, the *praetorium*)."

15:22   "And they brought him to the place called *Golgotha*."

15:46   "And he bought a linen shroud, and taking him down, wrapped him in the linen shroud, and laid him in *a tomb*."

Details of People

The following people are named in these chapters:

Peter	11:21; 13:3; 14:29-72 (passim); 16:7
James, John, and Andrew	13:3
Pontius Pilate	15:1-44 (passim)
Barabbas	15:6-15
Simon of Cyrene	15:21
Mary of Magdala	15:40–16:10 (passim)
Mary, mother of James	15:40–16:10 (passim)
Salome	15:40–16:10 (passim)
Joseph of Arimathea	15:43-46

As we reflect on Mark's references to people, we cannot help noticing the important and specific roles of a small number in this narrative. In particular, we observe Mark's interest in Peter (the apostate); Pontius Pilate (the Roman governor); Mary of Magdala, Mary mother of James and Joses, and Salome (witnesses to the location of and emptiness of the tomb); and Joseph of Arimathea (whose tomb it was).

Apart from Pilate, these characters are brought together in the final scene on the first day of the week. The women come to Joseph's tomb and upon finding it empty are told, "Do not be amazed; you seek Jesus of Nazareth, who was crucified. He has risen, he is not here; see the place where they laid him" (16:6). Furthermore, they are given a message by the angel from the Risen One: "But go, tell his disciples *and Peter* that he is going before you to Galilee; there you will see him, as he told you" (16:7).

By his narrative Mark establishes two vital facts. First, the tomb in which the crucified Jesus of Nazareth had been laid was empty because he had risen from the dead, and second, the Lord had reinstated Peter as leader of the disciples, notwithstanding his apostasy.

In short, it seems likely that chapters 11–16 originated as an independent composition or compositions, because (i) the passages are longer and organically connected, with (ii) concentrated details of time, place, and people, in which (iii) a small number of persons play important roles, and (iv) they establish as vital the realities that Joseph's tomb was empty, because Christ had risen, and that he had returned the leadership to the apostate Peter. It is difficult, then, to escape the conclusion that Mark is narrating a single coherent story in his latter chapters, especially 14:1–16:8.

This, however, raises critical questions. Where, when, and from whom did this discrete narrative (or narratives) originate? Throughout the greater part of the critical era scholars have dated Mark's gospel after A.D. 70, based on the *vaticinium ex eventu* principle whereby Mark was putting the *history* of the fall of Jerusalem into the mouth of Christ as *prophecy*. As discussed earlier, however, his prophecy of the destruction of the temple (13:14-18) differs significantly from Josephus's eyewitness description of the event.[13] There are substantial reasons not to tie Mark 11–16 to a post-70 date, as many now realize.

Furthermore, G. Theissen argues persuasively that certain elements in the Olivet Discourse apply well to the era of the emperor Gaius ("Caligula"),[14] who in A.D. 40 decided to install a statue of himself in the temple, provoking a crisis that brought Jews and Romans to the brink of war. "Gaius dispatched Petronius as his legate to Syria. . . . His orders were to lead a large force into Judea and, if the Jews consented to receive him, to set up an image of Gaius in the temple of God. If, however, they were obstinate he was to subdue them by force of arms and to set it up."[15]

Jesus' words as relayed by Mark, "when you see the desolating sacrilege[16] set up where *he*[17] ought not to be," sound an urgent warning

---

13. Barnett, *Birth of Christianity*, 156-57. Cf. the important discussion in J. A. T. Robinson, *Redating the New Testament* (London: SCM, 1976), 13-30.

14. G. Theissen, *The Gospels in Context* (Minneapolis: Fortress, 1991), chapter 4.

15. Josephus, *Ant* 18.261 LCL.

16. Dan 9:27; 11:31; 12:11.

17. Because the antecedent of the pronoun is neuter gender, we must assume Mark

that the lector *(ho anaginōskōn)* must explain to the church assembly. Here, by deliberately changing the pronoun from "it" (relating to its neuter antecedent "desolating sacrilege") to "he" *(hestēkota)*,[18] Mark was directing the church reader to address a church crisis that was current and that was precipitated by a *man*. Furthermore, Mark's words "then let those who are *in Judea* flee to the mountains" identify Judea (not Rome) as the location of the crisis. Mark's pointed reference to *"he* [standing] where he ought not to be" and his admonition to "those who are in Judea [to] flee" apply directly to a *local church crisis in Judea* in A.D. 40 (created by Gaius) but not to Rome in the post-70 situation.[19]

Several other elements in Mark 11–16 point to an early date of composition. One is Mark's use of specific chronological connectors that tie the narrative 11–16 (or narratives 11–13 and 14–16) together, as noted above. By contrast, chapters 1–10 are composed by a small number of sections that are chronologically connected (e.g., 1:21-32; 4:1–5:1; 6:30-53; 8:27–9:2 — see below) and the greater part of the text where the connectors are indefinite, indicated by, for example, "after some days" (2:1), or such vague words as "then," "when," or "and." Consequently, most of chapters 1–10 give us little sense of the passage of time, apart from the four examples just given. By strong contrast, however, the narrative (or narratives) in chapters 11–16 is chronologically tightly connected. It is reasonable to conclude that these connected passages were originally discrete and coherent entities. Since chapters 11–16 are the most detailed and closely connected and coherent of such passages, we think it more likely than not that they were committed to written form first. But when, where, and by whom?

A second characteristic of Mark 11–16 is the noticeable anonymity of the high priest, the more so since lesser figures are named (e.g., the two Marys and Salome and Joseph). The high priest was the most prominent person in Jerusalem and the chief offender in the mistrial of Jesus and the subsequent transference of the prisoner to Pilate for crucifixion (14:53, 54, 60, 61, 63; cf. 15:1). Yet Mark does not name the high priest. This is the more striking since Matthew in a parallel passage does name him (Matt 26:57).

---

has deliberately violated the grammar to make a point that the lector must explain to the assembled believers.

18. Technically called *constructio ad sensum*.

19. Perhaps, too, it inspired Paul to write a few years later about "the man of lawlessness . . . [who] takes his seat in the temple of God, proclaiming himself to be God" (2 Thess 2:3-4).

This omission would be explained if the early composition of Mark 11–16 were allowed. That is to say, if Mark 11–16 were composed before Caiaphas was deposed (as he was in A.D. 37), there would be no need to mention him by name since everyone would know. Besides, mentioning by name the Jewish archvillain responsible for the killing of the leader of the messianic movement in Judea could bring even more trouble for the disciples in Jerusalem (see Acts 4:1-22; 5:17-40). It would not matter that the Gentile Pilate was named and therefore blamed for the crucifixion in Judea in the early 40s; everybody hated him anyway! It was otherwise with the Jewish high priest, whose sacred office was respected despite the brutality of the Annas dynasty and suspicions of its complicity with Rome.

Likely significant is also Mark's reticence in naming some prominent figures who actively supported Jesus. It is possible to detect in these passages an element of "protective secrecy"[20] whereby the identity of three people appears to have been suppressed. The owner of the colt upon whom the Messiah rode into the city (Mark 11:1-7) could have been regarded as a political subversive. The woman who anointed the Messiah might also have been regarded as complicit in a messianic plot (14:3-9). The disciple who severely assaulted "*the* servant" of the high priest, i.e., a key figure in the arrest of Jesus, would likely have been a wanted man if only his identity were known. Mark does not identify this sword-wielding disciple (14:47); John reveals that it was none other than the *leader* of the movement, Peter (John 18:10).

These two opposite characteristics of Mark 11–16 — a narrative that names some of the characters but treats others anonymously — call for explanation. Most likely, in our view, is the hypothesis that these chapters were of early origin and were written in Jerusalem. But written by whom?

Reenter the naked man! "And they [the disciples] all forsook him [Jesus], and fled. And a young man followed him, with nothing but a linen cloth about his body; and they seized him, but he left the linen cloth and ran away naked" (Mark 14:50-52).

This much-discussed passage appears only in Mark's gospel. Evidently the young man was a disciple who had been present in Gethsemane when Jesus was arrested but, unlike the other fleeing disciples, followed along after Jesus and the arresting party. When the officials attempted to

---

20. Bauckham, *Jesus and the Eyewitnesses*, 187-97, depending on Theissen, *The Gospels in Context*, chapter 4.

seize him, they succeeded only in grasping his simple *sindōn* (sleeveless gown) so that memorably he fled naked into the night.

It is striking that the author does not reveal the name of the young man, though he writes in the expectation that the readers/hearers will know who he is.

Why did the author suppress the name of the young man? Was it to protect him since he too was a wanted man? Alternatively, if the young man himself was the author, as many believe, he may have suppressed his name for self-protection. Or did he do so as a literary convention in modesty to hide his identity, as the author of the Gospel of John appears to have done (John 1:35-42; cf. 21:21-24)?

In my judgment, the only reason the author included this short section was to identify himself as the author. Otherwise, this is an entirely gratuitous and useless piece of information adding nothing to the narrative overall.

If the young man was the author, did he write *only* the discrete final chapters 11–16, an author who forever remains anonymous for us? Or was the young man Mark, who initially wrote this independently and later incorporated it as part of the whole gospel, as reported by the Elder John to Papias? I see no substantial reason to doubt that Mark himself, in collaboration with Peter, wrote Mark 11–16 in Jerusalem quite early, as a narrative of Jesus' last days in Jerusalem. We note that Peter and his faction (as opposed to James and his "brothers") met in the house of Mark's mother (Acts 12:12-17). Later Peter calls Mark "my son" (1 Pet 5:13). These details, when considered along with the elder's connection of Mark with Peter, tend to support the notion of an early collaboration of the two men in a venture like the writing of Mark 11–16.

Such an explanation would be consistent with the need for written texts in the newly formed messianic congregations in the land of Israel that are attested in both the letters of Paul (Gal 1:22 — "the churches of Christ in Judea"; 1 Thess 2:14 — "the churches of God in Christ Jesus which are in Judea") and the Acts of the Apostles (Acts 9:31-32 — "So the church throughout all Judea and Galilee and Samaria had peace and was built up; and . . . it was multiplied. Now as *Peter* went here and there among them all . . ."). It would make good sense for Peter and the apostles quickly to create written texts for *reading* and teaching in these new churches, especially a text that narrated the Lord's last days in Jerusalem, along with an account of the institution of the Eucharist, a narrative-based explanation of Christ's death as a "saving" act (Mark 15:31), and the demonstration of his resurrection from the dead based on the emptiness of Joseph's tomb.

We must not miss the momentous significance of this. If Mark 11–16 (or 14–16) was written in the early 40s, it would mean that these "Jerusalem" chapters are very early indeed, and are most likely the first words for the early church to be committed to writing.

Peter in Mark: Explicit References

The elder reported to Papias that Peter's teaching was the source of what Mark wrote, based on his recollection of that teaching, which Mark had earlier interpreted (or translated). Is there any evidence within Mark's gospel that Peter was its wellspring?

Upon examination, we discover that Peter enjoyed a special role within Mark's gospel.[21]

The first disciple Mark has Jesus meet is Peter (1:16; he is called Simon until 3:16), and the last disciple we hear of is Peter (16:7). The references to Peter at the beginning and the end are striking and create a "frame" around the whole gospel.[22] Bauckham notes that according to a literary convention of the time, "the most authoritative eyewitness is one who was present at the events narrated from their beginning to their end and can therefore vouch for the overall shape of the story as well as for specific key events."[23] According to that convention, Mark is identifying Peter as the key witness for his narrative.

Consistent with Peter as the main witness, we also find that Mark has Peter present throughout the greater part of his narrative. Peter's name (as "Peter" or "Simon") occurs remarkably often in Mark, no fewer than twenty-six times. In relative terms "Peter" occurs more frequently in this short gospel than in the other two synoptic gospels.[24] After Peter, the

21. See further M. Hengel, *The Four Gospels and the One Gospel of Jesus Christ* (London: SCM, 2000), 82-86; Bauckham, *Jesus and the Eyewitnesses,* 124-27.

22. Bauckham, *Jesus and the Eyewitnesses,* 132-45, explores evidence from Lucian and Porphyry where the *inclusio* device is utilized to focus the readers' attention on a key character in the work, especially as an eyewitness source.

23. Bauckham, *Jesus and the Eyewitnesses,* 146.

24. Bauckham, *Jesus and the Eyewitnesses,* 126, supplies the following statistics. The

Zebedee brothers James and John appear next most frequently, nine times in all. But in all but two cases they are mentioned with Peter. Apart from the list of the Twelve (3:16-19), the only other disciples Mark mentions are Peter's brother Andrew (three times) and Judas Iscariot (once). In short, Peter is a dominating presence as the prime eyewitness in Mark's gospel, though his shortcomings are not glossed over (8:32; 14:29-72). This observation provides powerful support for the testimony of the elder to Papias that Peter was the eyewitness source for the gospel that Mark wrote.

The implications for the quest for the historical Christ are considerable. Source criticism has demonstrated to the satisfaction of most authorities that Matthew and Luke based their respective narratives on Mark's gospel. Since that gospel is based on the witness of Peter, it means that he has directly or indirectly shaped the entire synoptic narrative tradition. True, the gospels are not "straight" history in that each also seeks to secure the allegiance of the reader to Christ in ways that few other biographies do. Nonetheless, each gospel is identifiably a genuine *bios Iēsou,* as many now recognize. Due to the witness of a prominent "eyewitness and minister" as expressed initially through his amanuensis Mark, we have significant access to the historical Christ.

Peter in Mark: Implicit References

Numerous details in the "Galilee" chapters of Mark's gospel (1–10) support the elder's report to Papias that an eyewitness (i.e., Peter) is the source of this gospel. As noted above, the greater part of Jesus' ministry in Galilee (and the north and east) is narrated in units (pericopes) that are only loosely connected and in which the details of people and place are often likewise imprecise.

This, however, is what we would expect, based on the elder's account. Mark was a Jerusalemite, not a Galilean. His grasp of the topography of Jerusalem is confident, whereas for Galilee it is otherwise. Furthermore, he was (in our judgment) a witness to some of the events in Jerusalem, whereas he had to depend on his memory of Peter's teaching to write the earlier chapters. We recall that the elder said Mark "wrote as many things

---

name Peter or Simon or Simon Peter occurs once in Matthew for every 654 words, once in Luke for every 670 words, and once in Mark for every 432 words.

as he remembered" and "some things as he remembered them," implying that he did not remember everything he heard from Peter. The indefinite character of much of chapters 1–10 is consistent with Mark's honest attempt but less than perfect result.

That said, however, a number of more precise elements in chapters 1–10 support an eyewitness source for Mark's gospel.

Chronologically Connected Blocks

In Capernaum (1:21-32)

1:21   "And they went into Capernaum; and immediately on the sabbath he entered the synagogue."

1:29   "And *immediately* he left the synagogue, and entered the house of Simon and Andrew."

1:32   "*That evening*, at sundown, they brought to him all who were sick or possessed with demons."

1:35   "And *in the morning*, a great while before day, he rose and went out to a lonely place."

The activities of this day in Capernaum are followed by the events of the next morning.

Crossing the Lake (4:1–5:1)

4:1   "Again he began to teach beside the sea."

4:35   "*On that day*, when evening had come, he said to them, 'Let us go across to the other side.'"

5:1   "*They came* to the other side of the sea."

Mark intends us to see these events as occurring in the one day.

Another Lake Crossing (6:30-53)

6:31   "And he said to them, 'Come away by yourselves to a lonely place, and rest a while.'"

6:45   *"Immediately* he made his disciples get into the boat and go before him to the other side."

6:53   "And *when they had crossed over,* they came to land at Gennesaret."

Once again, the events of a particular day are on view.

In the North (8:27–9:2)

8:27   "And Jesus went on with his disciples, to the villages of Caesarea Philippi."[25]

9:2   "And *after six days* Jesus took with him Peter and James and John, and led them up a high mountain."

Unlike the other connected passages, Mark 8:27 and 9:2 describe the longer period of a week.

It could be argued that Mark has engaged in contrived verisimilitude. But why would Mark do this in these few instances rather than cast the whole narrative like this? It is more likely that Mark has specifically remembered these sequences from Peter's narration of them and that the more vague sequences are due to the limitations of Mark's memory.

Nazareth and Capernaum

Mark's references to Capernaum and Nazareth are sufficiently coherent to answer the claim that his gospel is merely a haphazard collection of episodes.

The "house" in Capernaum was home to Simon and Andrew and their direct and extended families. It was to this "house" that Jesus came (1:29), where he initially stayed (1:33, 35-36), and to which he returned after various journeys elsewhere (2:1; 3:20; [7:17]; 9:33). These Capernaum "house" references span the various episodes throughout the Galilee chapters.

25. After circa 54 Caesarea Philippi was renamed Neronias (Josephus, *Ant* 20.211). Mark's retention of the earlier name that was current during Jesus' ministry supports the general historicity of this gospel.

According to Mark, Jesus left Nazareth to be baptized by John in the Jordan (1:9), sometime after which he came to Capernaum (1:29; cf. Matt 4:13). He is routinely called "Jesus of Nazareth" (1:24; 10:47; 16:6) or "the Nazarene Jesus" (14:67). When he returned at last to Nazareth, the people were so skeptical that it provoked his famous aphorism that "a prophet is . . . without honor . . . in his own country" (6:4). Those who did not honor this prophet were "those of his own country" (district), "his own kin" (extended family), and "his own house" (immediate family including mother, brothers, and sisters — 6:3).

This skepticism in Nazareth was not new. Earlier his "family" (3:21), that is, his mother and brothers (3:31), set out from Nazareth to Capernaum to "seize" him (3:21). On arrival they were "outside" (3:31 — the house?), whereupon Jesus commented that his true mother and father were those who did the will of God (3:35).

This linkage between these two villages spans four chapters and consistently points up the unbelief of his biological family in contrast with the welcome of the new "family" in Capernaum.

This Capernaum-Nazareth distinction is not a major theme in Mark. But in a quiet way it does support the idea of Mark's dependence on a reliable witness, who saw things from a Capernaum viewpoint.

Evasive Withdrawals

One of the features of the Galilee chapters is that Jesus frequently withdraws from situations and people. Harold Hoehner lists these evasive movements in his biography of Herod Antipas,[26] and observes that frequently these withdrawals make "good historical sense."

1:45   In rural regions to escape the crowds.

3:7   From Capernaum and the synagogue to evade Pharisees and Herodians.

6:31-32 To the eastern shore of the lake, to evade Herod Antipas (secondary motive).

---

26. H. W. Hoehner, *Herod Antipas: A Contemporary of Jesus Christ* (Grand Rapids: Zondervan, 1980), 317-30.

6:45, 53   To Bethsaida and Gennesaret, following the feeding of the five thousand, to evade Herod Antipas (because the people tried to make Jesus "king" — John 6:15).

7:24   To Tyre, to withdraw from the possible menace of local Pharisees and scribes from Jerusalem (Mark 7:1).

7:31   To Sidon, the Sea of Galilee, Decapolis, a circuitous and uncertain (and debated) route, most likely to avoid crowds and Antipas's tetrarchy.

8:10   To Dalmanutha (briefly because it was close to Tiberias), to escape the crowds on the western side of the lake (following the feeding of the four thousand).

8:22   To Bethsaida then Caesarea in Philip's tetrarchy from the western side, most likely to evade Herod Antipas

9:30, 33   From Philip's tetrarchy, a secret journey through Galilee to Capernaum and south toward Jerusalem.

Mark's narrative is characterized by the often-bewildering references to Jesus' movements. Sometimes these involve crossing the lake and sometimes crossing borders into Tyre or Sidon or into Philip's tetrarchy or to the Decapolis. It is not always possible to account for the reason or the route taken. Yet the movements can be explained in part by the nature of Jesus' ministry, which provoked on one hand crowd interest in his healings and on the other the hostility of the Pharisees and more particularly of the tetrarch and his faction (the "Herodians"). Once more, the appearance of these details is consistent with Mark's recollection of Peter's teachings.

Vivid Details

Mark's gospel contains numerous examples of vivid detail. Where do these details come from? If they were present in all the stories in the Galilee, we might be inclined to view them as examples of contrived verisimilitude. Their haphazard occurrence, however, tends to support their authenticity.

That evening, at sundown, they brought to him all who were sick or possessed with demons. And the whole city was gathered together about *(pros)* the door. (1:32-33)

The Sabbath was now passed and the incapacitated can be brought to him; the whole city was, as it were, gathered expectantly facing the door of the house. This dramatic scene is beyond literary invention.

And leaving the crowd, they took him with them in the boat, just as he was. And other boats were with him. And a great storm of wind arose, and the waves beat into the boat, so that the boat was already filling. But he was in the stern, asleep on the cushion. (4:36-38)

The details "just as he was," the "other boats," and Jesus "asleep on the cushion" are at the same time so vivid and so gratuitous as to defy a fiction-based imagination.

There met him out of the tombs a man with an unclean spirit, who lived among the tombs; and no one could bind him any more, even with a chain; for he had often been bound with fetters and chains, but the chains he wrenched apart, and the fetters he broke in pieces; and no one had the strength to subdue him. Night and day among the tombs and on the mountains he was always crying out, and bruising himself with stones. (5:2-5)

Mark's images of this disturbed man who was prodigiously strong, with broken chains hanging from wrists and ankles, are potent and, again, credibly written out of an eyewitness's recollection.

When they came to the house of the ruler of the synagogue, he saw a tumult, and people weeping and wailing loudly. And when he had entered, he said to them, "Why do you make a tumult and weep? The child is not dead but sleeping." And they laughed at him. But he put them all outside, and took the child's father and mother and those who were with him, and went in where the child was. Taking her by the hand he said to her, "Talitha cumi"; which means, "Little girl, I say to you, arise." (5:38-41)

The name of the *archisynagōgos* (Jairus), the sounds of wailing, the laughter, and the Aramaic words all contribute to a strong sense of an eyewitness account.

Then he commanded them all to sit down by companies upon the green grass. So they sat down in groups (*prasiai prasiai,* "garden beds"), by hundreds and by fifties. (6:39-40)

This is an almost photographic image of people seated in ordered groups, their colorful gowns giving the appearance of garden beds set in green grass.

The words from these passages in Mark's gospel leap from the page. Most likely they spring from the memory of someone who was struck by the scene or the drama of the moment or the impact of the sounds. If such details were constant throughout, we could explain them as literary invention. Their occasional appearance, however, speaks against that explanation. A storyteller who was an eyewitness is the most likely reason for the appearance of these striking details.

Jesus' Emotions

Prominent among the vivid details in Mark's gospel are Jesus' emotional responses in various situations. These are some examples.

And a leper came to him beseeching him, and kneeling said to him. . . . Moved with *pity (splanchnistheis),*[27] he . . . touched him. . . . And he *sternly (embrimēsamenos)* charged him, and *sent him away (exebalen)* at once. (1:40-43)

Again he entered the synagogue, and a man was there who had a withered hand. And they watched him, to see whether he would heal him on the sabbath, so that they might accuse him. . . . And he looked around at them *with anger, grieved (met' orgēs syllypoumenos)* at their hardness of heart. (3:1-2, 5)

As he went ashore he saw a great throng, and he had *compassion (esplanchnisthē)* on them, because they were like sheep without a shepherd. (6:34)

And they were bringing children to him, that he might touch them; and the disciples rebuked them. But when Jesus saw it he was *indignant*

27. Some ancient authorities have "moved with wrath," which is not so well attested.

(*ēganaktēsen*), and said to them, "Let the children come to me, do not hinder them; for to such belongs the kingdom of God." (10:13-14)

And he took with him Peter and James and John, and began to be greatly distressed and troubled (*ekthambeisthai kai adēmonein*). And he said to them, "My soul is very sorrowful (*perilypos*), even to death." (14:33-34)

Are these observations the result of Mark's imagination or of his recollection of Peter's words? If the former, we would expect a more systematic development of these emotions. The writer's passing mention of them points rather in the direction of his recall of Peter's own reactions to Jesus in these situations.

Furthermore, on five occasions Mark observes that Jesus "looked around," as in a circle (*periblepomai*):

3:5   in the synagogue when they watched if he would heal on the Sabbath

3:34   in the house in Capernaum, with mother and brothers outside

5:32   at the crowd to see who touched him

10:23   to the disciples when he said how hard it was for the wealthy to enter the kingdom of God

11:11   on his arrival in the temple

Each of these was a dramatic occasion, and Jesus' manner of "looking right around" left its imprint in Peter's memory. Matthew does not use this word and Luke does so only once (Luke 6:10).

The "They" Passages

On twenty-one occasions Mark uses a third-person plural pronoun ("they") without an explicit subject, usually in passages to describe the movements of Jesus and his disciples, followed by a singular verb or pronoun referring to Jesus alone. Bauckham calls this "the plural-to-singular narrative device."[28] For example:

---

28. Bauckham, *Jesus and the Eyewitnesses*, 156-81. Bauckham acknowledges the influ-

They came to the other side of the sea, to the country of the Gerasenes. And when he had stepped out of the boat . . . (5:1-2)

They came to Bethsaida. And some people brought to him a blind man. (8:22)

They went to a place which was called Gethsemane; and he said to his disciples . . . (14:32)

When we compare Mark with Matthew and Luke, we find that these dependent Evangelists frequently remove references to the disciples ("they") and narrate the incident as if between Jesus and the other person(s) (to be healed or addressed). Matthew and Luke stand removed from the events, which they narrate as historians; Mark, however, remains close to the events. C. H. Turner, and Bauckham on whom he depends, points out how easy and simple it is to render the "they" as "we," reflecting Peter's presence as an eyewitness. Mark, however, who was not an eyewitness, naturally (and honestly) expresses the eyewitness Peter's "we" as a narrator's "they."

Consider, for example, how easily Mark's text retroverts to Peter's eyewitness testimony. "And immediately he left the synagogue, and entered the house of Simon and Andrew, with James and John. Now Simon's [my] mother-in-law lay sick with a fever, and immediately they [we] told him of her. And he came and took her by the hand" (1:29-31).

This hypothesis resists ultimate confirmation. Nonetheless, it remains an interesting possibility, especially when added to the other indications of Petrine influence, noted above.

Rabbi Jesus

Despite contrary arguments,[29] there are good reasons to regard Jesus as a rabbi. It is recognized, of course, that the era of the ordained rabbinate would not be reached for a century or more. Nonetheless, it is likely that the more formal office evolved from a looser understanding of that minis-

---

ence of C. H. Turner, "Markan Usage: Notes Critical and Exegetical, on the Second Gospel V; The Movements of Jesus and His Disciples and the Crowd," *JTS* 26 (1925): 225-40.

29. So M. Hengel, *The Charismatic Leader and His Followers* (Edinburgh: T. & T. Clark, 1981), 42-60.

try, as from times earlier than Jesus. The Mishnah refers to Jesus' contemporary Gamaliel as rabbi, implying that the office was current in the first century (cf. Acts 5:34 — "Gamaliel, a teacher of the law, held in honor by all the people").

Furthermore, it is acknowledged that to limit Jesus' role to that merely of a rabbi would scarcely do justice to the complex and multiform character of his *messianic* mission.[30] Nonetheless, evidence points to Jesus as "rabbi," even if he was an unusual and unorthodox rabbi, whose activities defy neat classification.

First, in each gospel, including Mark's, Jesus is often addressed as "rabbi" (9:5; 10:51; 11:21; 14:45) or its likely synonym "teacher" (4:38; 5:35; 9:17; 10:17, 20, 35; 12:14, 19, 32; 13:1), or referred to as "the teacher" (5:35; 14:14). That Jesus was addressed as "rabbi" and "teacher" in Mark suggests that he was a *teaching* rabbi, and that rabbi was not merely a respectful term of address.[31]

Second, the gospels describe Jesus the teacher in technical rabbinic terminology. The use of the word "disciple" for those who "followed" (1:16-20) him, "learned from him," and had taken his "yoke" upon them (Matt 11:28-30) implies that Jesus was a rabbinic teacher. A woman even sat at his feet like the pupil of a rabbi (Luke 10:39).

Third, Mark repeatedly recounts occasions where Jesus had given instruction in public that he then explained to his immediate disciples in private.

1:29　　　"And immediately he left the synagogue, and entered the house *(eis tēn oikian)* of Simon and Andrew."

4:10　　　"And when he was alone *(kata monas)*, those who were about him *(hoi peri auton)* with the twelve asked him concerning the parables."

4:11　　　"And he said to them, 'To you has been given the secret of the kingdom of God, but for those outside *(tois exō)* everything is in parables.'"

4:33-34　"With many such parables he spoke the word to them, as they were able to hear it; he did not speak to them without a para-

---

30. Hengel, *Charismatic Leader*, 67-71.
31. Hengel, *Charismatic Leader*, 43-44.

ble, but privately *(kat' idian)* to his own disciples he explained everything."

7:17   "And when he had entered the house *(eisēlthen eis oikon)*, and left the people, his disciples asked him about the parable."

9:28   "And when he had entered the house *(eiselthontos autou eis oikon)*, his disciples asked him privately *(kat' idian)*, 'Why could we not cast it out?'"

The Q logion "I thank thee, Father, Lord of heaven and earth, that thou hast *hidden* these things from the wise and understanding and *revealed* them to babes" (Luke 10:21/Matt 11:25) supports Mark's portrayal of Jesus' *private* ministry to his disciples, a ministry that is consistent with a rabbinic ministry of some kind. Mark's account of Jesus' "call" and "appointment" of the Twelve "to be with him" (Mark 3:13-14) gives further support to the notion of an *esoteric* ministry.[32]

Fourth, Jesus made extensive use of parables: more than forty are reported in the synoptic tradition.

Mark (and parallels)	11
Q	9
M	10
L	15

It is beyond dispute that rabbis of the general era told parables.[33] In fact, some of Jesus' parables employ similar cultural referents and story lines.[34] As parable teller, Jesus is identified as a rabbi.

Fifth, Paul's language for Jesus' institution of the Lord's Supper is *rabbinic:* "For I *received* from the Lord what I also *delivered* to you" (1 Cor 11:23). Paul intends his readers to understand that the Lord Jesus on the night he was betrayed "delivered" words to his original disciples, which they "received," and which were later "delivered" to Paul (who, in turn, "delivered" them to the churches). The ex-Pharisee Paul did not formulate these words; the original disciples formulated them. Their preservation *in this form* suggests that Jesus' original disciples "received" them from him, as from a rabbi.

32. B. F. Meyer, *The Aims of Jesus* (London: SCM, 1979), 111-13.
33. See, e.g., McArthur and Johnston, *They Also Taught in Parables.*
34. See chapter 9 below.

Jesus' own (likely) use of rabbinic language is consistent with the Mishnah's portrayal of the transmission of the Torah.[35] "Moses *received* Torah from Sinai [i.e., God] and *delivered* it to Joshua, and Joshua [*delivered* it] to the elders, and the elders [*delivered* it] to the prophets, and the prophets *delivered* it to the men of the great synagogue. These said three things: be deliberate in judging, and raise up many *disciples*, and make a hedge for the Torah."[36]

Jesus was at home with this language of "receiving" and "delivering," as his rebuke of the Pharisees makes clear ("You have a fine way of rejecting the commandment of God, in order to keep your *tradition*" — Mark 7:9). Jesus' complaint on this occasion, however, was not directed to the *practice* of "delivering" instruction (which he also practiced); his objection was with the Pharisees' employment of the corban formula to subvert the wellspring of the Torah tradition, Moses.

In short, the evidence points to Jesus as a rabbi who created a rabbinic fellowship by calling and instructing his disciples, so long as we understand that the total picture of Jesus is rather larger. Even Jesus' final commission to the disciples is cast in these terms: "*make disciples* of all nations . . . *teaching* them to *observe* all that I have *commanded* you" (Matt 28:19-20). He had "discipled" them by teaching them; and in turn they were to "disciple" others from the nations by delivering his *teaching* to them.

The rabbinic-style fellowship that existed between Jesus and the Twelve anticipated earliest Christianity in Jerusalem. Their fellowship did not cease with his death, but continued despite his physical absence from them. Jesus' "school" continued without interruption into the new community of faith in Jerusalem. The "tradition" they had "received" from Jesus they "handed over" to those who responded to Peter's proclamation and who were baptized. This now-enlarged group continued in the apostles' "teaching" (*didachē* — Acts 2:42; cf. 5:38).

In a short time the converted persecutor Saul of Tarsus would "visit" the apostle Peter in Jerusalem (Gal 1:18-19). The kerygmatic tradition and the Lord's Supper tradition (1 Cor 15:1-7; 11:23-26), which Paul "received"

---

35. See P. S. Alexander, "Orality in Pharisaic-Rabbinic Judaism at the Turn of the Eras," in *Jesus and the Oral Gospel Tradition*, ed. H. Wansbrough (Sheffield: JSOT, 1991), 159-84, and in the same volume, R. Riesner, "Jesus as Preacher and Teacher," 185-210.

36. *Pirqe 'Aboth* 1.1.

(and in turn "delivered"), óriginated from the apostles in Jerusalem, and were "delivered" to him — whether indirectly in Damascus circa 34 or directly in Jerusalem circa 36. The language of the rabbinic school will become prominent in his letters, with related terminology in other NT writings.[37] In other words, after the first Easter Rabbi Jesus' teachings to his original disciples were disseminated to new communities of disciples in Jerusalem initially, and throughout the land of Israel subsequently. Within a few years Saul/Paul began disseminating the Lord's teachings among Gentiles, initially among synagogue-connected Godfearers and then among rank idolaters.[38]

Naturally, it cannot be denied that Jesus was a public figure in Israel, both as a prophet announcing the kingdom of God to the people and as a leader who was sufficiently notable as to justify crucifixion as a pretended messiah. No less, however, was Jesus *a rabbi* who created a rabbinic school. Much of the subsequent history of early Christianity will not make sense unless this is understood.[39]

The point is that Peter was the most prominent member of the "school" of Rabbi Jesus, who after the first Easter became the leading apostle in both Jerusalem and the land of Israel for the next seven or eight years (Gal 1:18; 2:7-8; Acts 9:31-32). And, according to the elder's report to Papias, this Peter's teaching, as heard and remembered by his "interpreter" Mark, became the basis of the gospel Mark wrote.

Verbal Kerygma and Written Gospel

The documents of the NT confront us with two forms of "gospel." One expression of gospel is the record of what the apostles *preached* (*to kērygma* — 1 Cor 1:21), and the other is the *written* gospel (Mark 1:1). As noted in the previous chapter, Paul summarizes his kerygma (or proclamation) in 1 Corinthians 15:3-7 in terms that broadly conform to the "Jerusalem" section of Peter's message in Caesarea Maritima, as summarized in Acts 10:39-43. This was tradition that Paul and the Jerusalem apostles shared (1 Cor 15:11; Acts 13:16-41).

---

37. See P. Barnett, *Jesus and the Logic of History* (Leicester: Inter-Varsity, 1997), 142-44.
38. See Barnett, *Paul,* 140-42.
39. Barnett, *Logic,* 144-58.

Peter's message in Caesarea is the last of a series of five summarized messages scattered throughout Acts 1–10. Peter's earlier messages focus on Christ's death and resurrection in Jerusalem, whereas the Caesarea message begins with John the Baptist and Jesus' ministry in Galilee and concludes with his death and resurrection in Jerusalem. Nonetheless, all of Peter's messages, as summarized in Acts, are *formulaic* in character and in this are similar to Paul's "received" outline that he cites in 1 Corinthians 15:3-7 (cf. Acts 13:16-41). Likewise formulaic is Paul's citation of the Lord's Supper *paradosis*/"tradition" (1 Cor 11:23-26).

This observation prompts an important question. What is the relationship between the formulaic kerygma in Acts 10:36-43/1 Corinthians 15:3-7/Acts 13:16-41 as *verbally* proclaimed and the small units (pericopes) in Mark's *written* gospel? To what extent, if at all, do the formulaic kerygmatic summaries contribute to the biographical details in the pericopes in Mark?

To answer this we need to consider Mark's gospel from its two aspects, its overall narrative sweep and its detailed components (pericopes). In regards the first, Mark's gospel (and consequentially Matthew's and Luke's) broadly follows the sequence of events set out in the Acts formulaic summary of Peter's Caesarea and Paul's Antioch sermons. This is widely recognized and needs little further discussion.[40]

Formulaic versions of the kerygma occur in Paul's letters (notably 1 Cor 15:3-7, as above) but also in fragmentary passing references in other NT letters (see, e.g., Heb 6:1-4; 1 Pet 1:18-21). It is clear that brief references to the incarnation, death, resurrection, and reappearance of Christ replay repeatedly within the NT letters, whether as echoes of mission preaching or as baptismal confessions or early hymns. Again, this is not disputed among NT authorities.

It is otherwise, however, with the component pericopes in Mark's gospel. The specific deeds and words of Jesus in Mark's small units do not appear to be part of the formulaic outlines, as Bauckham observes: "The very broad outline of the story could well have been adopted by Mark from the type of 'kerygmatic summary' that is found in the speeches of Peter and Paul in Acts and that, in my opinion, existed in early Christian tradition as *a distinct form of the gospel traditions themselves, that is, from the individual stories and sayings.*"[41]

40. Barnett, *Birth of Christianity*, 153-54.
41. Bauckham, *Jesus and the Eyewitnesses*, 243, emphasis added.

True, Paul's letters have echoes of Jesus' teaching from an embryonic Markan tradition that will appear later in Mark's gospel, as set out below. But so far as we can tell from the following examples, these echoes do not arise from the formulaic kerygmatic outlines.

Paul	*Echoing*	*the "Mark" Tradition*
1 Thess 4:15-16	(sound of the trumpet)	13:37 (a loud trumpet call)
1 Cor 7:10-11	(a wife not separate)	10:9 (let not man put asunder)
Rom 13:7	(pay . . . their dues)	12:17 (render to Caesar)
Rom 13:8	(he who loves neighbor)	12:31 (love your neighbor)
Rom 14:13	(a stumbling block)	9:42 (one . . . to stumble)
Rom 14:14	(nothing is unclean)	7:15 (nothing . . . can defile)
Rom 14:20	(everything . . . is clean)	7:19 (all foods clean)

It appears that the elements of the embryonic "Mark" tradition that Paul adapts are distinct from the kerygmatic outlines, implying the existence of two related but discrete traditions, the kerygmatic and the pericope traditions.

This observation prompts two related questions. First, who was responsible for creating the pericope tradition? Most likely it was a Petrine tradition arising from Peter's instructions in church meetings, likely articulated through Mark as his "interpreter." Second, since the kerygmatic tradition was *oral*, it raises the question whether the pericope tradition was also oral, or was it written (or both oral and written)? We defer addressing this question until the next chapter.

The Past and the Present in Mark

During the years redaction criticism was in vogue, there was a tendency to downplay the distinction between the past in Mark's gospel (his Jesus biography) and the existential circumstances of Mark's readers at the time he wrote his gospel (the *Sitz im Leben* of the Markan community).[42] That is

---

42. See, e.g., T. J. Weeden, *Mark — Traditions in Conflict* (Philadelphia: Fortress, 1971); W. Marxsen, *Mark the Evangelist: Studies in the Redaction History of the Gospel* (Nashville: Abingdon, 1969), 131-38. For a contrary view see E. E. Lemcio, "The Intention of the Evangelist, Mark," *NTS* 32 (1986): 187-206.

to say, in this view the gospel reflected the totality of what Mark and his audience believed. In other words, Mark's narrative essentially mirrored the present ecclesial circumstances of Mark and his circle, but not the historic past of Jesus of Nazareth.

More recently the scholarly interest in the reader (better, "hearer") of Mark's narrative has helped distinguish the present (*when* Mark wrote) from the past (*about which* he wrote).

This is most obviously evident in Mark's direction to the church lector, "Let the reader *(ho anaginōskōn)* understand" regarding Jesus' words about the "desolating sacrilege set up where it ought not to be" (Mark 13:14). Here the distinction between Jesus' original words and their present application is carefully preserved.

Mark also appeals to two past events that he implies are known to his present readers, so that no additional comment is warranted.

> And a young man followed [Jesus], with nothing but a linen cloth about his body; and they seized him, but he left the linen cloth and ran away naked. (14:51-52)

> And they compelled a passer-by, Simon of Cyrene, who was coming in from the country, the father of Alexander and Rufus, to carry his cross. (15:21)

Mark carefully preserves the distinction between past ("a young man" and "Simon of Cyrene") and present (the hearers' present knowledge of both the young man and Simon).

Mark's gratuitous "Thus he declared all foods clean" (7:19; cf. Rom 14:20) is his present gloss on Jesus' original declaration about the nature of purity (Mark 7:9-16). Mark the pastor is driving home the current application of Jesus' *historic* utterance about purity.

True, at several points Mark so constructs his narrative that Jesus appears to speak directly to Mark's hearers in the churches.

> "All things are possible to him who believes." (9:23)

> "The gospel must first be preached to all nations." (13:10)

> "So also, when you see these things taking place, you know that he is near, at the very gates." (13:29)

"And what I say to you I say to all: Watch." (13:37)

"And truly, I say to you, wherever the gospel is preached in the whole world, what she has done will be told in memory of her." (14:9)

By giving Jesus a present voice, has Mark erased the past so that it is the timeless ascended Lord who is now addressing his people? By no means: Mark manages to portray the present Lord speaking from his authentically historic past.

In short, Mark wrote as one who knew the difference between the past of Jesus and the present circumstances of his audience. Furthermore, implicit in his narrative is his concern to explain *how* the past of Jesus and the present of his hearers happened. It was by means of the kerygma, which was verbal initially but is now written, and which his hearers have apprehended.

Conclusion — Whose Memory?

It is time to draw together the threads of our argument. We subscribe to the widely held view that Mark's was the earliest synoptic gospel and that it was written by about 70, if not earlier.

In response to the critical question, How do we span the forty or so years between Jesus and Mark's written text? we note various theories of memorized oral transmission. In our view, those associated with Bultmann and Bailey do not explain the nature of the original didactic ethos in the land of Israel nor the nature of early Christian ministry. Gerhardsson's rabbinic explanation accounts for the original remembering of Jesus' parabolic teaching and for the "rabbinic" character of the "receiving" and "delivering" of kerygmatic and other formulae reflected in the Acts sermons and in sections of Paul's letters. His hypothesis, however, is less convincing when applied to shorter narrative units (pericopes) in Mark 1–10 or to the longer, connected narrative(s) in chapters 11–16.

The best explanation for these longer and shorter narratives is the first-century report of the Elder John that Papias writes about early in the second century. The ambivalent nature of Papias's account actually helps secure our confidence in its authenticity. Put simply, the elder reported that the first disciples of the Lord said Mark wrote his gospel based on his memory of the things Peter taught, which Mark had "interpreted" to Peter's hearers.

Upon examination, chapters 11–16 appear to have been written in the early 40s, as a connected and coherent discrete work. There are good reasons to believe that John Mark wrote this text in collaboration with Peter for local church use in Judea and Galilee.

The first ten chapters focus on Galilee and consist of mainly shorter episodes that are not usually so closely connected as those in the Jerusalem narratives. These, too, were likely originally Peter's "stories" about Jesus that Peter formulated in the land of Israel for Mark to articulate and later write down for us.

The prominence of Peter as the first-mentioned and last-mentioned disciple and as one present throughout the narratives supports the elder's account of this gospel as *Petrine*. The numerous vivid descriptive details that occur irregularly in this gospel are consistent with Mark's partial recollection of Peter's stories, as acknowledged by the elder/Papias. Evidently Jesus engaged in a private ministry in the manner of a rabbi to Peter and other disciples, explaining both the rabbinic character of aspects of early Christianity and also Peter's authority as the leading teacher of the words and works of his master in public and in the churches in the land of Israel in the earliest years of Christian history.

A Scenario

Let me propose a scenario. It is based in Jerusalem and it focuses on the period A.D. 33-40. Since the tradition shared by Peter (Acts 10:41-42) and Paul (Acts 13:31-32) refers to Christ's direction that his disciples "witness" to him, it is imaginable that they quickly created a summary of his life story (as related to his saving works — Acts 2:22), beginning with John the Baptist, pointing to what Jesus did in Galilee, and ending with his death and resurrection in Jerusalem. This summary became the basis of Peter's preaching in Jerusalem and later in Caesarea. Persecuted disciples took this message to Damascus where it became the basis of Paul's baptismal instruction and subsequent preaching, which we glimpse in 1 Corinthians 15:3-7 and Acts 13:16-41.

Around A.D. 40, following Gaius's threat to desecrate the temple, Mark and Peter collaborated in writing a narrative of Jesus' last days in Jerusalem. This narrative was used for instruction and worship in the churches in Jerusalem and in the land of Israel that grew up under Peter's apostolate. Later Mark incorporated this "Jerusalem" narrative in his completed gospel.

SIX

Earliest Window (Luke 1:1-4)

This prologue contains all that we really know respecting the composition of early narratives of the life of Christ, and it is the test by which theories as to the origin of our Gospels must be judged.

Alfred Plummer[1]

Since the gospels make remarkable claims about Jesus of Nazareth, it is important that we know whether or not their portrayal reasonably corresponds to the person as he was *historically.* It was possible for people alive during the life span of his immediate followers to speak to the authors directly and to evaluate their testimony, but all others since that era have one principal source of information, the gospels.

So we must ask, how historically credible are those gospels? To find an answer we must further ask, by which means did the information about Christ in the gospels come to be written in the gospels? This in turn brings us back to an issue we raised in the previous chapter: Was the data that found its way into the gospels transmitted orally or in writing?

In our earlier discussion about the time frame in which the gospels were written and used, we argued that the four gospels were in circulation and use by the end of the century of Christ, that is, within six decades of

---

1. A. Plummer, *St. Luke,* ICC (Edinburgh: T. & T. Clark, 1901), 2.

his life span.[2] This effectively seals off the period in which the gospels were written and facilitates the inquiry into their prehistory.

One of those gospels itself gives us a window on the process by which the author wrote his book, his two-volume work, Luke-Acts.[3] Luke 1:1-4, the author's prologue to Luke-Acts, uniquely reveals the situation between the historical Christ and when Luke began to write, when a believer like Theophilus, the dedicatee, was dependent on oral instruction and fragmentary and incomplete texts.

Luke 1:1-4 and the Genre of Luke-Acts

Considerable attention has been directed to the prologue to Luke-Acts. Scholars have been interested in the author's "stately" tone and have rightly supposed that he was using recognizable literary conventions.[4] Some have discerned hints that a technical treatise will unfold after these solemn opening lines, perhaps a medical excursus.[5] With greater probability others think the prologue is identifying the book that follows as a historical work but written with pastoral intent.[6]

---

2. See chapter 1 above.

3. The author wrote Luke-Acts as one work, necessarily divided into two parts of equal length, due to the length limits of papyrus scrolls. See Barnett, *Birth of Christianity,* 189-90.

4. The following words appear in "classical" texts as well as in some other Lukan passages: *epeidēper* ("since"), *epicheirein* ("undertake" — see also Acts 9:29; 19:13), *anatassomai* ("draw up"), *diēgēsis* ("narrative"), *kathexēs* ("orderly" — Luke 8:1; Acts 3:24; 11:4; 18:23). Writers of prologues in antiquity were sometimes guilty of investing these prefaces with overlong, overblown rhetoric in contrast with a less than impressive text that followed. The second century A.D. critic Lucian referred to such prologues as having "the head of a colossus on the body of a dwarf" (*On How to Write History* 23).

5. There is an interesting parallel in the preface to Dioscorides' *Materia Medica:* "Although not only many ancient but also many modern writers have composed works on the preparation, the power and the testing of drugs, my dearest Areios, I shall try to prove to you that no empty or unreasonable impulse has moved me to undertake this work." Dioscorides was a first century A.D. army physician who wrote about the properties of plants and drugs. L. Alexander, *The Preface to Luke's Gospel,* SNTSMS 78 (Cambridge: Cambridge University Press, 1993), has argued that Luke's preface most closely resembles introductions to technical or professional works, rather than specifically historical works.

6. See R. Bauckham, *Jesus and the Eyewitnesses: The Gospels as Eyewitness Testimony* (Grand Rapids: Eerdmans, 2006), 117-19.

Reference to the dedicatee Theophilus in the prologue in the gospel is picked up in the opening sentence of the Acts of the Apostles.

Luke 1:3-4   "It seemed good to me . . . to write . . . for you, *most excellent Theophilus*, that you may know the truth concerning the things of which you have been informed."

Acts 1:1   "In the first book, *O Theophilus*, I have dealt with all that Jesus began to do and teach."

This finds a parallel in the opening sentences of the first and second books of Josephus's *Against Apion* (written in the 90s in Rome).

Book 1   ". . . *most excellent Epaphroditus*, I . . . devote a brief treatise . . . in order to . . . instruct all who desire to know the truth concerning the antiquity of our race."

Book 2   "In the first volume of my work, *my most esteemed Epaphroditus . . .*"

Both texts (a) have a named dedicatee, (b) state a need to be addressed, and (c) assure the reader of the writer's competence to provide accurate information. Yet Luke is not literarily dependent on Josephus, nor vice versa, because the vocabulary is quite different. Moreover, the circumstance of the addressees is dissimilar. Josephus must convince Epaphroditus about Judaism's antiquity whereas Theophilus does not need further assurance about his new faith; he is already a Christian catechumen.[7] Furthermore, *Against Apion* is a polemical work, as its title implies, whereas Luke-Acts is a didactic narrative of the things Jesus *began* to do and to teach (in the gospel) and *continued* to do and to teach through his servants (in Acts). Despite these and other differences, Josephus and Luke are observing an established convention about their prefaces in a genre of literature that is broadly historical in character.

---

7. Based on Greek *katēchoun* (= "to instruct") as in Acts 18:25; 1 Cor 14:19; Gal 6:6.

Luke 1:1-4: The Situation

It is time to look more closely at Luke 1:1-4.

> Since many have undertaken to draw up a narrative about the things
> that have been fulfilled among us, just as they delivered [them] to us,
> (who from the beginning were eyewitnesses and servants of the
> word) it seemed good to me also (having investigated everything
> from the first) to write accurately and sequentially to you, most ex-
> cellent Theophilus, in order that you may know the certainty of the
> matters about which you have been instructed. (Luke 1:1-4, my trans-
> lation)

i. Luke appears to be making a distinction between the "many" who
wrote their "narratives" and those "eyewitnesses and servants of the word"
who "delivered" them to him. Yet this may not be an ironclad distinction.
"Eyewitnesses and servants of the word" may have been among those who
"delivered" their texts to the author.

The "eyewitnesses and servants of the word" are the original
disciples-become-preachers of the word[8] who (rabbi-like) have "delivered"
the *writings* of the "many" to Luke, thereby effectively validating these as a
basis for his more comprehensive work. The technical-sounding "delivered" *(paredosan)* is usually applied to "handing over" oral tradition,[9] giving these *texts* a greater sense of weight.

ii. It follows that these "eyewitnesses and servants of the word"
were still alive when they "delivered" their "narratives" to Luke. Scholars
debate the dating of Luke-Acts. I see no reason to locate Luke-Acts later
than the mid-70s, based on the sense that Acts "fits" the political ar-
rangements of Roman provinces in the middle of the century, but not
much later.[10] The point to make here, though, is not so much the dating
of authorship, but that Luke received the "narratives" of the "eyewitnesses" *while they were still alive* and their memory of the historical
Christ was current.

---

8. The book of Acts could be characterized as a chronicle of the "word" *(logos)*
preached, taught, and believed (e.g., Acts 2:41; 4:4, 29, 31; 6:2; etc.).

9. Mark 7:13; 1 Cor 11:2; 15:3; cf. Mark 7:3, 5, 8, 9; Gal 1:14; 2 Thess 2:15; 3:6.

10. Classically argued by A. N. Sherwin-White, *Roman Society and Roman Law in the
New Testament* (Oxford: Clarendon, 1963), 172-85.

The qualification of these eyewitnesses is impressive. They were "eyewitnesses *from the beginning*" *(ap' archēs)*, that is, from the time the word of God came to John the Baptist (Acts 1:21-22) and onward throughout Jesus' ministry up to and including his death, resurrection, and exaltation. In the years since his exaltation these "eyewitnesses" were "servants of the word" (cf. John 15:27 — "And you also are witnesses, because you have been with me *from the beginning*"). In other words, these "eyewitnesses" of Christ are now "servants of the word" and leaders of early Christianity who are able to validate the texts relating his earthly ministry.

iii. Unfortunately, Luke does not indicate when or where these texts were delivered to him. His "we" passages and other references, however, give us a series of possibilities. The first possibility locates Luke at Troas circa 49 (Acts 16:11), where he is already a disciple and a missionary (so it seems) and someone known to Paul (why else would he go with him immediately?). If, as appears likely, he was from Antioch-on-the-Orontes,[11] he was a disciple there in the 40s and would have had opportunity to meet Barnabas and Paul and likely Peter as well (Gal 2:11-14).

Second, it appears that he spent the next eight years (49-57) in Philippi engaged in mission work (Acts 16:16; 20:6), where he may have been the unnamed emissary to Corinth from the Macedonian churches "whose praise in the gospel[12] is throughout all the [Macedonian] churches."[13] Be that as it may, he must have kept in contact with Paul throughout those years since he traveled with him in 57 from Philippi to Jerusalem (Acts 20:6; cf. 2 Cor 8:19). It is probable that Paul had contact with him in Philippi during the writing of 2 Corinthians in about 56 (2 Cor 7:5; 8:18).

Third, from about 57 to 60 Luke was with or near Paul, from their return together to Jerusalem (57), and also in Israel while Paul was imprisoned in Caesarea (57-60 — Acts 20:6–27:1).

Fourth, throughout 60-62 Luke was in Rome while Paul was imprisoned there (Acts 28:31).

Fifth, circa 64 Luke was in Rome while Paul was imprisoned awaiting

11. See Barnett, *Birth of Christianity*, 191-92.

12. The words "in the gospel" *(en tō euangeliō)* find parallels in 2 Cor 2:12 and Rom 15:19 and point to comprehensive mission work, including preaching and gathering, instructing and ordering a new congregation.

13. An ancient opinion going back to Origen but not shared by, e.g., V. P. Furnish, *II Corinthians* (New York: Doubleday, 1984), 435-36.

execution (2 Tim 4:11). Of particular importance here are Paul's requests to Timothy in Ephesus. He asked Timothy to bring Mark to Rome "for service" *(eis diakonian),* and with him "the scrolls" *(ta biblia* — LXX texts?) and "the parchments" *(tas membranas* — superior writing material?). Clearly these were not for Paul's use (since he faced death — 2 Tim 4:6), which must mean Paul was securing these for Luke in Rome ("Luke alone is with me" — 2 Tim 4:11). The arrival of Timothy and Mark in Rome together with the scrolls and the parchments allows us to imagine the human and material resources converging in Rome for Luke to commence writing his magisterial work.

We may sum up the known possibilities when and where "the eyewitnesses and ministers of the word" had opportunity to hand over "narratives" to Luke. One possibility is (a) Antioch in the 40s (Peter was there circa 49 — Gal 2:11-14). Another is (b) Jerusalem and Caesarea circa 57-60 (Acts 20:15; 27:1). Yet another is (c) Rome circa 60-62 (Acts 28:30). And finally there is (d) Rome circa 64 (2 Tim 4:11), where Peter and Mark were also present (1 Pet 5:13; cf. 2 Tim 4:11). Of these possibilities, the most likely are (c) and (d), that is, circa 60-64 in Rome.[14]

We thus conclude that Luke was an experienced minister who had ample opportunities to receive written traditions upon which he would base his own two-volume history. The precise information about when and where the narratives were delivered to him may elude us, but these details are less important than the *fact* that the "eyewitnesses" of Christ who became "servants of the word" *did* "hand over" these texts to the major contributor to the New Testament. Without his two-volume history we could make little sense of the relationship between the historical Christ and the rise of Christianity. But that two-volume history rests on sources that had been validated by the highest authorities, the original disciples of Jesus.

iv. Just as Luke gives the qualification of the traditors ("from the beginning . . . eyewitnesses") who "delivered" the texts to him, so now he gives his own qualification to write. He has "investigated everything from the first" *(parēkolouthēkoti anōthen pasin).*

As noted, Luke had extensive associations with Paul, considerable contact with Mark, and opportunity to meet Peter (in Rome — 2 Tim 4:11; 1 Pet 5:13). As the traveling companion of Paul for many years (ca. 57-62),

---

14. We must not assume that Luke collected these texts on only one occasion.

as indicated by the "we" passages,[15] Luke was able to hear about Paul's life and ministry, and through Paul to learn about Peter and James, and through them to have thirdhand information about Christ (Gal 1:18-19). Furthermore, Luke was present with Mark when Paul wrote Colossians (Col 4:10, 14), so that Luke had access to yet another leader in the early church, Mark, through whom he was able to know about Peter and through him to have thirdhand knowledge about Christ.

Peter < Paul < Luke (Gal 1:18/"we" passages)
Christ <
James < Paul < Luke (Gal 1:19/"we" passages)
Christ < Peter < Mark < Luke (Col 4:10; Acts 12:12-13)

In short, Luke had extensive direct access to Paul and Mark, and through them indirect, secondhand access to Peter and James, and through them at third hand, to Christ himself. Luke, the major contributor to the NT and its primary historian, was not isolated from the historical Christ by a wall of ignorance. On the contrary, his extensive contact with Paul and Mark gave him considerable information about the original eye-witnesses and their witness to Christ.

Yet, Luke is careful not to say or imply that he was an eyewitness.

Luke may have known other lesser figures, as sources for his inquiries, as he hints in Luke-Acts. Among such lesser figures is Manaen (= Menachem), one of the prophets and teachers in the church of Antioch in the 40s, who had been a member of the court *(syntrophos)* of Herod Antipas (Acts 13:1). Since Luke likely had been part of the church of Antioch,[16] he would have known Manaen, and had opportunity to inquire about Manaen's remarkable life-change from Herodian courtier to Christian leader (about which we may only speculate) and to solicit Manaen's own observations about Jesus of Nazareth. Tiberias, the tetrarch's capital, is only a few miles from Capernaum, Jesus' base of operations.

Furthermore, it may be no coincidence that Luke says so much about someone else in Herod Antipas's circle in Tiberias, Joanna the wife of Chuza the tetrarch's estate manager *(epitropos)*. Joanna accompanied Christ and the disciples in Galilee and came to Jerusalem where she witnessed the empty tomb (Luke 8:3; 24:10). It is likely no coincidence that

15. Acts 16:10-18; 20:6–21:17; 27:1–28:31; cf. Col 4:14; 2 Tim 4:11.
16. See Barnett, *Birth of Christianity,* 191-92.

Luke alone of the four Evangelists mentions Joanna, suggesting some personal contact.

Luke appears to have been in Palestine circa 57-60 while Paul was in prison in Caesarea Maritima. This extended period would have offered him the chance to visit places where key events took place and to speak to people like Joanna who would appear in his narratives. It is by no means inconceivable that Luke also had opportunity to speak to the aged Mary, as hinted by the words, "Mary kept all these things, pondering them in her heart" (Luke 2:19).

In short, in making his claim to have "investigated everything from the first," it is evident that Luke had opportunities to do so through his certain contact with Paul and Mark and likely contact with Manaen and Joanna.

v. Does Luke exaggerate when he speaks of "many" who undertook to write a "narrative"? Our ancient writer does not indicate the identities of these "many" writers. The modern discipline of source criticism, however, when applied to the synoptic gospels, has revealed that Luke (1,149 verses) used (i.e., adapted, often abbreviating) a number of texts.

Mark	380 verses
Q — the source common to Matthew and Luke	250 verses
L — source(s) peculiar to Luke	580 verses

These three do not quite add up to "many" who wrote a "narrative," yet it is possible that L represents multiple subsidiary sources, including a nativity narrative (Luke 1–2),[17] records of miracles and parables peculiar to Luke, his own distinctive details of Jesus' last days in Jerusalem, and the special account of the resurrection appearances (Luke 24). Additionally, we have to consider that Luke may also be referring to the sources underlying the book of Acts (though it is difficult to identify the sources of Acts). It may be no hyperbole for Luke to refer to "many" texts that the traditors "delivered" to him.

As noted, we may only speculate when and where the "eyewitnesses and servants of the word . . . delivered" these "narratives" to Luke. For example, various authorities[18] have proposed that (in Caesarea) Luke first

17. The nativity chapters are characterized by Hebraic and archaic tones, including in the Magnificat, Benedictus, and Nunc Dimittis (1:46-55; 1:68-79; 2:29-32).

18. See, e.g., V. Taylor, *The Four Gospels* (London: Epworth, 1960), 36-43. The proto-Luke hypothesis originated with B. H. Streeter.

created a proto-gospel from Q and (some of) his L material, which commenced with the elaborate sixfold chronological intersection that marked the beginning of John's prophesying (Luke 3:1-2).[19] Then, to these he attached at the beginning the nativity narrative and at the end the Emmaus narrative. Subsequently (so it is proposed) Mark's gospel came to hand (in Rome), assisting Luke to fill in the otherwise missing parts of Jesus' ministry in Galilee, so that he added in whole blocks of Mark, alternating with material from his initial proto-gospel. According to this theory, Luke created most of his gospel by a "banding" process, as he alternated blocks of material from proto-Luke (PL) and Mark (Mk).

Luke 1–2 Infancy Stories
   PL   3–4
   Mk   4:31; 4:44
   PL   5:1; 5:11
   Mk   5:12; 6:11
   PL   6:12; 8:3
   Mk   8:4; 9:50
   PL   9:51; 18:4
   Mk   18:5; 18:43
   PL   19:1; 19:28
   Mk   19:28; 19:36
   PL   19:37; 19:48
   Mk   20:1; 22:13
Luke 24 Resurrection Stories

In favor of this "proto-Luke" theory, we note that Luke 3:1-2 does read like the beginning of a gospel; that Luke makes surprisingly little use of Mark (compared with Matthew's strong dependence), consistent with Luke's later access to it; and that Luke appears to make Mark fit in with his other entity (proto-Luke), rather than vice versa.

19. It is difficult to avoid the conclusion that Luke was aware of the similar-sounding and critical time note in Thucydides, *The Peloponnesian War* 2.6 that marked the beginning of the Peloponnesian War: "In the fifteenth year [of the truce], in the forty-eighth year of the priestess of Chrysis at Argos, in the ephorate of Aenesias at Sparta, in the last month but two of the archonship of Pythodorus of Athens, and six months after the battle of Potidaea, just at the beginning of spring, a Theban force . . . made an armed entry into Plataea" (Everyman's Library).

Against this reconstruction is the possibility that Mark's gospel (or an earlier draft) predates Paul's early letters. We refer to Paul's awareness of teaching peculiar to Mark, as noted previously,[20] including references to the trumpet sound (1 Thess 4:15-16/Mark 13:37), a wife's duty to not separate (1 Cor 7:10-11/Mark 10:9), the requirement to pay taxes (Rom 13:7/Mark 12:17), the call to love the neighbor (Rom 13:8/Mark 12:31), warnings against being a stumbling block (Rom 14:13/Mark 9:42), the assertion that nothing is unclean (Rom 14:14/Mark 7:15) but that everything is clean (Rom 14:20/Mark 7:19). Paul was not making systematic use of these words of the Lord, but he used them only insofar as they were applicable to the pastoral circumstances in the churches.

If these logia of the Lord came to Paul as oral tradition, this would cast no light on the question of his companion Luke's early access to a *written* text of Mark (since it did not yet exist). If, however, by the early 50s Paul was alluding to a written text of Mark (or an earlier draft) — which is more likely than less likely — it raises the possibility that Luke also had access to Mark (or an earlier draft) by the time he came to Palestine in 57-60. In this case, the hypothesis of an early proto-Luke text into which Luke added sections of Mark seems implausible.[21]

In the end, therefore, there is no scientific way to establish when Luke "received" these narratives nor the sequence or means by which he incorporated them into his global two-volume narrative. We may, however, agree that source criticism has confirmed Luke's statement in his prologue that he had access to preexistent texts, which the critics have isolated as Mark, Q, and L.

vi. Luke's prologue prompts the question of his attitude to the "narratives" that the "eyewitnesses" delivered to him. Unlike Josephus's explicit rejection of information that had come to Epaphroditus, Luke writes positively about his sources. These had been "delivered" to him by the highest authorities, the eyewitnesses *(autoptai)* of Christ.

Nonetheless, Luke hints at a number of shortcomings that his proposed work will rectify. (a) His "investigation" of "everything *from the first*" *(anōthen)* may point to a deficiency in the Gospel of Mark that provided no information about Christ's early life. (b) Further, that Luke's nar-

---

20. See the previous chapter.

21. For further arguments against a full proto-Luke hypothesis, see G. N. Stanton, *The Gospels and Jesus* (Oxford: Oxford University Press, 1989), 90.

rative would be "sequential" *(kathexēs)* may imply that the texts that came to him were fragmentary, somehow incomplete (lacking in accuracy? — *akribōs),* so that he must give a more comprehensive record. (c) Moreover, his connecting of the narratives of Christ (the gospel) with those of the "servants of the word" (the Acts) indicates that he saw the "fulfilled" purposes of God extending beyond the earthly life of Christ into his exalted life and the work he did through these "servants." (d) In particular, Luke's written account will provide Theophilus with a "certainty" *(asphaleia)* that is lacking from his present circumstance as a catechumen dependent on oral tradition.

vii. What, then, do we see of early Christianity through Luke's window? We see five things. First, we see a number of scrolls in which are written "narratives" of the deeds and words of Jesus of Nazareth. Second, we glimpse "eyewitnesses" of Christ engaged in "serving" (i.e., preaching) the gospel-word. Third, we see these "eyewitnesses and servants of the word" giving these texts to Luke, a trusted colleague of Paul's, thereby validating these scrolls. Fourth, we see Luke, with scroll opened and stylus in hand, writing his comprehensive history. Fifth, we see a man of distinction, Theophilus, who has become a Christian-under-instruction.

In particular, through Luke's window we observe the concurrent currency of two sources of information about Christ, *oral* tradition and *written* "narratives."

Theophilus was probably instructed *(katēchēthēs)* by oral tradition, most likely at baptism, a practice hinted at throughout the NT (e.g., Rom 6:3, 17; 10:8-11; 1 Cor 12:3, 13; 1 Pet 3:21; cf. also 1 Thess 4:1-8).

Those who composed the various "narratives" that were "delivered" to Luke wrote them to be *read aloud* in the nascent church gatherings in the land of Israel, as Mark 13:14 ("Let the [church] reader understand") indicates. The original writers and hearers of these texts were Jews accustomed to hearing the Law and the Prophets read and expounded in the synagogues. It was entirely fitting that sacred texts should be written, focused on the Christ who fulfilled the Law and the Prophets. Furthermore, merely oral traditions, including formulae like 1 Corinthians 15:3-7 and invocations like "Lord, come"/*Maran atha* (1 Cor 16:22), were limited in their didactic scope. The creation eventually of four extensive biographical narratives of Christ in the gospels expressed the felt need for comprehensive, permanent records for teaching purposes. This biographical process in embryo may have begun quite soon after the first Easter.

Unfortunately, we have no objective means of establishing a time frame for the appearance of these pre-Lukan narratives. There is no reason, however, why they might not have appeared in the 30s or 40s. We have earlier suggested that Mark 11–16 (or 14–16) was created in the early 40s.[22]

viii. The creation of these early "narratives" (including Mark and Q) arose from the original authors' concern for the preservation of *biographical* information about the historical Christ, information that would be used for instruction and worship in the early church gatherings in Israel. There is a sense in which Luke, by writing his gospel, merely continued and refined that process. The shortcomings he rectified (absence of a "beginning" to these texts and their fragmentary character) are in no way a censure of early efforts at Christian historiography, but rather an endorsement and an improvement of them.

Christ Biography in the Pre-Lukan Sources

Do Luke's sources Mark, Q, and L help us find the historical Christ? Clearly Mark is biographical in character, but what about Q and L?

Mark

Mark's gospel languished throughout the greater part of Christian history until modern times. It appeared to be a merely briefer version of Matthew, omitting the critically important Sermon on the Mount and other teachings. This perception changed dramatically with the rise of source criticism in the eighteenth century. The source critics established Mark's as the first-written of the synoptic gospels, and furthermore, they posited that Matthew and Luke followed Mark's sequence and incorporated large amounts of his text in their own gospels, often closely following Mark's words. Some scholars have insisted on Matthew's priority and that Mark is a shortened version of Matthew. The overwhelming majority, however, are convinced that Mark's is the earliest of the three.

Historical analysis depends on primary and underived sources that

22. See chapter 5 above.

are as close as possible to the object of inquiry. Since we have no extant antecedent to Mark's gospel, his gospel is of special interest in discovering biographical information about Jesus of Nazareth. It follows that the material from Mark that Matthew and Luke replicate is not useful to the historian, unless the later writer had superior information and corrected Mark, as Matthew and Luke do (for example) in calling Herod a "tetrarch" in place of Mark's reference to him as "king."[23]

Our best early evidence is that Peter the eyewitness of Christ was the source of all that Mark wrote. Mark accompanied Peter as his interpreter and later, based on his memory of Peter's preaching, wrote this gospel. As discussed earlier, numerous elements in Mark's gospel support this evidence from the Elder John, from around A.D. 80.[24]

Mark's gospel, then, is based on Peter's verbal biographical sketch of Christ's public ministry. It begins with John's baptism of Christ in the Jordan and ends with the empty tomb in Jerusalem. In the first half of the narrative Jesus announces the arrival of the kingdom of God, as attested by his expulsion of the unclean spirits, and his call and dispatch of twelve missioners to the villages of Galilee. Midway in the narrative, when Jesus is forced out of Herod Antipas's jurisdiction, at Caesarea Philippi the disciples formally recognize Jesus as the Christ. To this point they have struggled to identify his role and vocation, and even at Caesarea Philippi their expectations of the messianic role are militaristic. From this point Jesus moves resolutely toward Jerusalem, repeatedly calling himself the Son of Man, speaking in dire terms of his fate there, and instructing his disciples in critical patterns of behavior for the future. In Jerusalem, events quickly take their dramatic course; Jesus is crucified at the request of the temple authorities. But the tomb is empty.

We sense that many aspects of Mark's narrative are infused with his kerygmatic and pastoral intent, including Christ's stark call to follow him, regardless of cost, and the necessity to confess him publicly (e.g., 1:16-20; 8:34–9:1). As well, Mark seems to recognize that some of his readers/hearers, like the original disciples, may be slow in acknowledging Jesus as the Christ. As many have noted, Mark's is a kerygmatic biography.

Nonetheless, it *is* a biography, or we should say, it is biographical in character. Many elements in Mark cannot satisfactorily be explained only

23. Mark 6:14; Matt 14:1; Luke 9:7-9.
24. See chapter 5.

as kerygmatic and pastoral. There is no reason to question that Jesus came from Nazareth and made Capernaum his base, that he was frequently forced away from that base, that he called and sent twelve disciples, that he had to withdraw from Galilee after the feeding of the five thousand, that the messianic recognition at Caesarea Philippi marked the moment when he moved to Jerusalem. These and many other items in Mark's gospel are historical and biographical in character, and plausibly originate with Peter the disciple and eyewitness.

At the same time, of course, we cannot forget that Mark is the author who shaped Peter's biographical sketch for his intended readers/hearers and who at many points can be "heard" speaking to them. Mark's own "voice" can be heard at many points:

7:19   "Thus he declared all foods clean."

13:28-29   "'From the fig tree learn its lesson: as soon as its branch becomes tender and puts forth its leaves, *you* know that summer is near. So also, when *you* see these things taking place, *you* know that *he* is near, at the very gates.'"

13:32-37   "'But of that day or that hour no one knows, not even the angels in heaven, nor the Son, but only the Father. Take heed, watch; for you do not know when the time will come. It is like a man going on a journey, when he leaves home and puts his servants in charge, each with his work, and commands the doorkeeper to be on the watch. Watch therefore — for you do not know when the master of the house will come, in the evening, or at midnight, or at cockcrow, or in the morning — lest he come suddenly and find you asleep. And what I say to you I say to *all:* Watch.'"

14:9   "'And truly, I say to you, wherever the gospel is preached in the whole world, what she has done will be told in memory of her.'"

14:51-52   "And a young man followed him, with nothing but a linen cloth about his body; and they seized him, but he left the linen cloth and ran away naked."

15:21   "And they compelled a passer-by, Simon of Cyrene, who was coming in from the country, *the father of Alexander and Rufus,* to carry his cross."

Most prominent of all is Mark's direction to the person reading his text to a church gathering, "Let the reader [lector] understand" (13:14). This, together with references above, gives us a sense that Mark knows or knows of his readers and has fashioned his gospel with their circumstances in mind. By no means, however, does this indicate that Mark is writing exclusively to a particular church. His gospel is too global and comprehensive for that. Once again, though, Mark's shaping of his text for the needs and circumstances of readers/hearers does not of itself preclude an underlying biographical thread running through this gospel.

In short, the Gospel of Mark, which arose from Peter's preaching as interpreted by Mark, is sufficiently biographical in character to give us confidence that in it we encounter Christ as a genuinely historical figure.

Q

When we remove from Matthew and Luke the Gospel of Mark and their own distinctive material (L and M), we are left with about 250 verses, which are commonly called Q.[25]

While a majority of authorities agree that there is such a common source, there is considerable debate about the nature or limits of Q. This is because of the differing relationships between common or apparently common texts. While some passages boast almost verbatim agreement (e.g., Luke 3:7-9 and Matt 3:7-10), other, similar-sounding passages have significant differences (e.g., Luke 11:9-13 and Matt 7:7-9, where Luke has "will your Father . . . give the Holy Spirit" and Matthew has "will the Father . . . give good things"). In some passages the differences are considerable (e.g., Luke 11:2-4 and Matt 6:9-13, where in so important a matter as the Lord's Prayer the versions are quite different).

Various solutions have been offered, including that Luke and Matthew had access to different versions of Q or that they gave, or had access to, different translations of an Aramaic version of Q.[26] It is difficult to see

25. See Barnett, *Birth of Christianity,* 138-49.

26. Scholars have drawn attention to Papias's statement about the origins of Matthew: "So then, Matthew compiled the oracles *(logia)* in the Hebrew language *(Hebraidi dialectō);* but everyone interpreted *(hērmēneuse)* them as he was able" (Eusebius, *HE* 3.39.16). Because these words do not apply to Matthew's Greek text (which does not readily

that final consensus will be reached after several centuries of close scrutiny of these texts.

Most authorities, however, are agreed that Q consisted almost entirely of the sayings of Jesus and that it was in effect a collection of the words of the Lord, with little or no narrative. There are no birth narratives and, strikingly, no crucifixion and resurrection narratives. It appears that the early disciples compiled Q as a manual for teaching Jesus' words. Perhaps once Matthew and Luke were written there was no further need for Q, which would explain its disappearance.

Given its lack of narrative structure, is Q of any use for biographical purposes? We might easily suppose that since Q generally does not mention Jesus' movements, place-names, or time notes, its value is limited to the teachings of Jesus. But this is not so.

The following examples indicate that even within the sayings of Jesus there is biographical information.

Passages	*Historical or Biographical Information*
Luke 3:7-9 = Matt 3:7-10	Preaching of John the Baptist
Luke 3:21-22 = Matt 3:16-17	Baptism of Jesus
Luke 7:22-23 = Matt 11:4-6	Jesus' reference to his miracles
Luke 7:24-29 = Matt 11:7-11	Jesus' contrast of John with Antipas
Luke 10:13-15 = Matt 11:20-24	Jesus' miracles in northern towns
Luke 10:2-16 = Matt 10:7-16	Jesus' (Galilean) mission charge
Luke 13:34-35 = Matt 23:37-39	Jesus' lament over Jerusalem
Luke 14:27 = Matt 10:38	Jesus' cross saying

Biographically speaking, Q is consistent with Mark in connecting the preaching and baptizing of John with the commencement of the public ministry of Jesus; in emphasizing the extent of Jesus' miracles; in pointing to the fact and mission of the disciples in Galilee; in mentioning the miracles of Jesus in local towns Bethsaida, Chorazin, and Capernaum; in noting Jesus' implied contrast of John the Baptist with Herod Antipas; in

---

retrovert into a Semitic text), some have wondered if an Aramaic version of Q is intended, and further if Matthew and Luke have each used a separate Greek translation of an Aramaic original. For this see, e.g., T. W. Manson, *The Sayings of Jesus* (London: SCM, 1961), 17-20. A problem with this view is that some of the Q material in Luke and Matthew is almost verbatim, which is not what we would expect; we would expect greater idiosyncratic differences.

pointing to the cross of Jesus that those who follow him must bear; and in recording Jesus' grief over unrepentant Jerusalem.

This list, though not long, is nonetheless impressive. It begins with John and (by implication) ends in Jerusalem, while along the way confirming the reality of the miracles, the call and mission of the disciples, and the imprisonment of John by the tetrarch. On its own, Q's biographical details are somewhat haphazard. But when set alongside Mark, they prove to be authentic. In short, we reasonably infer that the early Christians had a secure understanding of the main outlines of the Jesus story that are innocently confirmed in various references in the Q tradition.

L

In my consideration of the L source I am not including the nativity narrative, whose Hebraic tone and archaic character point to an origin independent of other parts of this source.

The L source is noted for parables and miracles that contribute to the special character of the Gospel of Luke.

Miracles	*Parables*
The miraculous catch	The two debtors
The raising of the widow's son	The Good Samaritan
The healing of the bent woman	The friend at midnight
The healing of the man with dropsy	The rich fool
The healing of the ten lepers	The barren fig
	The rash builder/reckless king
	The lost coin/sheep/son
	The unjust steward
	The rich man and Lazarus
	The farmer and his servant
	The unjust judge
	The two men in the temple

These miracles and parables are often set in historical or geographical contexts, but not those that are distinctly identifiable with an overall Jesus biography. So the question arises whether the L source, minus the nativity chapters and the miracles and parables, coheres with other known aspects of the historical Christ. In fact, it does, as the following passages indicate.

The mission of John	3:1-6, 10-14, 18-20
Rejection at Nazareth	4:16-30
Journey to Jerusalem via Samaria	9:51-56
Arrival in Jericho	19:1-10
Approach to Jerusalem	19:11-27
Arrival in Jerusalem	19:28-44
Resurrection appearances	24:13-49

The evidence in L coheres with the broad sweep we have in Mark and is confirmed in Q. That is to say, John the Baptist is the forerunner to the Messiah, Jesus, who began his ministry in Galilee. From there he traveled to Jerusalem, where he was killed and rose again from the dead, to be seen alive by numbers of witnesses. In asserting a broad confirmation of Mark's chronology, we must acknowledge that the L source appears to omit altogether Mark's record of Jesus' extensive travels to the north and the east of Galilee (Mark 7:24–10:1). The explanation for this "great omission" is twofold. First, Luke uses Jesus' direct and intentional journey to Jerusalem (Luke 9:51–19:44) as a paradigm for the disciples' intentional cross-centered lives; the narrative of Jesus' travels to the north and east would defeat this purpose. Second, Luke understood that he needed to omit material to fit in with the available space on his scroll.

L is of special value for dating the preaching of John the Baptist to circa 28/29 (Luke 3:1-2), establishing thereby an approximate date for Jesus' public ministry that began soon afterward.

Christ Biography in the Pre-Lukan Sources: Conclusion

We may summarize our discussion with a table. Where Mark provides specific narrative information, the Q and L sources, as primarily sayings sources, often confirm Mark indirectly, as noted above. The square brackets [] indicate biographical details that may be reasonably inferred.

	Mark	*Q*	*L*
John preaching, baptizing	x	x	x
John's baptism of Jesus	x		
Jesus' Galilee ministry	x	x	
including miracles	x	x	
Mission of the disciples in Galilee	x	[x]	
Journey to Jerusalem	x	[x]	x
Death in Jerusalem	x	[x]	
Resurrection appearances	[x]		x

Q and L, while briefer than Mark and primarily consisting of "words of the Lord," nonetheless agree with the broad biographical outline of Mark. It needs to be emphasized that Q and L are certainly independent of Mark, though it is possible that L was influenced by exposure to Q. This independence of sources is critical for historical analysis and points to the reasonable conclusion that we are able to reconstruct the broad outlines of a Christ biography, at least for the years of his public ministry. Although L is generally the least helpful biographically, the dating of John's ministry to circa 28/29 is particularly important (Luke 3:1-2).

Christology in the Pre-Lukan Sources

Independent sources can also be used to establish the identity and sense of vocation of Jesus of Nazareth. I have limited the following references from Mark to those where Jesus himself is the speaker and omitted those where the Evangelist attributes an identity marker to Jesus (e.g., Mark 1:1 — "The beginning of the gospel of Jesus Christ, the Son of God"). In Q and L the identity references are also limited to recorded sayings of Jesus.

I will concentrate on a selection of Jesus' references to himself as the Son of Man, the Christ, and the Son as they appear in Mark, Q, and L. My survey does not need to be exhaustive since I merely seek to establish in principle Jesus' sense of his identity in his vocation from God from these sources.

Mark

From Mark's account it is clear that Jesus' most distinctive self-reference is as "the Son of Man," especially at and after the Caesarea Philippi incident.[27]

In the vernacular Aramaic form(s) the words "son of man" meant only "a man" and were used as a circumlocution for "I." Accordingly, it has been proposed that Jesus' self-reference as "the Son of Man" was merely a Semitic idiom for himself, speaking as a man.[28] It is more likely, however, that Jesus is echoing Daniel's dream vision of "one like a son of man" who comes to the Ancient of Days (Dan 7:13-15). The invariable presence of the article in Jesus' references pointedly elevates Daniel's "one *like* a son of man" into a title, "*the* Son of Man." Moreover, as we review the occasions that Mark records Jesus using this terminology, we are struck by the way Jesus consistently saw his destiny in terms of Daniel's vision. In short, the idiomatic "man" explanation has little to commend it, whereas Daniel's vision proves to be a significant quarry for Jesus' self-designation as "the Son of Man."

On twelve occasions Mark records Jesus speaking of himself as "the Son of Man," although he uses the term only twice before Caesarea Philippi.

2:10   "'The Son of Man has authority on earth to forgive sins.'"

2:28   "'The Son of Man is lord even of the sabbath.'"

8:31   "The Son of Man must suffer many things, and be rejected by the elders and the chief priests and the scribes, and be killed, and after three days rise again."

8:38   "'The Son of Man [will come] in the glory of his Father with the holy angels.'"

9:9   ". . . until the Son of Man should have risen from the dead."

9:31   "'The Son of Man will be delivered into the hands of men,

27. For discussion of Son of Man terminology in the OT as background for the Son of Man tradition in the NT, see P. Stuhlmacher, "The Messianic Son of Man: Jesus' Claims to Deity," in *The Historical Jesus in Recent Research*, ed. J. D. G. Dunn and S. McKnight (Winona Lake, Ind.: Eisenbrauns, 2005), 336-44.

28. See S. Y. Kim, *The Son of Man as the Son of God* (Grand Rapids: Eerdmans, 1985), 32-37, summarizing the debate involving C. F. D. Moule, G. Vermes, and J. A. Fitzmyer.

and they will kill him; and when he is killed, after three days he will rise.'"

10:33-34   "'The Son of Man will be delivered to the chief priests and the scribes, and they will condemn him to death, and deliver him to the Gentiles; and they will mock him, and spit upon him, and scourge him, and kill him; and after three days he will rise.'"

10:45   "'The Son of Man also came not to be served but to serve, and to give his life as a ransom for many.'"

13:26   "'They will see the Son of Man coming in clouds with great power and glory.'"

14:21   "'The Son of Man goes as it is written of him, but woe to that man by whom the Son of Man is betrayed.'"

14:41   "'The Son of Man is betrayed into the hands of sinners.'"

14:62   "'I am [the Christ]; and you will see the Son of Man seated at the right hand of Power, and coming with the clouds of heaven.'"

Jesus alone uses the term "the Son of Man," and he does so with remarkable concentration from the time he begins his final journey to Jerusalem in Caesarea Philippi. The question whether or not Jesus is "the Christ" is the setting for three of his references to "the Son of Man."

Before the Sanhedrin (14:61-62)

This is the only occasion in Mark when Jesus explicitly acknowledged that he was "the Christ, the Son of the Blessed."[29] This he did by saying "I am" to the high priest's question. However, Jesus immediately identified himself as "the Son of Man seated at the right hand of Power, and coming with the clouds of heaven" (14:61-62). By this Jesus defined himself as "the Christ," but not in terms of current nationalistic messianic expecta-

---

29. The "Blessed One" is a contraction for the common expression "the Holy One, blessed be he." By asking whether he was "the son of the blessed," the high priest was not referring to the Christ's *filial* sonship. "Son of God" was a title for the Messiah (Ps 2; 2 Sam 7:14; cf. 1QSa 2.1 and 4Q Florilegium).

tions, but radically differently, as "the Son of Man." The Christ is "the Son of Man" who combined in himself the persons of David's "Lord" (Ps 110:1, "The LORD says to *my lord: /* 'Sit at my right hand'"; cf. Mark 12:35-37) *and* the heavenly Son of Man (Dan 7:13 — "one like a son of man," coming "with the clouds of heaven").[30] According to Jesus, the Christ is the Son of Man, a figure exalted to the place of ultimate authority in heaven.

With the Disciples at Caesarea Philippi (8:29-31)

Earlier, at Caesarea Philippi in response to Jesus' direct question, Peter addressed him as "the Christ." As he would do before the Sanhedrin, Jesus spoke of himself as "the Son of Man" (8:29-31), though in dramatically different terms from that later occasion. At Caesarea Philippi he declared that "the Son of Man must *suffer* many things . . . *be killed, and* after three days *rise again.*" Yes, he was "the Christ," but not as the one who would liberate Israel from her Gentile occupiers and reinstate a Davidic theocracy based on the temple and the Torah (as hoped for in the *Psalms of Solomon*). From now on Jesus will speak repeatedly of the betrayal, sufferings, and death of the Son of Man, but also of his resurrection (9:12, 31; 10:33, 45; 14:21, 41).

This Son of Man was not the liberator Christ of contemporary Jewish hopes. For Jesus the Christ is the Son of Man who *must* suffer, die, and rise again on the third day. But he will suffer as "a ransom for many" (*lytron anti pollōn:* 10:45 — evocative of LXX Isa 53:11-12); he will pour out his blood to inaugurate "the [new] covenant . . . for many" (*enchynnomenon hyper pollōn:* 14:24 — evocative of Jer 31:31, 34). These texts do not elucidate the effects of this all-pervasive suffering theme that runs throughout Mark's narrative, beginning with the Herodian-Pharisee conspiracy in Galilee (Mark 3:6), repeatedly foreshadowed by Jesus from Caesarea Philippi to the arrival in Jerusalem (8:31–10:52), and narrated extensively in the Jerusalem chapters (11:1–15:47). Rather, Mark's explanation for the sufferings of the Christ must be discerned within his narrative where Jesus is crucified as "king of the Jews" and where the chief priests mock him: "He saved others; he cannot save himself" (15:31). Mark does

---

30. In *1 Enoch* 48.2-10, one like a Son of man is a "messianic" figure. See further W. Horbury, "The Messianic Associations of 'The Son of Man,'" *JTS*, n.s., 36 (1985): 34-55.

not teach his atonement theology by direct statements, but indirectly through the narrative.

The Christ (the king of the Jews) died redemptively, but it was not for the political redemption that had been expected and hoped for.

Also with the Disciples at Caesarea Philippi (8:38)

"The Son of Man [will come] in the glory of his Father with the holy angels."

This is the first of three occasions when Jesus connects "the Son of Man" with the verb "come" (also 13:26; 14:62). The same connection occurs in Daniel 7:13, where "one like a son of man" is coming *to* the "Ancient of Days" (= God), where he is "given dominion and glory and kingdom." If, as appears likely, Jesus is echoing Daniel 7:13, he is not referring to a coming back to earth but to a *going to* God as the glorified man whose kingship is eternal and whom men will worship.

We rightly infer from the words of Jesus that his exaltation as the Son of Man was the consequence of his resurrection after three days. We conclude that from Caesarea Philippi until his arrival in Jerusalem Jesus accepted from both disciple and accuser that he was the expected Christ, but that he spoke of himself in unexpected ways. As the Christ he is the Son of Man who will suffer, be killed, rise again on the third day and come in glory to the Ancient of Days as the vicegerent over human history.

When Jesus asserted his authority as the Son of Man to forgive sins and to abrogate the Sabbath (Mark 2:10, 28), it was in anticipation of the authority he would assume following his death and resurrection. Most likely the authority he exercised over unclean spirits also anticipated his coming authority as the heavenly Son of Man (see, e.g., 1:21-27).

This *going to* God does not mean, however, that Jesus did not anticipate his physical return, his *coming back* whence he went. True, it is difficult to find a specific text to say that in Mark. Yet that is exactly Jesus' teaching in the parable of the secretly growing seed (4:26-29). The parable speaks of the seed of the gospel-word growing secretly and coming to fruition unaided, as witnessed by the sower's carefree attitude. When, however, the grain is ripe, it transpires that the reaper is none other than the sower, come to gather the harvest. The Son of Man who is the sower will return as reaper (so also Rev 14:14).[31]

Easy to miss are the words in which the Son of Man refers to God as "his Father." In other words, the Christ who is the Son of Man is the *filial* Son of "his Father," whom Daniel had called "the Ancient of Days." Jesus' words reveal the hitherto hidden character of the Lord as the Father of the Christ, his Son. This is clear also from Matthew 16:13-20, the Matthean parallel to Mark 8:27-30, where Peter's confession of Jesus as the Christ has the additional "the Son of the living God," and where Jesus also speaks about God as "my Father."[32]

This, too, becomes a recurring theme from Caesarea Philippi onward. Jesus teaches the chief priests in Jerusalem that, like the prophets, he is "sent" from God (Mark 12:2, 4-6), but in distinction from them he is "a *beloved* Son," whom God sees as "*my* son" (12:6). He calls himself "*the* Son" and refers to God as "*the* Father" (13:32), where the repeated definite articles point to a unique relationship between the Son and the Father. In Gethsemane he prays to God with intimacy and confidence as "Abba, Father" (14:36). The Christ, who is the Son of Man, is the filial Son of God.

It should be evident that "*the* Son of Man" was Jesus' dominant mode of self-reference in Mark's gospel. Moreover, while he did not reject being identified as the Christ, Jesus preferred to express his messiahship as the Son of Man. From Mark 14:61-62 and 8:29-31 we learn that the Christ who is the Son of Man (a) is the filial Son of his Father; (b) will suffer, be killed, yet be raised on the third day; and (c) will be exalted to the side of God as ruler of the kingdoms of the world.

This observation, however, raises the question of historicity. How confident can we be that the historical figure, Jesus of Nazareth, spoke of himself as the Son of Man? We mention several reasons for believing this was indeed Jesus' mode of self-expression.

First, Jesus' redefinition of the Christ as the Son of Man who must suffer and be vindicated by resurrection and exaltation is radically unlike streams of thought among the Jews in that era. It is not possible to explain Jesus' complex self-disclosure as Christ/the Son of Man/the Son of

---

31. See Stuhlmacher, "Messianic Son," 339-40.

32. Stuhlmacher, "The Messianic Son of Man," points out that Matt 16:13-20 can easily be retroverted into Aramaic and that the terminology has many echoes in Qumranic and OT texts (333).

God/the Servant of the Lord in terms of existing categories of thought. E. Schweizer was correct in saying that Jesus was "the man who fits no formula."[33]

Second, the absolute absence of "the Son of Man" references from the letters of Paul and Peter suggests that the early church did not create and then retroject that identity back onto Jesus in the gospel records. This absence is the more noteworthy since both Paul and Peter had in their friendship with Mark the opportunity to do so. This points to the care taken by the early Christians to preserve the integrity of the gospel traditions.

Third, since Mark's narrative was written out of his recollections of Peter's teaching, we argue that "the Son of Man" references are another example of historical authenticity based on an eyewitness report. Furthermore, the concentration of the Son of Man references after Caesarea Philippi as he and his disciples approached Jerusalem, with their revelation of Jesus' identity as the Christ, who is the filial Son but must suffer before he will be vindicated, is readily imaginable.

Q

Here we need only summarize an earlier discussion.[34] First, in response to the question from John the Baptist, "Are you *he who is to come?*" Jesus combined a number of messianic texts from Isaiah, concluding, "Blessed is he who takes no offense at *me*" (Luke 7:23/Matt 11:4-6).

Second, Jesus exercised messianic authority in his "I say to you" form of speech that occurs fourteen times in Q texts, and in the various "woes" he pronounces against religious leaders (Luke 11:43/Matt 23:16) and the villages of Galilee (Luke 10:13/Matt 11:21).

And third, Jesus promises a "messianic" banquet, informing his disciples: "You are those who have continued with *me* in my trials; and I assign to you, as *my* Father assigned to *me*, a kingdom, that you may eat and drink at *my* table in my kingdom, and sit on thrones judging the twelve tribes of Israel" (Luke 22:28-30/Matt 19:28).

---

33. E. Schweizer, *Jesus* (London: SCM, 1971), 13.
34. See "The Christology of Q," in Barnett, *Birth of Christianity*, 143-45.

In sum, the sayings of Jesus preserved in Q powerfully establish that Jesus was convinced he was the Christ, though in ways that were unexpected.

Do we find "the Son of Man" references in the Q source? There are several.

"The Son of Man has come eating and drinking; and you say, 'Behold, a glutton and a drunkard, a friend of tax collectors and sinners!'" (Luke 7:34/Matt 11:19)

"Foxes have holes, and birds of the air have nests; but the Son of Man has nowhere to lay his head." (Luke 9:58/Matt 8:20)

"And every one who speaks a word against the Son of Man will be forgiven; but he who blasphemes against the Holy Spirit will not be forgiven." (Luke 12:10/Matt 12:32)

It could be argued that "the Son of Man" in these passages represents a circumlocution for "I" or "a man." Each text, however, is a weighty saying about "*the* Son of Man" and is consistent with the texts from Mark that are more identifiable with Daniel 7:13-15.

L

Son of Man References

There are five "the Son of Man" references in the L source, four of which are in the same passage. These appear to foreshadow the return of the Son of Man, an expectation not articulated (apparently) among the Son of Man texts in Mark.

Luke 17:22 "And he said to the disciples, 'The days are coming when you will desire to see one of the days of the Son of Man, and you will not see it.'"

Luke 17:24 "'For as the lightning flashes and lights up the sky from one side to the other, so will the Son of Man be in his day.'"

Luke 17:26 "'As it was in the days of Noah, so will it be in the days of the Son of Man.'"

Luke 17:30   " 'So will it be on the day when the Son of Man is revealed.' "

The fifth occurrence in the L source is Jesus' word to Zacchaeus: "The Son
of Man came to seek and to save the lost" (Luke 19:10).

Initially, these words may appear to be a Lukan construction, spring-
ing from Luke 15 where Jesus relates three parables in which the lost
(sheep, coin, son[s]) are found and where Jesus defends himself to the
Pharisees and scribes for "receiving and eating" with sinners (15:1-2). Likewise, in Luke 19:10 Jesus justifies entering the house of a tax collector to
those who complain that he has become the guest of a sinner. Clearly Luke
15:1-2 and 19:1-10 are so integrally connected that the genuineness of 19:10
may be doubted. On the other hand, however, the notion of the "lost sheep
of the house Israel" for whose sake Jesus came is found in non-Lukan passages (Matt 10:6; 15:24). I conclude that Luke 19:10 is a genuine dominical
oracle that has been colored by Luke's parallel narrative and parables in
Luke 15.

Christ

The L source appears to lack specific references to Christ. Yet it contains
"kingdom" references that are by implication messianic.

> "Nor will they say, 'Lo, here it is!' or 'There!' for behold, the kingdom
> of God is in the midst of you." (Luke 17:21; cf. Luke 11:20/Matt 12:28)

> "For I tell you that from now on I shall not drink of the fruit of the
> vine until the kingdom of God comes." (Luke 22:18)

The Son

The L source has only one specific "sonship" passage. However, it also has
"*my* kingdom" (Messiah) references and, by inference, mention of the call
of the twelve disciples who will judge the twelve tribes. "You are those who
have continued with me in my trials; and I assign to you, as *my Father* assigned to me, a *kingdom*, that you may eat and drink at *my* table in *my*
kingdom, and sit on thrones judging the twelve tribes of Israel" (Luke
22:28-30).

Christ and Son

In the parables in Luke 15 Jesus implies that he is both the Christ and the Son of the Father. In the parable of the lost sheep Jesus *himself* is the shepherd who searches for the lost sheep, thus justifying to the Pharisees his "welcome" of sinners (15:2). By his parable Jesus appears to cast himself in the role of the Davidic/messianic shepherd prophesied by Ezekiel (Ezek 34:23). In his story of the lost son, where the father welcomes home the lost boy, Jesus is again justifying his welcome of sinners (Luke 15:2). However, since in Jesus' story the welcoming father depicts God, Jesus is implying that in his welcome of sinners he is depicting the welcoming God. In other words, Jesus' story is asserting a functional sonship of God: the Son welcomes sinners because the Father welcomes sinners.

Christology in the Pre-Lukan Sources: Conclusion

Our brief survey has established that Jesus repeatedly referred to himself in Mark's gospel as "the Son of Man," and that this self-reference was deeply influenced by Daniel 7:13-15. Contrary to contemporary messianic hopes, Jesus portrayed the Christ as the Son of Man who would suffer for others and be vindicated by resurrection and exaltation. As well, the Christ who is the Son of Man is the filial Son of God who while on earth exercises by anticipation the future heavenly authority of the Son of Man.

When we examine the independent sources Q and L, we find references to the Son of Man, to the Christ, and to the Son, as in the table following. In addition, I have included some examples of Jesus' "I have come to . . ." sayings[35] and evidence for his calling of *twelve* disciples, both of which are messianic in character.

	Mark	Q	L
"I came to . . ." sayings	2:17; 10:45	Luke 12:51 = Matt 10:34	12:49; 19:10
Call of twelve disciples	3:14, 16	Luke 22:28-30 = Matt 19:28	[22:30]

35. See A. H. I. Lee, *From Messiah to the Preexistent Son*, WUNT 192 (Tübingen: Mohr Siebeck, 2005), 181-201.

Son of Man	2:10; 8:38	Luke 12:40 = Matt 24:44	19:10
Christ	8:29-31; 12:35; 14:61	[Luke 7:22 = Matt 11:4-6][36]	[22:30]
The Son	13:32; 12:6 (beloved Son)	Luke 10:21-24 = Matt 11:25-27	
His Father	8:38; 14:36 (*abba*)	Luke 10:21-24 = Matt 11:25-27	
My Father			22:29

Earliest Window: Final Reflection

In the few words of his prologue, Luke gives us a unique window through which we see him collecting various "narratives" from those who were Jesus' original disciples who are now "servants of the word." Although Luke endorses these texts, he must rectify their incomplete character by writing his own, more comprehensive narrative. This he will do for his dedicatee, a catechumen, who has been dependent to date on oral instruction, for the sake of his greater certainty.

Through the work of the source critics we are able to isolate at least three "narratives," Mark, Q, and L. These sources are especially important to the biographer-historian since they appear to be both independent of each other and without extant antecedent. That is to say, they are *primary* sources for reconstructing a Christ biography and for gaining a sense of who Jesus thought he was. Jesus of Nazareth regarded himself as the Christ, the Son of Man, and the Son of God, his Father.

36. See Barnett, *Birth of Christianity,* 143-45.

SEVEN

Is the Witness of John Historical?

The Gospel of John "is profoundly untrue."

Maurice Casey[1]

Does the Gospel of John assist us in our search for the historical Christ?

The immediate problem is the scale of differences between John and Mark (and therefore between John and Matthew and Luke). If, as I have argued, Mark is a "written-up" version of his recollections of Peter's preaching, the differences we find in John present significant issues for our use of this gospel for historical research.

In the modern era scholars have distinguished John from the synoptics. While there are close parallels between Mark, Luke, and Matthew, both in sequence of passages and in verbal similarities between passages, it is not possible to include the Gospel of John in these close comparisons between the synoptics. We rightly regard the Gospel of John "unsynoptic."

Furthermore, it is well known that John omits key events that are prominent in Mark, Matthew, and Luke.

The temptations
Jesus' public "kingdom" proclamation in Galilee
    harvest parables
    exorcisms

---

1. M. Casey, *Is John's Gospel True?* (London and New York: Routledge, 1996), 229.

table fellowship with "sinners"
Jesus' formal appointment of twelve disciples
Peter's messianic confession at Caesarea Philippi
The transfiguration of Jesus
The institution of the Eucharist
Jesus' Gethsemane prayer
The Sanhedrin trial

These omissions are quite striking and contribute to the sense of difference between John and the synoptics.

The most prominent difference, however, is John's location of the story of the clearing of the vendors from the temple near the beginning of his gospel whereas in Mark it occurs during Jesus' final visit to the Holy City. So is one or the other account incorrectly located, or did Jesus clear the temple twice? The various options have their advocates.[2] Whatever the truth is about John's location of the incident,[3] it is difficult to doubt that Mark's placement of it at the time of Jesus' final arrival in Jerusalem is correct since it is the catalyst of the ensuing events of the arrest, trial, and execution of Jesus.

According to Mark, Jesus was condemned by the Sanhedrin as a false messiah, based on the testimony of those who reported him saying, "I will destroy this temple that is made with hands, and in three days I will build another, not made with hands" (Mark 14:57-59). Mark nowhere attributes these words directly to Jesus, nor do the (false) witnesses claim that Jesus spoke these words when he cleared the temple. Remarkably, however, John connects Jesus' act of clearing the temple with his words "Destroy this temple, and in three days I will raise it up" (John 2:19). Without John's account we would not connect Jesus' *act* (of clearing the temple) with his *word* ("Destroy this temple . . ."); Mark does not make the connection. Thus, although John's placement of the incident is problematic in relation to Mark's, his connection of *act* and *word* is invaluable historically.

2. For argument that John has the location right, against Mark, see J. A. T. Robinson, *The Priority of John* (London: SCM, 1985), 127-31. D. A. Carson, *The Gospel according to John* (Grand Rapids: Eerdmans, 1991), 177-78, contends that Jesus cleared the temple twice.

3. It seems likely that John has relocated the incident and the logion to fit thematically with a series of other "replacement" items that occur near the beginning of his gospel (2:1-11 — wine replaces purificatory water; 2:12-22 — new "temple" replaces old temple; 3:1-14 — new birth replaces old birth; 4:4-26 — new worship replaces old worship).

The problems associated with John are not new. As early as Clement of Alexandria (late second century) similar concerns were expressed. "But that John, last of all, conscious that the outward facts *(ta sōmatika)* had been set forth in the Gospels, was urged on by his disciples, and, divinely moved by the Spirit *(pneumati)* composed a spiritual *(pneumatikon)* Gospel" (Eusebius, *HE* 6.14.7 Loeb).

According to Clement, John wrote after the other gospels had been completed, and the gospel he wrote was more spiritually interpretative. Had Clement said that John derived his gospel from the earlier written gospels, it would indeed call into question, historically speaking, John's account of the "outward facts." Clement does not do this, yet his assertion that John came after the other gospels does weaken our sense of his significance as a historical source.

Be that as it may, the modern observations (as noted) do tend toward a lesser view of John as a reliable source for historiography.[4] But how well based is this view, and what can be said in defense of John?

Global Agreement between Mark and John about Major Incidents

Despite these differences, broad agreement exists between Mark and John about the overall sequence of events concerning Jesus.

John baptizing in the Jordan
John baptizes Jesus
Jesus calls disciples
Arrest of John
Jesus in Galilee
Feeding of five thousand
Triumphal entry to Jerusalem
Jewish trial of Jesus
Roman trial of Jesus
Crucifixion of Jesus and two others
Burial of Jesus in Joseph's tomb

4. For a comprehensive survey of modern scholarship on the historical character of the Gospel of John, see C. L. Blomberg, "John and Jesus," in *The Face of New Testament Studies,* ed. S. McKnight and G. R. Osborne (Grand Rapids: Baker Academic, 2004), 209-26.

Discovery of empty tomb on first day of the week

Resurrection appearances[5]

The occurrence of these events in the same sequence is quite significant and must be kept in mind to maintain a sense of historical perspective.[6] Both Mark and John begin with John's baptisms (including of Jesus)
and end with the empty tomb and the resurrection appearances.

Surprising and Credible Detail in the Above Passages in John

John's narrative, where it runs parallel with Mark's (as above), often supplies details not present in Mark (or Matthew and Luke). Let us assess the
credibility of these details.

1:28   The location where John baptized was Bethany-beyond-Jordan
(cf. 10:40).

1:35   Two (at least) of those who followed Jesus had been disciples of
John.

1:44   The city of origin of Philip, Andrew, and Simon was Bethsaida
(cf. 12:21).

2:19   John connects Jesus' *act* of clearing the temple with his *word*
about raising it.

3:22   Jesus' disciples were baptizing in parallel with John's disciples.

3:24   Whereas Mark indicates that Jesus began in public only after
John was arrested (Mark 1:14), John shows that the ministry of
the two ran in parallel, with a considerable overlapping period.

6:15   John's detail that the crowd sought to impose the kingship upon
Jesus coheres with Mark's otherwise inexplicable detail of Jesus
forcing his disciples to leave (Mark 6:45-46).

11:47   Caiaphas decided to remove Jesus before the triumphant entry.[7]

---

5. Implicit in Mark 16:7 where the angel says to the women, "Go, tell his disciples and
Peter that he is going before you to Galilee; there you will see him, as he told you."

6. So J. D. G. Dunn, "John and the Oral Gospel Tradition," in *Jesus and the Oral Gospel Tradition*, ed. H. Wansbrough, JSNTSS 64 (Sheffield: JSOT, 1991), 351-79.

7. E. Bammel, "Ex illa atque die consilium fecerunt," in *The Trial of Jesus*, ed.
E. Bammel (London: SCM, 1970), 11-40; B. Chilton, "The Whip of Ropes in John 2:15," in *Je-*

Accordingly, Judas appears to have consulted early with the temple authorities.

18:13   Annas was Caiaphas's father-in-law (a detail not found elsewhere).

18:13   Former high priest Annas was still a powerful figure (cf. 18:24, 28).

Each of these details has an intrinsically high claim to accuracy. If it were possible to account for these by appeal to John's special interests, it would weaken their credibility. But nowhere can this be demonstrated. Clearly, this writer is well informed and has an eye for detail.

Most detailed of all, and strikingly so, is John's account of the *Romans'* involvement in the arrest and trial of Jesus.[8]

18:3   A cohort (*speira*)[9] of Roman soldiers arrest Jesus in the Kedron garden.

18:12   The *speira* is led by a Roman captain (*chiliarchos*).

18:13   The soldiers and Jewish attendants bring Jesus bound to high priest Annas.[10]

18:15   A disciple who followed is known to Caiaphas[11] and admitted to his house.

18:28   Jewish chief priests convey Jesus from Caiaphas's house to the praetorium. They refuse to enter for fear of defilement at Passover time.

---

sus in Context: Temple, Purity, and Restoration, ed. C. A. Evans and B. Chilton (Leiden: Brill, 1997), 454.

8. See F. F. Bruce, "The Trial of Jesus in the Fourth Gospel," in *Gospel Perspectives: Studies in the History and the Tradition of the Four Gospels,* vol. 1, ed. R. T. France and D. Wenham (Sheffield: JSOT Press, 1980), 7-20.

9. A *speira* was a tenth of a legion, which seems excessive for the task of arresting one man!

10. Annas was the patriarch of his dynasty and likely a continuing dominant influence (Josephus, *Ant* 18.26; 20.197-198; Luke 3:2). See further E. M. Smallwood, "High Priests and Politics in Roman Palestine," *JTS* 13 (1962): 14-34.

11. Caiaphas is referred to by Josephus (*Ant* 18.35, 95). See further H. K. Bond, *Caiaphas in Context: Friend of Rome and Judge of Jesus* (Louisville: Westminster John Knox, 2004).

18:29 Pilate asks what is their accusation *(katēgoria)*[12] against this man.[13]

18:30 The Jews assert that Jesus is an evildoer *(kakon poiōn),* without being more specific.[14]

18:31 The Jews observe that it is "not lawful" *(ouk exestin)* for them to execute anyone.[15]

18:33 Pilate "calls" *(ephōnēsen)* Jesus.[16] We infer that the chief priests' accusation is that Jesus claimed to be "king of the Jews" *(basileus tōn Ioudaiōn).*[17]

18:39 Pilate asks about the "paschal privilege" to release Jesus.

18:40 Barabbas is a political insurgent *(lēstēs).*[18]

19:1-3 Pilate hands Jesus to the soldiers for flogging.[19]

19:6 Pilate declares that he finds no "charge" *(aitia)* against Jesus.

19:10 Pilate refers to his "authority" *(exousia/imperium)* to execute Jesus.

19:12 Chief priests appeal to Pilate as "friend of Caesar" *(amicus Caesaris).*[20]

12. The process was called *cognitio:* the judge establishing the charge he must adjudicate.

13. Josephus narrates a trial by Governor Florus some years later that illuminates Pilate's trial process: "Florus lodged at [Herod's] palace, and on the following day had a tribunal *(bēma)* placed in front of the building and took his seat; the chief priests, the nobles and the most eminent citizens then presented themselves before the tribunal. [These] implored a pardon for the individuals who had acted disrespectfully" (*War* 2.301-304).

14. The accusers, called *delatores,* were the temple authorities.

15. Only the Roman governor, who bore the emperor's imperium, had the *ius gladii.* See Josephus, *War* 2.117; Bruce, "Trial," 12-14. The synoptics presuppose that the temple authorities had to hand Jesus over to the Romans for their trial procedures, but only John explains this. See Robinson, *The Priority of John,* 255; A. N. Sherwin-White, "The Trial of Jesus," in *Historicity and Chronology in the New Testament,* ed. D. E. Nineham et al. (London: SPCK, 1965), 108.

16. The technical term for charging a person.

17. Only the Roman emperor appointed a "client king."

18. Josephus's frequent use of the word *lēstēs* suggests that it had political associations; a *lēstēs* was not a mere robber.

19. Torture of the victim *(addidta ludibria)* routinely accompanied and preceded the act of crucifixion. See M. Hengel, *Crucifixion* (London: SCM, 1977), 25-30.

20. "Friend of Caesar" *(amicus Caesaris)* was a technical term for someone who en-

19:13　Pilate mounts the magistrate's bench *(bēma)* and formally passes sentence.

19:13　The *bēma* is located on the stone pavement *(lithostrōton:* in Aramaic: *Gabbatha).*[21]

19:20　The superscription *(titlon)* of Jesus' crime is written in Aramaic, Latin, and Greek.[22] Golgotha[23] is near the city walls.

19:23　There are four soldiers in the execution squad.

19:31　Jews break legs so bodies do not remain on the cross on Passover-Sabbath.[24] The next day was to be a special Sabbath.[25]

19:34　The soldier thrusts his spear to ascertain death.

19:41　Joseph's family tomb is in a garden.

None of these details appears in Mark's account of the Jewish and Roman trials or the Roman execution. The question of their origin thus arises. Generally speaking, John's information is consistent with the practices of the Jews (e.g., avoidance of contamination by going indoors with Gentiles) and with the likely continuing power of Annas. More pointedly

---

joyed the patronage of the emperor and who may have benefited by an imperial appointment, e.g., to the lucrative position of provincial governor. See generally, Bruce, "Trial," 16-18; M. Goodman, *Rome and Jerusalem: The Clash of Civilizations* (London: Allen Lane, 2007), 81-82, 232-33, 375-76. Tacitus wrote, "whoever was close to Sejanus [praetorian prefect] had a claim on the friendship with Caesar [Tiberius]" *(Annals* 6.8). Pontius Pilate likely held his office through Sejanus's patronage, so that when Sejanus fell from imperial favor in 31 his "friend" Pilate became vulnerable to the threat that he was not a "friend of Caesar."

　　21. *Gabbatha (lithostrōtos)* may mean a large raised stone platform within Herod's palace (now the prefects's praetorium), which, although so specifically referred to, has not been located by archaeologists.

　　22. The Romans attached a placard *(titulus)* to the cross bearing the charge *(aitia)* against the felon, which for Jesus was treason based on the accusation that he was "king of the Jews." See E. Bammel, "The Titulus," in *Jesus and the Politics of His Day,* ed. E. Bammel and C. F. D. Moule (Cambridge: Cambridge University Press, 1984), 353-64.

　　23. *Golgotha* transliterates an Aramaic word meaning "skull," perhaps because it was a place where executions occurred. Only John calls it "place of the skull" (19:17; cf. Matt 27:33; Mark 15:22).

　　24. See Deut 21:22-23.

　　25. Literally, "for great was the day of that Sabbath." That day was both a Sabbath and the 15th of Nisan, the first day of Passover.

still, John displays easy familiarity with Roman military structure: a *speira* led by a *chiliarchos,* a Roman governor's authority *(exousia)* in the province, the Roman (not Jewish) authority for capital punishment, Roman trial processes *(katēgoria, aitia, bēma),* and Roman crucifixion practices *(titlon,* the leg breaking and spear thrust).

More broadly, John makes explicit what Mark and Matthew and Luke assume about the relationships between the Jewish sacral authorities and the Roman jurisdiction. That is to say, under Roman administration the high priest had no authority to execute Jesus; he had to send him to the prefect. Jewish trial processes could not achieve the desired outcome. The case had to be tried again in the only tribunal that could achieve this. It is John's account, not Mark's, that makes this clear. At the same time, John discloses that it was still the Jews' case; the Romans did not initiate it.

Furthermore, John alone supplies the reason the chief priests had their way despite the opposition of the otherwise omnipotent Roman prefect. It was due to the "patronage" factor. Pilate held his office for one reason only: he was *philos tou Kaisaros* (19:12). Evidently Pilate knew that the high priest had some hold over him in this.[26]

So, has John contrived these details to create the impression of reality, or do they arise innocently and genuinely from the events as they happened? True, the details about Jesus' unbroken bones could be accounted for theologically (19:31), but such a redactional explanation is not applicable to the mass of other information as noted above and expanded in the footnotes. We conclude that these details are gratuitous and authentic and contribute significantly to our sense of the historical integrity of the fourth gospel. There appears to be no good reason to disparage or explain away these details, not least since they significantly exceed those found in Mark and the synoptic parallels.

Nonetheless, we still face the question why John gives such an extensive account of the *Roman* engagement with Jesus in his gospel, beginning with the Romans' arrest of Jesus and ending with their crucifixion of him as "king of the Jews."

---

26. If the crucifixion occurred in 33 (not 30), then Pilate's patron Sejanus was no longer there, having been executed in 31. By 33 Tiberius had regained the reins of power and was attempting to rectify Sejanus's anti-Semitic policies around the empire, including in Judea under his protégé Pilate. See further Robinson, *The Priority of John,* 265-66.

Mark	John
	Roman soldiers arrest Jesus.
	Roman soldiers escort Jesus to Annas.
	Roman soldiers [?] escort Jesus to Caiaphas.
The Jews accuse Jesus to Pilate.	The Jews bring Jesus to Pilate.
	Pilate outside the praetorium: speaks to the Jews.
	Pilate inside the praetorium with Jesus.
Pilate offers Passover release.	Pilate outside the praetorium, offers Passover release.
Soldiers mock and torture Jesus.	Soldiers mock and torture Jesus.
	Pilate outside the praetorium: speaks to the Jews.
	Pilate inside the praetorium with Jesus.
	Pilate takes Jesus outside, mounts the *bēma*.
Soldiers lead Jesus to the cross.	Pilate hands Jesus to soldiers for crucifixion.
Soldiers crucify Jesus.	Soldiers crucify Jesus.

So why does John narrate at such length the Roman engagement with the last part of Jesus' life? S. van Tilborg explains this phenomenon, but he is likely incorrect.[27] Building on the work of S. J. Friesen, S. R. F. Price, and others, van Tilborg establishes the ubiquity and potency of the emperor cult in Ephesus throughout the first century. Then, however, he seeks to explain the Roman elements of John's narrative in terms of the *Sitz im Leben* in Ephesus created by the omnipresence there of the imperial cult. To do so he must engage in speculative allegory of several sections of John's narrative, in particular the soldiers' "ridicule" of Jesus (which is really the soldiers' enthronement of Jesus!) and Pilate's presentation of Jesus to the people (which is really the epiphany of the Son of God!).

All this is to miss the point. John's intention in narrating the Romans' extensive involvement is to establish them — Pilate in particular — as a foil against which the darkness of "the Jews" may be seen. "The Jews" in the Gospel of John are the "rulers" in Jerusalem (7:26), that is, the Pharisees and

27. S. van Tilborg, *Reading John in Ephesus* (Leiden: Brill, 1996), 165-219.

the chief priests (7:32, 45).[28] In chapters 18–19, where the term occurs many times, the *Ioudaioi* are the temple authorities led by the high priest. From the beginning of his gospel John established the malevolence of the Jews and their intention to kill Jesus.[29] John's account of the trial of Jesus has one tenacious theme: the determination of the *Ioudaioi* to get rid of Jesus and the vain attempts of Pilate to release him. There is one main purpose in John's detailed account of the trial of Jesus: to demonstrate that the *Ioudaioi* had their way against the sometimes halfhearted attempts of Pilate.

Is this, then, an expression of a contrived Johannine anti-Semitism? By no means! John's ascription of blame for Jesus' death to the temple hierarchy (and not to the Jews in general) is consistent with the other gospels and should be regarded as historically based. John's contribution to our historical knowledge has been to provide an impressively detailed narrative of the Roman trial as a means to display the evil determination of the *chief priests* to remove Jesus.

John's Literary Independence from Mark

Does John make use of the text of Mark?[30] If it could be established that John merely reproduces (and embellishes) the text of Mark, it would expose a fatal flaw in the historical integrity of the fourth gospel. Precisely this view has been widely held, a view that if correct would rightly regard John's historicity negatively. But is it demonstrably correct? Where does the truth lie?

The resolution of this question is relatively straightforward and depends on two actions. The first is to establish a list of incidents that both John and Mark narrate in broadly similar terms. The second is to compare closely their respective texts to determine the likelihood that one has depended on the other.[31]

28. For discussion on the meaning of "the Jews" in the Gospel of John, see Barnett, *Birth of Christianity*, 177 n. 35, and for a defense of John against the charge of anti-Semitism, see S. Motyer, *Your Father the Devil? A New Approach to John and "The Jews"* (Carlisle, U.K.: Paternoster, 1997).

29. 1:9-11; 2:23-25; 3:19-20; 4:1-3; 4:43-45; 5:15-18; 6:67-71; 7:1, 10; 7:32-34; 8:20; 8:37-41; 8:56-59; 10:33-40; 11:45-47; 12:10-11; 12:19.

30. For more on John's literary independence from Mark, see Barnett, *Birth of Christianity*, 165-69.

31. The classical study arguing for John's literary independence was P. Gardner-Smith,

There are nine common incidents.

	Mark	John
The dovelike descent of the Spirit upon Jesus	1:10	1:32
The temple-clearing incident	11:15-19	2:13-22
Feeding the five thousand	6:34-44	6:1-15
Triumphal entry	11:1-10	12:12-19
Anointing at Bethany	14:3-9	12:1-8
Arrest of Jesus	14:43-50	18:1-11
Peter's denials	14:66-72	18:15-18;
		18:25-27
Soldiers' mockery of Jesus	15:16-20	19:1-3
Burial of Jesus in Joseph's tomb	15:42-47	19:38-42

When we compare these texts we discover the following:

Passages Where the Wording Is Quite Similar

The Dovelike Descent of the Spirit upon Jesus (Mark 1:10; John 1:32)

Both texts have the Spirit descending as a dove, but in Mark 1:10 Jesus *sees* this and in John 1:32 it is John the Baptist's *testimony* to what he saw. The literary-dependence model is not sustainable from these passages.

Soldiers' Mockery of Jesus (Mark 15:16-20; John 19:1-3)

Both passages refer to a purple gown, a crown of thorns, mock homage, and the striking of Jesus' face. Mark's account is more detailed. Again, comparison of texts appears to preclude direct borrowing or adaptation by one or another of these writers.

Saint John and the Synoptic Gospels (Cambridge: Cambridge University Press, 1938), whose views lay dormant during the war years but were revived by J. A. T. Robinson, "The New Look on the Fourth Gospel," in *Studia Evangelica*, vol. 1, ed. K. Aland et al. (Berlin: Akademie-Verlag, 1959), 338-50; see also L. L. Morris, *Studies in the Fourth Gospel* (Exeter: Paternoster, 1969), 15-63.

Passages Where the Story Line Is Similar and the Wording Is Minimally Similar

Triumphal Entry (Mark 11:1-10; John 12:12-19)

The only common wording is limited to the citation "Blessed is he who comes in the name of the Lord" (Ps 118:26). Jesus rides a colt *(pōlon)* in Mark but a donkey *(onarion)* in John; in Mark the people cut branches *(stibas)* and in John palm branches *(ta baia tōn phoinikōn)*; in Mark the people go before and come after Jesus and in John they meet him. John appears to depend on an oral source that he overwrites as part of his narrative.

The Temple-Clearing Incident (Mark 11:15-19; John 2:13-22)

It is instructive to compare the texts.

Mark	John
Jesus cast out those who sold and bought.	Jesus found those who sold oxen, sheep, doves; and money changers.
He would not allow passage through temple.	Jesus made a whip and cast out all, sheep and oxen.
	Scattered coins.
Overturned tables of money changers.	Overturned tables of money changers.
And benches of those who sold doves.	Cast out those who sold doves.
My house, a house of prayer.	*Do not make my Father's house a market.*

Most likely Mark and John are narrating the same incident even though it could be argued that any temple clearing would involve these actions (allowing the possibility of two such incidents). On the other hand, however, in both we find that Jesus casts out sellers of animals, overturns tables of money changers, and refers to the temple as a "house" (pointing to the same incident). John's account is far more detailed (a whip to drive out people and animals; scattering of coins; casting out of dove sellers), and Mark describes Jesus barring access through the temple.

The vocabulary and detail in John are so different that it is hard to accept that he based his account on Mark's.

Arrest of Jesus (Mark 14:43-50; John 18:1-11)

The vocabulary is different but the general story line is similar: Jesus and the disciples are in an olive grove/Gethsemane when Judas brings an arresting party who seize Jesus and take him away. The major differences are that: in Mark Judas identifies Jesus by a kiss and the disciples flee, deserting Jesus; in John it is a detachment of *Roman* soldiers, with temple attendants, that arrests him. In Mark an unidentified disciple cuts off the ear of the high priest's servant; John identifies the disciple as Peter and gives the name of the servant (Malchus).

The extensive differences preclude dependency.

Burial of Jesus in Joseph's Tomb (Mark 15:42-47; John 19:38-42)

In both accounts Joseph of Arimathea asks Pilate for the body of Jesus, which he receives. Using different vocabulary, both Mark and John report that Joseph wraps the body in linen and lays Jesus to rest in a rock tomb. John has extra details about Nicodemus, the burial spices, and the location of the new tomb near a garden.

Again, the dependency model is problematic.

Passages Where Story Line Is Similar but Wording Is Dissimilar

Feeding the Five Thousand (Mark 6:34-44; John 6:1-15)

This is the most significant incident reported by both gospel writers. Analysis of these texts, more than any others, will determine the question of literary dependence.[32]

The theological setting differs. In Mark Jesus is the shepherd-king who teaches the people and who feeds them (through the Twelve). John

---

32. See, e.g., P. W. Barnett, "The Feeding of the Multitude in Mark 6/John 6," in *Gospel Perspective 6*, ed. D. Wenham and C. Blomberg (Sheffield: JSOT, 1986), 273-93; I. D. Mackay, *John's Relationship with Mark*, WUNT 182 (Tübingen: Mohr Siebeck, 2004).

presents Jesus as the Mosaic prophet-Messiah who feeds the people in the wilderness at the paschal season.

The story line is different at the beginning but then is broadly similar:

i. The setting (on the east side of the lake). In Mark the crowd, excited by the mission of the Twelve, reaches the anticipated destination on foot before Jesus and the disciples, who arrive by boat; in John the crowds follow Jesus because of his "signs upon the sick," but he is already seated on a mountain and sees them approaching.

ii. Recognition of the crowd's hunger. In Mark the disciples recognize the crowd's hunger whereas in John Jesus asks where he and the disciples can purchase food for the crowd.

iii. A financially impossible task. In Mark Jesus tells *them* to feed the crowd, which, *they* say, is financially impossible (200 denarii needed); in John Jesus asks where *we* can purchase food, which the disciples say is financially impossible (200 denarii needed).

iv. The loaves and fish. In Mark the disciples discover five loaves and two fish, but John adds that Andrew has found a boy with five loaves and two fish.

v. The seating. In both gospels Jesus directs the disciples to seat the people; in Mark they do this in groups of hundreds and fifties.

vi. The blessing. In both gospels Jesus takes and blesses the loaves. Mark adds that he "looked up to heaven" and "broke the loaves."

vii. The distribution. In Mark the disciples distribute the food while in John Jesus distributes the food.

viii. The collecting. In both gospels the disciples gather up twelve baskets of uneaten food.

ix. The conclusion. In both gospels Jesus withdraws alone to a mountain.[33]

The agreement in the narratives is noteworthy. The differences noted in (ii), (v), and (vi) are minor and could be explained by the redactional

---

33. Both accounts have dramatic but different conclusions that may, however, explain one another. John narrates the attempt to force the kingship on Jesus whereas Mark says Jesus forced the disciples into the boat while he withdrew to a mountain to pray. It is likely that these details are complementary. That is to say, that Jesus compelled the disciples to leave because the crowd attempted to make him a king. Did Mark discreetly omit the kingship bid for apologetic reasons, not wishing the Roman authorities to think that believers were part of a politically active sect? See H. W. Montefiore, "Revolt in the Desert?" *NTS* 8 (1962): 135-41.

interests of the authors. The differences in (i), however, are substantial and not so easily explained.

There is also remarkable agreement in arithmetical detail: there were *five thousand* men; *two hundred* denarii were needed to feed the men; there were *five* loaves and *two* fish; there were *twelve* baskets of uneaten food.

Based on a common story line and the agreement in arithmetical details, it might appear that one text has depended on the other. Against this, however, there are differences in detail that defy explanation. Why does Mark refer to "green grass" and John to "much grass"? Why does Mark give his vivid description of the neatly ordered groups of fifties and hundreds, which John omits?

Furthermore, differences in vocabulary caution against a too-ready theory of literary dependence. Mark refers to "bread and fish" *(artous, ichthyas)* while John has "barley loaves" and "small pickled fish" *(artoi krithinoi, opsaria)*. In the blessing of the food Mark has "bless" *(eulogeō)* while John has "thank" *(eucharisteō)*. Different words are used for the satiation of the crowds (Mark: *chortazō;* John: *empiplēmi*). In Mark the disciples "take up" the uneaten food while John says they "filled twelve baskets." It is noteworthy that Matthew and Luke follow Mark relatively closely, including his vocabulary, whereas John diverges significantly.

How can we explain the phenomenon of striking numerical agreement in accounts that follow a similar story line but diverge significantly at one point in their respective story lines (the setting) and use different vocabulary?

Two conclusions are warranted. One is that Mark and John are describing the one event, as the common story line and the agreed numbers imply. The other is that neither text has depended on (copied from or adapted) the other; the divergent vocabulary prevents that conclusion.[34]

The implications for history are considerable based on this judgment, for we are positing two independent accounts of the one event, thereby enhancing the probability of its historicity.

---

34. Barnett, "Feeding," 273-93.

Passages Where Story Line Is Similar and Some Wording Is Similar

Anointing at Bethany (Mark 14:3-9; John 12:1-8)

Although Mark locates this incident two days before Passover and John six days beforehand (Mark 14:1-3; John 12:1), the story line is (broadly) similar:

   i. The setting: a meal in Bethany.
   ii. A woman anoints Jesus with valuable perfumed ointment.
   iii. Those present express indignation at this waste.
   iv. Jesus speaks, endorsing the woman's action.
   v. The aftermath: the chief priests decide that Jesus must die.

Likewise, the vocabulary and detail are similar. The valuable perfumed ointment is described in identical terms *(nardou pistikēs polytelous)* and said to be worth "more than three hundred denarii." In both passages Jesus contrasts "the poor" who "are always with" them with himself, who is "not always" to be "with" them, and on that account the woman has anointed his body ahead of its "burial" *(entaphiasmon)*.

At the same time, however, the names of those involved are different. In Mark the only name given is the host's, Simon the leper. In John, however, the meal occurs in the house of Lazarus, where Martha is serving and the woman who anoints Jesus is Mary (see also 11:2). John identifies the complainant as Judas Iscariot. It appears that John has introduced known named people who are important in his unfolding narrative.

Another difference is that in Mark the woman anoints Jesus' *head* whereas in John she (Mary) anoints his *feet* and wipes them with her hair (Luke 7:37-38). This, too, might be explained by John's special narrative interests. That is to say, John's accounts of the crucifixion (the unbroken bones, the spear thrust, the body fluid) and of the Easter evening resurrection appearance ("he showed them his hands and his side") are quite *visceral*. Anointing Jesus' feet in anticipation of the burial of his body is more appropriate than anointing his head.

John's version of this incident reveals his own special narrative interests. What is going on here? There are several options. Is John redacting Mark's text that is in front of him? Or is he adapting a version of the incident that he knows Mark has written about (but without the specific text in front of him)? Or is he adapting a known oral tradition of this incident?

We may eliminate the first option. The general wording of the two incidents is quite dissimilar and there are numerous divergent details. The case for literary dependence is weak. The second option is likewise unlikely because the identical references are too identical: the "expensive pure perfume" *(nardou pistikēs polytelous)* worth more than "three hundred denarii" *(triakosiōn dēnariōn)* and Jesus' words about the omnipresent "poor" *(ptōchoi)* and that the anointing was done for his "burial" *(entaphiasmon)*. These are too exact, too precise to have been known on the basis of merely knowing *about* the existence of Mark's gospel. The third option, then, is the more likely since these precise references are probably the prominent memorable parts of an oral tradition that John knew and overwrote in its present distinctly Johannine form.

Conclusion

On the basis of the foregoing analysis, we are able to reach a number of conclusions about the relationship between John's and Mark's gospels.

First, it cannot be demonstrated that John has depended for his version of these incidents on the text of Mark's gospel. Most authorities agree that the literary-dependence model is unsustainable.[35]

Second, it is likewise unlikely that John wrote these narratives in the knowledge that Mark had also written about these incidents. Many authorities, however, take precisely this view.[36]

Against that, however, is the argument of many that while John did not copy from or adapt Mark's account, he did know of it and wrote his gospel in the knowledge of its existence and content.[37] Yet, apart from identifiable literary dependence, how would we establish this? If we could clearly show that John corrected or endorsed Mark, it might point to John's knowledge of Mark. On the contrary, however, John develops his narrative entirely from within his own intellectual and spiritual universe. There is no hint of either John's approval of or criticism of any other gospel, including Mark's.

35. Morris, *Studies*, 23-38.

36. R. Bauckham, "John for Readers of Mark," in *The Gospel for All Christians: Rethinking the Gospel Audiences*, ed. R. Bauckham (Grand Rapids: Eerdmans, 1998), 147-71; Mackay, *John's Relationship with Mark*, 158, 300-303.

37. Mackay, *John's Relationship with Mark*, 158, 300-303.

In any case, even if we allow that John knew about Mark, how is that relevant, especially since John has confidently written his own idiosyncratic gospel, aloof from any demonstrable influence from the synoptics, whether direct or indirect?

In short, the contention that John knew of Mark must remain hypothetical, and in any case is irrelevant.

Accordingly, thirdly, there is a strong case for the equal nonposteriority for both texts. That is to say, each was created independently of the other. Mark's text belonged to the oral and written stream associated with Peter that emptied eventually into Mark's written text, and John's text was the end point of a tradition, oral or written, that began earlier and ran its course in parallel with Peter's, to reach its finality in the Gospel of John.

Because we have two independent written narratives for the nine parallel events, we conclude that the case for the historicity of those events is to that extent enhanced.

The Credibility of Passages Found Only in John

When we remove from John the passages that are in direct parallel with Mark, we find that the greater part of John's gospel is independent of Mark (and Matthew or Luke).

2:1–4:54	Jesus' circular journey from Cana to Cana, via Capernaum, Jerusalem, Judea, and Samaria
5:1–47	Disputation following the healing of the invalid at Bethzatha Pool
7:10–12:1	Jesus' six months' disputations in Jerusalem (from Tabernacles to Passover), with brief withdrawals to Bethany-beyond-Jordan and Ephraim
13:1–17:26	Jesus' farewell discourses on the eve of Passover
21:1–23	The reinstatement of Peter by the Sea of Tiberias

These passages present significant problems for the historian since there is nothing to match them or measure them against. Are they John's invention, with no basis in real events?

Several factors may be considered in support of these texts. First, several passages depend on *details* also found more broadly in the Gospel of Mark. John's farewell discourses depend on Judas's betrayal and Peter's denials, both of which are deeply rooted in Mark's narrative of the final meal (14:17-31).[38] Similarly, Jesus' reinstatement of Peter in Galilee (21:15-19) depends on Peter's earlier failure in Jerusalem, which is also narrated in Mark (Mark 14:66-72).

Second, the passages found only in John (chapters 2–5; 7–11; 13–17; 21) are dotted with extensive, authentic-sounding detail, as summarized below.[39] The impressive selection following will serve to underline the historical, geographical, and religious-cultural awareness of the author of the Gospel of John.[40]

2:1-11   Wedding in Cana of Galilee.

2:1   Cana is located near Nazareth, making Jesus' mother's presence at the wedding credible.

2:6   Stone jars for water for purification (cf. Mark 7:3-4).

---

38. Both Mark and John agree that Jesus and the disciples ate a meal together on the Thursday evening before Jesus was arrested in Gethsemane/an olive grove. According to Mark 14:12-25, it was a Passover meal during which Jesus instituted the Eucharist. The Passover, however, was not due to be celebrated until the next evening following the sacrifice of the lambs earlier in the day. Some explanation is needed for why Jesus and the disciples celebrated the Pesach a night early. Perhaps Jesus knew that his arrest was imminent and the opportunity for a Passover meal and the institution of the Eucharist would soon pass. Equally curious is John's failure to mention that the meal was a Passover meal (though there are hints it may have been planned for later in the evening — John 13:29) or to refer to the institution of the Eucharist. Since this gospel is permeated with the Passover theme as signaled early by the Baptist's "Behold, the Lamb of God" (1:29) and climaxed by John's narration of the death of the *unbroken* lamb of God (19:36), John may have felt that the point would have been diminished by including a narrative of the Passover meal. Likewise, he may have felt that his powerful exposition of participating by faith in Christ's death as the "bread" and "drink" for eternal life (6:53-58) would have been weakened by a deflecting reference to the institution of the Eucharist.

39. See M. Hengel, *The Johannine Question* (London: SCM, 1989), 110-13; P. W. Barnett, "Indications of Earliness in the Gospel of John," *RTR* 64 (2005): 61-75.

40. For detailed analysis passage by passage of this gospel that demonstrates its claim to be regarded as historical in character, see C. L. Blomberg, *The Historical Reliability of John's Gospel* (Leicester: Apollos, 2001), and for an overall survey of John see S. S. Smalley, *John Evangelist and Interpreter* (Downers Grove, Ill.: IVP, 1998).

2:9	The unusual title of chief-steward *(architriklinos)*.
2:13	Jesus went "up" to Jerusalem (as the characteristic way of reference).
3:1-14	Nicodemus.
3:1	Nicodemus from a well-known aristocratic[41] family?
3:22–4:1	Baptizing in Jordan
3:23	Aenon near Salim.[42]
3:25	An imaginable dispute of the validity of rival baptisms.
4:1	We note two groups baptizing (a unique Johannine detail).
4:4-42	Jesus in Samaria.[43]
4:5	Geographical conjunction of Sychar (modern 'Askar) and nearby Joseph's field (Gen 48:22) and nearby (traditional) Jacob's well (cf. Gen. 33:18-20).[44]
4:9	Jews will not share drinking vessels[45] with Samaritans.
4:20	"This mountain," that is, Mount Gerizim (location of the Samaritan temple and cult), is opposite Sychar.
4:25	Samaritans were expecting a messiah, known as *Taheb* ("Restorer"), likely based on the prophecy of Deuteronomy 18:15-19 of a coming Moses-like prophet-revealer (note that the woman said, "He will show us all things" — 4:25).[46]
4:46-54	Cana in Galilee.
4:46	The "royal official" *(basilikos)* from Capernaum and likely

---

41. Josephus, *Ant* 14.37, refers to an aristocratic Jew named Nicodemus a century earlier. Possibly from the same family was Naqdimon ben Gorion, a wealthy Jew at the time of the siege of Jerusalem (*b. Ta'anit* 19b-20a; *b. Gittin* 56a; *b. Ketubbot* 66b). See R. Bauckham, "Nicodemus and the Gurion Family," *JTS* 47 (1996): 1-37.

42. There were two places named Salim that were within the region of Samaria (where Jesus went next); "Aenon" is transliterated Aramaic, meaning "many waters." This would mean that John the Baptist had moved up the Jordan from Bethany.

43. T. Okure, *The Johannine Approach to Mission: A Contextual Study of John 4:1-42*, WUNT 2.31 (Tübingen: Mohr, 1988), 188-91.

44. Carson, *John*, 216-17.

45. Greek: *synchraomai*. See J. P. Meier, "The Historical Jesus and the Historical Samaritans," *Bib* 81, no. 2 (2000): 229.

46. Cf. M. F. Collins, "The Hidden Vessels in Samaritan Traditions," *JSJ* 3 (1972): 97-116.

one of the senior courtiers of Herod Antipas, tetrarch of Galilee (4 B.C.–A.D. 39).[47]

4:47   The "royal official" requests Jesus to "come *down*" *(katabainō)* from Cana to Capernaum (also 4:49, 51). Cana was an uplands village and Capernaum was 200 meters below sea level.

5:1-16   Healing at the Pool of Bethzatha in Jerusalem.

5:1   Jesus went "up" to Jerusalem from Galilee, a topographically correct reference.

5:2   A deep pool *(kolymbēthra)* with five covered colonnades *(stoa)*, near the "Sheep Gate," has likely been identified as adjacent to St. Anne's Church near the eastern wall of the city.[48]

5:7   "When the waters are stirred *(tarachthē)*" is cogently explained by intermittent bursts of water from springs or aquifers.

5:35   Jesus' commendation of John the Baptist as a light to the nation is confirmed by Josephus's positive comments about John *(Ant* 18.116-117). According to this gospel, John the Baptist was the prime witness at the beginning of Jesus' ministry (1:6-8, 15, 19-36; cf. 5:33; 10:40-41), who matches the Evangelist John's witness throughout and at the end of Jesus' ministry.

6:1-70   The feeding of the five thousand and the accompanying disputation.

6:1   John is the only NT writer to refer to the city of Tiberias, founded in A.D. 17 by Herod Antipas as his new capital (cf. 6:23; 21:1).[49]

6:14   The crowd's recognition of Jesus as the expected prophet (Deut 18:15-19) is consistent with the well-documented inter-

---

47. Like those present at Antipas's birthday banquet (Mark 6:21). Josephus mentions the "respectable persons" *(andrōn euschēmonōn)* who were closest to the tetrarch in Tiberias, including two named Herod, members of the royal family *(Life* 33). These and other courtiers were likely represented by the group known as *Hērōdianoi* (Mark 3:6; 12:13).

48. See further J. Wilkinson, *Jerusalem as Jesus Knew It* (London: Thames and Hudson, 1978), 95-104.

49. Josephus, *Ant* 18.36.

est in prophetic figures of the era who presented themselves as a new Moses or Joshua (cf. John 1:21, 25; 7:40).[50]

6:1-59   Underlying Jesus' "bread of life" discourse and dialogue is a Haggadah based on the manna God provided in the wilderness.[51]

7:1–8:12   Disputation in Jerusalem at the Feast of Tabernacles.

7:22   Jesus observes that it was lawful to circumcise a boy on the Sabbath, as it was according to the Torah (*m. Shabbat* 18:3; 19:2; *m. Nedarim* 3:11).

7:23   In arguing that it is likewise lawful to heal a man totally on the Sabbath, Jesus is employing the rabbinic *qal wahomer,* "lesser to greater" argument.

7:37   The Feast of Tabernacles had a "last and greatest day" (*m. Sukkah* 4:8; Josephus, *Ant* 3.345).

7:37-39;   Jesus' references to water and light at the Feast of Tabernacles
8:12   cohere with Jewish practices where these elements are central to the ceremonies (*m. Sukkah* 4:9–5:4).

7:49   The Pharisees' dismissive "this crowd, who do not know the law, are accursed" finds many echoes in rabbinic literature where the scribes scathingly referred to "the people of the land" (*'am hā'arets*).[52]

8:13   The Pharisees complain that Jesus' testimony to himself is against teaching that would appear in the Mishnah (*m. Ketubbot* 2:9; cf. John 5:13).

8:20   The location of Jesus' dispute with the Pharisees was the "treasury" (*gazophylakion*), the set of thirteen trumpetlike funnels ("Shofar-chests") into which worshipers placed their gifts (cf. Mark 12:41 — same word). The treasury containers

---

50. Cf. P. W. Barnett, "The Jewish Sign Prophets," *NTS* 27 (1980): 679-97.

51. P. Borgen, *Logos Was the True Light and Other Essays on the Gospel of John* (Trondheim, Norway: Tapir Publishers, 1983), 21-46; P. Anderson, *The Christology of the Fourth Gospel: Its Unity and Disunity in the Light of John 6*, WUNT 2.78 (Tübingen: Mohr, 1996).

52. Some years later Yohanan ben Zakkai wrote, "Galilee, Galilee you hate the Torah" (*b. Bava Qamma* 50a).

were located at the wall of the Court of Women (*m. Sheqa-lim* 6:5) where the ceremony of lights was held.

9:1–10:22   Jesus heals a blind man at the Feast of Dedication.

9:2   The disciples' question whether a man's sin or his parents' sin caused the man's blindness is echoed in the opinions of the rabbis, some of whom held that a child in the womb was already involved in sin (e.g., *Gen Rab* 63.6 in *Midrash Rabbah* [London: Soncino Press, 1961], 2:559-60).

9:6   Jesus' act of making a poultice of mud (for application to the eyes of the blind man) was a specific breach of the Sabbath (*m. Shabbat* 7:2).

9:7   The Pool of Siloam's water was "sent" to it from Gihon Spring and conveyed via Hezekiah's tunnel (cf. 2 Kings 20:20).[53]

9:22   The fear of the parents of the blind man of being excluded from the synagogue (*aposynagōgos* — cf. 12:42; 16:2) is not an anachronistic reference dating from the Jamnia Conference (ca. 80) but refers to long-established practice.[54]

10:22-40   Jesus discusses himself with the Jews.

10:22-23   John describes the credible conjunction of a place of shelter (Solomon's Porch — see also Josephus, *War* 5.184-185) and a cold season (winter) that occurs at the Feast of Dedication *(ta enkainia/Hanukkah).*[55] The earliest Christians assembled there (Acts 3:11; 5:12), perhaps in memory of Jesus teaching there.

10:31   One guilty of uttering the Tetragrammaton (YHWH) was guilty of blasphemy and eligible for stoning (*m. Sanhedrin* 7:5). While this is not Jesus' crime, claiming to be the Son of God was likely viewed as equally offensive.

10:40   Jesus and his disciples return to Bethany-beyond-Jordan, the place John originally baptized (1:28; cf. 3:23, Aenon near Salim), which is on the east side of the Jordan River. This is in the jurisdiction of Herod Antipas, tetrarch of Galilee-Perea, by whom he was executed.

---

53. See Wilkinson, *Jerusalem*, 104-8.
54. See Barnett, *Birth of Christianity*, 170-71.
55. 1 Macc 4:56; Dan 3:2.

11:1-55   Jesus raises Lazarus.

11:18   Bethany, fifteen stadia (two miles) from Jerusalem, is differentiated from Bethany-beyond-Jordan (10:40).[56]

11:39   Martha protests against opening Lazarus's tomb since he had been there for four days and there would be the stench of decomposition. The Mishnah tractate *Yevamot* 16:3 declares that evidence of a corpse's identity could be given only within three days of death.

11:49   According to Josephus, Caiaphas had been the high priest since circa 18 (*Ant* 18.35, 95). He was, however, son-in-law of the dynastic patriarch Annas (see John 18:12-13), who may periodically have reasserted his leadership. Luke brackets together the names of Annas and Caiaphas, suggesting some kind of co-pontificate. Five of Annas's sons became the high priest.

11:54   The "town called Ephraim" to which Jesus withdrew has been identified with Ephron (2 Chron 13:19), about twelve miles from Jerusalem (far enough away for safety, yet near enough for the return to Jerusalem).

11:55   John refers to the pilgrimage of country folk to Jerusalem for purification ahead of Passover (also 12:12, 20).

12:1-49   Jesus returns to Jerusalem six days before Passover.

12:20   The "Greeks" who came "up" (i.e., to Jerusalem) to "worship at the feast [of Passover]" most likely were Jews from the Diaspora (cf. 7:35; 10:16). The dedicatory inscription (in Greek) for a synagogue in Jerusalem that also served as an inn for those who came from abroad provides confirmation of such pilgrimages.[57]

12:21   For linguistic reasons the Greek Jews seek out Philip (a Greek name), who came from Bethsaida (in Gaulanitis, a Greek-speaking region).

13:1–17:26 Jesus' teaching at the final meal.

13:5   The washing of feet upon entry to a house prior to a meal is

---

56. On the location of Bethany (modern El Azariyeh), see Wilkinson, *Jerusalem*, 110.

57. See C. K. Barrett, *The New Testament Background: Selected Documents* (London: SPCK, 1987), 54-55.

tangentially confirmed independently (Luke 7:44). It was an established practice among the Jews, usually done by a slave or lesser member of the household.[58]

13:23   Reclining at meals with cushions (instead of sitting) was a Greek practice that became common among the Jews of the NT era (so also 6:11; 12:2). At Passover meals, however, it was obligatory since the Passover Haggadah said, "on all other nights we eat and drink either sitting or reclining, but on this night we all recline."[59] Perhaps this suggests that the meal in John 13 was a Passover meal after all (but celebrated later that evening — cf. 13:29).

16:2   Jesus' grim prediction of the disciples' synagogue-expulsion (*aposynagōgos*) and sacrificial killing fits the known *Sitz im Leben* of early Jewish Christianity at the hands of Saul of Tarsus (Gal 1:13, 23; 1 Cor 15:9; Phil 3:6). Others after him also persecuted the church in Judea (1 Thess 2:14-15).

21:1-14 Fishing in Lake Tiberias.

21:3   Peter and six disciples decide to go fishing in the lake, using two boats, one large, the other small (21:3 — *ploion*; 21:8 — *ploiarion*). Peter was fishing by the "cast net" method (21:6; Matt 4:18). The others were likely using the "veranda" net method, a dragnet between the two boats.[60]

The extensive list of selected credible historical, geographic, topographical, and religio-cultural details in the passages found only in John is impressive. True, these details are embedded in John's strongly interpreted theological text that he expresses from beginning to end in a homogeneous style. Yet the amount of such detail is greater in John than in the other three gospels combined.

Only in John do we meet Nicodemus, the woman of Samaria, the invalid at Bethzatha Pool, the blind man who washes in the Siloam Pool, and

58. J. C. Thomas, *Footwashing in John 13 and the Johannine Community*, JSNTSS 61 (Sheffield: JSOT Press, 1991).

59. Quoted in R. Michaels, *John*, New International Bible Commentary (Peabody, Mass.: Hendrickson, 1998), 251.

60. See M. Nun, *The Sea of Galilee and Its Fishermen in the New Testament* (Kibbutz Ein Gev, Israel: Kinnereth Sailing Co., 1989), 41-42.

(the resurrected) Lazarus. Since these individuals do not appear in the synoptics, we cannot by comparison validate them. Are they, then, fictitious characters created by John for theological effect?

That is unlikely, for three reasons. First, the author would lay himself open to ridicule if upon inquiry by the readers these persons proved not to be genuine. If, as many believe (following Westcott), John wrote his gospel in Palestine for Palestinian readers, it would have been possible to check John's narratives and potentially discredit his gospel in its entirety.

Second, none of the characters mentioned can be understood as a mere theological symbol. True, Nicodemus was a representative of an aristocratic class, the woman was typical of Samaritan peasantry, the invalid and the blind man were like many disabled folk of that era. Yet each appears as a lively and genuine individual. They may have been representatives of various groups, but each is a real person and no faceless symbol.

Finally, the immense amount of accompanying detail that finds considerable independent verification bears its own testimony to the likely truthfulness of the narratives overall. If the details we can check prove to be authentic, it enhances the likelihood that information we can't check is also reliable.

The Centrality of Jerusalem and Judea (Not Galilee) in John

We can explain some of our sense that John is "different" from Mark by the different perspectives from which the two authors write their gospels. In Mark's gospel Jesus goes (once) from Galilee and the north to Jerusalem in the south; his entire gospel is constructed around a north-to-south axis. In John, however, Jerusalem and Judea in the south are "his own country" where, as a prophet, he is not honored (4:44-45). Accordingly, Jesus comes *from* Judea *to* Galilee (1:43; 4:47). True, he is "Jesus of Nazareth" (1:45) in Galilee, but in John he spends the greater part of his time in Jerusalem and Judea (2:13–4:2; 5:1-47; 7:10–20:31), where the "sin of the world" is revealed and the redemptive drama is played out. John constructs his narratives around the great feasts of Passover, Tabernacles, and Dedication to demonstrate that Jesus fulfills their theological intentions *eschatologically* and thereby discontinues them.

This focus on Jerusalem and Judea is reflected in John's topographical references:

The deep pool at *Bethzatha* (5:2)
The treasury (8:20)
The *Siloam* Pool (9:7)
Solomon's Porch (10:23)
Bethany, two miles from Jerusalem (12:1)
The olive grove near the "wadi" *Kedron* (18:1)
Gabbatha (*lithostrōtos* — 19:13)
Golgotha (19:17)

These detailed references are consistent with John's preoccupation with Jerusalem.

Two connected facts need to be kept in mind here. One is that the original disciples of Jesus came with him from Galilee to Jerusalem, where they remained. Galilee was no longer their home. For the next decades they were firmly established in Jerusalem. The other is that for almost a decade after the first Easter John Zebedee was the second most senior apostle in Jerusalem (Acts 1:13; 3:1, 3, 4, 11; 4:13, 19; 8:14; cf. 12:2) and then (ca. 47) the third most senior leader (Gal 2:7-9). We lose sight of John in Palestine after about 47, but from 33 to 47 he was a very significant leader of Christianity in Jerusalem. Many hold that the John Zebedee who lived through those turbulent and eventful years in Jerusalem was the author of this gospel.[61] If so, there is a good argument that the Gospel of John, more than any other, reflects the troubled interface between the disciples and the Jewish authorities during those early years.

There is some evidence within the Gospel of John that Jerusalem from 33 to 47 was indeed the *Sitz im Leben* for this gospel. First, one passage that reflects the post-Easter setting is Jesus' dialogue with Nicodemus. At a critical point in the dialogue John has Jesus say, "*We* speak of what *we* know, and bear witness of what *we* have seen; but you (plural) do not receive *our* testimony" (3:11). This contrasts pointedly with Jesus' earlier "*I* say to you (singular) . . ." in verses 3, 5, and 11a, and the sharp "*I* said to you (plural), 'You (plural) must be born anew'" in verse 7. In other words, John writes with a double vision in which he *simultaneously* reports the historic words of Jesus to this distinguished leader of "the Jews" while also reporting the "witness" of the apostolic

---

61. For the view that he was John the Elder, see R. Bauckham, *Jesus and the Eyewitnesses: The Gospels as Eyewitness Testimony* (Grand Rapids: Eerdmans, 2006), 358-468.

community to "the Jews" and the failure of "the Jews" to accept their "witness" to Jesus in Judea.

Second, the farewell discourses and prayer (chapters 13–17) on the eve of the crucifixion envisage a situation that will soon occur, beginning with the betrayal (13:18-30), denial (13:37-38), and oblique references to Jesus' death and resurrection (13:33, 36; 14:1-3, 5, 18, 28-31; 16:16-24). Looking onward beyond his death and resurrection, Jesus speaks of his "going" or "departing" that will be matched by the "coming" of the Paraclete to "teach" and "remind" of everything he told them (14:25-26; 15:26; 16:7-15). This "remembering" points to the disciples' Spirit-led reflections on Jesus' pre-Easter works and words as fulfillment of OT prophecy (2:17, 22; 12:16). At the same time, the Paraclete will "witness" to Jesus as the disciples — who have been "with" him "from the beginning" (15:26) — will "witness" to the world about Jesus.

One way of reading these prospective acts of the "Paraclete" is that they began to be fulfilled soon after his coming, that is, soon after the first Easter, as the original disciples were engaged in their mission in the land of Israel.

Third, that mission would attract severe persecution (15:20; 16:1), including exclusion from the synagogue and death (16:2). Against this expected onslaught Jesus admonished his disciples to "remain" in him, the "true vine" who is the *true* Israel (15:4, 9). Jesus' absence will be replaced by the Paraclete's presence, but the persecution and hatred directed toward him by the Jews will continue to be directed toward them.

This would help explain the worldview of the Gospel of John that sees Jerusalem so negatively. Instead of acclamation in Samaria (4:42) and "welcome" in Galilee (4:45), the people of Jerusalem misread his signs (2:23-24) and the "rulers" in Jerusalem reject Jesus altogether and bring about his death. In this respect the "rulers" embody the "darkness" (1:5; 12:35) of "the world" (e.g., 8:23, 26; 15:18-19) that is subject to its murderous "father" and "ruler" (8:44; 12:31; 18:11).

Fourth, we are struck by John's thoroughgoing emphasis on Christ as the absolute fulfillment of Israel's past ("law" given "through Moses" — 1:17) as well as of her present religious life (as expressed in Judaism). Because Jesus is the "lamb of God" whose bones were unbroken in death (1:29; 19:33-37), John is implying that the Feast of Passover is now superseded and finished. Because Jesus is the source of divine "water" (7:37-39) and is the "light of the world" (8:12), he fulfills the Feast of Tabernacles, where the great ceremonial acts are centered on *water* and *light*. Like the Pesach, the Tabernacles festival is now overtaken and discontinued by Jesus the Christ. The water for purification in the stone jars is not only replaced; it is destroyed (2:6). According to John, Jesus is the "true light," the means to "true worship," the "true bread," and the "true vine" (1:9; 4:23; 6:32; 15:1), where the word "true" *(alēthinos)* implies his supersession of all previous understandings of "light," "worship," manna, and Israel (the "vine") herself.[62]

Are these assertions a mere Johannine construct, or are they rooted in the actual words of Jesus? The synoptic tradition offers several hints that support John's radical "fulfillment" emphases. One is Jesus' response to the challenge that his disciples do not fast. In the twin parables of new wine destroying old wineskins and his presence among them as the Bridegroom (an image for YHWH — Isa 62:5), he is implying an immediate finality of Israel's past (Mark 2:18-22). Likewise, Jesus' opposition to purity washing, and his assertion about the source of impurity, implies that he is replacing the Levitical approach with his own. Another example is found in the Q logion where Jesus declares that *he* is one "greater than Solomon" and "greater than Jonah" (Luke 11:31-32/Matt 12:41-42). Most significant of all, however, is Jesus' assertion that in the event of the temple being destroyed he will raise it after three days (Mark 14:58; John 2:19).

These examples from the synoptic tradition, upon which John does not depend, encourage us to believe that John's *discontinuity* emphases are not idiosyncratic and unhistorical. Once again, we must acknowledge that John has absorbed Jesus' teachings and actions and restated them in his own powerful idiom, which is homogeneous from first to last.

Therefore, this discontinuity theme throughout John's narrative reflects Jesus' radical teaching, which John and others radically continued in earliest Christianity. Here I am thinking of Stephen's attack on both Moses/the law and the temple (Acts 6:11-14). Was John radicalized by Stephen's insights (as Paul himself came to be)?

In short, elements within the Gospel of John suggest that Jesus' teaching and attitudes continued into earliest Christianity, including the

---

62. Contra J. Beutler, *Judaism and the Jews in the Gospel of John*, StudBib 30 (Rome: Editrice Pontificio Instituto Biblico, 2006), 154-57.

disciples' ongoing interface with Jewish leaders, the replacement of Jesus' "going" from them with the "coming" of the Paraclete, the witness of the disciples that inspired hatred and persecution, and Christ being deemed to have terminated the key festivals and various cultic aspects of Judaism.

The point is that the disciples' post-Easter circumstances are directly continuous with Jesus' pre-Easter circumstances. There is no hiatus between his circumstances and theirs. In terms of an early (Israel) or late (Israel or Roman Asia) historical setting for this gospel, the former is the more likely.[63]

Jesus Speaks through John in the Gospel of John

Jesus' reported words, like his reported deeds, are expressed in typically Johannine tones throughout. John's gospel is seamless, a consistent whole: his narratives of reported events and reported speech are virtually indistinguishable. Furthermore, parables, which are so much a part of the synoptic gospels, simply do not appear in John's book.

Nonetheless, Jesus in John often speaks figuratively:

3:8	The freely blowing wind
4:35-38	The harvest
5:19-20a	The apprenticed Son
8:35	Slave and son
10:1-5	The shepherd
11:9-10	Walk in the daylight
12:24	The grain of wheat
12:25	The riddle of life and death
12:35	Walk in the daylight
13:16	A servant is not greater than his master
14:2	The Father's house
15:1-9	The true vine
16:16-22	The woman in labor

---

63. See Barnett, *Birth of Christianity*, 170, for reasons to reject a post-Jamnia dating for John that is based on *Birkat ha-Minim* references and synagogue-exclusions in the Gospel of John (9:22; 12:42; 16:2).

Before we too quickly dismiss the reported words of Jesus in John as not typical of Jesus' manner of speech (in parables), we note several points: (1) The social and agricultural referents are small in number, as they are in the synoptic parables and also in the parables of the rabbis of that era.[64] (2) More specifically, there are synoptic parallels to several of John's figures: the harvest (Luke 10:2/Matt 9:37-38), the apprenticed Son (Matt 11:27), the slave and the son (Luke 11:11-13/Matt 7:9-11), the shepherd (Matt 10:16), the riddle of life and death (Mark 8:36-37), the servant/master (Mark 10:45), and the true vine (Mark 12:1-9).[65] (3) Jesus himself is the implied central figure in each of John's figures, as he is also in each of the synoptic parables.[66] According to Ernst Fuchs, "Jesus hides himself behind the parables, they are veiled self-testimony, and Jesus is the secret content,"[67] an observation that is as true of John's images as it is of the synoptic parables.

We must allow the possibility that Jesus, master of imagery that he was, actually did speak figuratively in ways that John notes but that do not occur within the synoptic tradition. In any case, John restates Jesus' words in his own idiosyncratic idiom, as he does in every other part of his gospel. Even so, it is possible to discern the words of Jesus behind John's version of them.

For the most part, however, John reports Jesus' speech in unbroken tracts of teaching (John 13–16) or long dialogues, whether "pastoral" (as with Nicodemus, the woman of Samaria, the invalid at Bethzatha, the blind man, the disciples, or Peter) or polemical with "the Jews" (as in the synagogue in Capernaum or the courts of the temple at the Feasts of Tabernacles and Dedication). Sometimes the dialogues elucidate the "sign" that Jesus has performed — e.g., about himself the Son of the Father who works always (5:16-47); as himself the bread of life (6:16-65); or as himself the good shepherd to the blind man (10:1-39). In the polemical sequence of dialogues in Jerusalem at the Feast of Tabernacles, Jesus is portraying himself as fulfilling the symbolism of the water and light of that festival (7:14–8:20).

---

64. See below.

65. For a list of Johannine parallels to synoptic sayings, see W. F. Howard, *The Fourth Gospel in Recent Criticism and Interpretation* (London: Epworth, 1955), 306-7 (also 216-27).

66. E. Schweizer, "What about the Johannine Parables?" in *Exploring the Gospel of John*, ed. R. A. Culpepper and C. C. Black (Louisville: Westminster John Knox, 1989), 209-19.

67. Quoted in A. M. Hunter, *According to John* (London: SCM, 1968), 88.

Are these long dialogues and discourses free creations of John? We may feel that they are since there is nothing quite like them in the synoptics. But several considerations prevent us from reaching that conclusion.

First, there are many examples of disputes between Jesus and the religious authorities in the synoptic tradition (see, e.g., Jesus' "woes" against the Pharisees in Matt 23). These were provoked by Jesus' radical attitude to the law in relation to the claims (implied or direct) he made about himself. Mark contains spirited disputes about (for example) Jesus' claim to forgive sins (Mark 2:1-12), his fraternizing with sinners (2:13-17), his failure to fast (2:18-22), his breaching of the Sabbath (2:23–3:6), and his rejection of purity practices (7:1-23).

These disputes are all between Jesus and the religious teachers, as they are in John. In John the Pharisees and temple authorities dispute with Jesus over healing on the Sabbath and his claims to divine Sonship (John 5:16-47), over the source of Jesus' authority to teach the people (7:14-36), over his explanation of himself as the true meaning of the symbolism of the Feast of Tabernacles (7:27–8:20), over the Jews' rejection of Abraham as their spiritual father (8:21-59), and over his identity as the messianic "good shepherd" (10:1-39).

In both Mark and John the presenting cause for the dispute was some aspect of the law (which Jesus and his disciples were breaking), but in each case the real issue was *Jesus himself* and his identity and role. John's account of these disputes is lengthy and Mark's, rather briefer (but see Mark 7:1-23), but John's longer versions may have been truer to the way things were[68] since the rabbis were ferocious debaters, as the Mishnah makes clear.[69]

Second, we need to be open to a breadth of modes of communication employed by Jesus. T. W. Manson classified Jesus' teaching in the synoptic sources as D (to disciples), G (to the general public), and P (polemical).[70] Further, he pointed out the uneven distribution of these classes of teaching

---

68. So N. T. Wright, *The New Testament and the People of God*, vol. 1, *Christian Origins and the Question of God* (Minneapolis: Fortress, 1992), 431.

69. In a private conversation with a leading Israeli rabbinic scholar, I asked whether he found offensive the tone of the Gospel of John. He replied that this was exactly the way rabbis argued and that he was quite untroubled by the disputes as recorded in the New Testament.

70. T. W. Manson, *The Teaching of Jesus* (Cambridge: Cambridge University Press, 1959), 20-21.

among the sources,[71] an observation that should make us pause before too quickly passing unfavorable judgment upon John's version of Jesus' speech. Furthermore, the wide variety of parable styles within the synoptics casts further doubt on our capacity to be dogmatic about the forms of speech that appear in John. The synoptic tradition contains parables that are two-line aphorisms, parables that are longer stories, parables that are allegories to be decoded item by item, and parables that have but one point to be noted. And, as we have already observed, in the synoptics we have numerous examples of Jesus engaged in rabbi-to-rabbi argument about the law in settings where the real point at issue is Jesus' messiahship.[72]

Third, we have distinctively Jewish elements evident within John's texts that are consistent with Jesus' manner of speech.

a. As already noted, Jesus employs lines of argument that appear in the Mishnah. For example, he uses the "lesser to greater" rhetoric much loved by the rabbis (e.g., 7:22-23; 3:12; 10:34-36). He points to the lawfulness of circumcising a boy on the Sabbath (7:22-23; *m. Shabbat* 18:3; 19:2; *m. Nedarim* 3:11). Jesus' references to himself as source of life and light (John 7:37-39; 8:12) pick up key symbols of the Feast of Tabernacles (*m. Sukkah* 4:9–5:4). The Pharisees point out that Jesus' self-testimony is against the law (John 8:13; cf. 5:13; *m. Ketubbot* 2:9). The disciples' question about the cause of the beggar's blindness (John 9:2) was part of a widespread dispute where some believed that the child *in utero* could sin. Making a mud poultice, as Jesus did (John 9:6), was an explicit breach of the Sabbath (*m. Shabbat* 7:2).

These and other references are consistent with *Jesus'* known disputes with the Pharisees and temple hierarchy as reflected in the synoptics. Furthermore (and very significantly), they do *not* reflect the issues the disciples had with the Jewish leaders in subsequent decades. Such a consider-

---

71. Manson, *The Teaching of Jesus*, 28.

	D	G	P
Mark	53.5%	23.0%	23.5%
Q	52.4%	36.9%	10.7%
M	66.3%	8.4%	25.3%
L	26.6%	34.9%	38.5%

72. See E. E. Ellis, *The Making of the New Testament Documents* (Leiden: Brill, 2002), who suggests some of Jesus' Old Testament motifs (e.g., 3:1-14 — dialogue with Nicodemus; 8:31-58 — "before Abraham was . . .") may have been based on the *yelameddanu rabbenu* ("let our master teach us")–type midrashim (173).

ation supports an early Palestinian rather than later Palestinian[73] or a later Asian provenance for this gospel.[74]

b. Examples of Jewish poetry within John's texts have parallels in the synoptics.[75]

Synonymous Parallelism

"That which we know we speak,
and that which we have seen we testify." (John 3:11; cf. Mark 10:38)

Antithetic Parallelism

"That which is born of flesh is flesh,
and that which is born of spirit is spirit." (John 3:6; cf. Matt 7:17)

Synthetic Parallelism

"But if you do not believe his writings,
how will you believe my words?" (John 5:47; Matt 23:5-10)

Step Parallelism

"He that receives whomsoever I send receives me;
and he that receives me, receives him that sent me." (John 13:20; cf. Mark 9:37)

Two connected observations are appropriate. On one hand Jesus employed poetic forms that were typically Semitic, and on the other, these also appear in the synoptic texts.

c. It has been demonstrated that John 6:31-58 is a unity along the lines of a Jewish midrash,[76] where a text is introduced (v. 31) and then ex-

---

73. As in W. D. Davies, "Aspects of the Jewish Background of the Gospel of John," in *Exploring the Gospel of John*, 43-64, who sees the disputes in John as post-Jamnian.

74. The identification of the synagogue exclusions (in 9:22; 12:42; 16:2) with the Jamnian *Birkat ha-Minim* urged by J. L. Martyn, *History and Theology in the Fourth Gospel* (Nashville: Abingdon, 1978), 37-62, has now been strongly opposed (for details see Blomberg, "John and Jesus," 222; E. W. Klink, "Expulsion from the Synagogue? Rethinking a Johannine Anachronism," *TynBul* 59, no. 1 [2008]: 119-34).

75. So C. F. Burney, *The Poetry of Our Lord* (Oxford: Oxford University Press, 1925), chapter 2; see also summary in Howard, *Fourth Gospel*, 307-9.

76. Borgen, *True Light*, 21-46.

plained and paraphrased (vv. 32-40). This is followed by a second, related scripture (vv. 41-44), which is expounded (vv. 45-47). Finally, the original text is returned to and expounded (vv. 45-58). There are parallels to this procedure in synoptic passages (e.g., Mark 12:1-12) and in sermons in Acts (e.g., Acts 13:16-41). As the synagogue preacher we know he was, it comes as little surprise that Jesus employed the rhetorical conventions of a rabbinic teacher.

d. Following is an example of an important synoptic saying (Q) that is echoed in John (in italics).

"All things have been delivered to me by my Father; *and no one knows the Son except the Father, and no one knows the Father except the Son* and any one to whom the Son chooses to reveal him." (Luke 10:22/Matt 11:27)

"I am the good shepherd; I know my own and my own know me, *as the Father knows me and I know the Father;* and I lay down my life for the sheep." (John 10:14-15)

The echo is unmistakable, even if abbreviated.[77] It does, however, serve as a further caution against too quickly assuming that John (not Jesus) was the source of teaching we find in this gospel, especially where (unlike in this instance) we know of no corroborating echo. If an utterance of Jesus appearing in John can be identified with a known oracle of Jesus in the synoptics, it enhances the likely integrity of other sayings of Jesus in John for which there is no matching word in the synoptics.

e. Jesus' reference to his "works," an important theme in John (see especially 4:34; 5:17, 19-20; 9:3-4; 17:4), is likely to have been authentic.[78]

---

77. According to A. Denaux, "The Q-Logion: Mt 11,27/Lk 10,22 and the Gospel of John," in *John and the Synoptics*, ed. A. Denaux, BETL 101 (Leuven: Leuven University Press, 1992), 163-99, this logion is echoed fifty-one times in the Gospel of John.

78. P. W. Ensor, *Jesus and His "Works": The Johannine Sayings in Historical Perspective*, WUNT 2.85 (Tübingen: Mohr, 1996); Ensor, "Johannine Sayings of Jesus and the Question of Authenticity," in *Challenging Perspectives on the Gospel of John*, ed. J. Lierman, WUNT 219 (Tübingen: Mohr Siebeck, 2006), 14-33. Ensor argues for "a sliding scale of possibilities . . . from the original Aramaic words of Jesus himself at one extreme to the loosest representation of them in a different language and cultural idiom at the other" ("Johannine Sayings," 23). Accordingly, Ensor refers to *ipsissima verba* (Jesus' actual words), *ipsissima dicta* (Jesus' words translated), and *ipsissima sententiae* (Jesus' notions, ideas).

In conclusion, based on our reflections on John's reports of Jesus' speech, we have noted that John's imagery, while not formally the same as Jesus' parables, uses a similar stock of social and agricultural referents. More important still, Jesus' use of figurative speech in John has the same effect as the synoptic parables in focusing attention on Jesus and the existential and end-time relationship with him.

Typical of Jesus' speech in John are the lengthy discourses and dialogues, which are both pastoral and polemical. While these are quite lengthy and markedly Johannine in expression, we must note that Mark and the synoptics also portray Jesus engaging in vigorous debate with the Pharisees and temple hierarchy. There is a sufficiently broad variety of Jesus' reported speech in the synoptics to allow for the Johannine speeches and dialogues also to be true to Jesus. Jesus evidently employed differing rhetoric for differing situations.

Furthermore, there are decidedly Jewish elements in John's reports of Jesus' words, whether disputes that echo the Mishnah or dialogues that are midrashic in style, or various forms of poetry.

We must acknowledge, as we have already, however, that John has processed the words of Jesus within his own spiritual psyche according to the circumstances of the churches for whom he wrote, and expressed those words in a remarkably consistent and homogeneous way.

The Historical Christ May Be Found in the Gospel of John

Throughout this chapter I have attempted briefly to demonstrate that the Gospel of John merits respect for its wealth of biographical, historical, topographical, religious, and cultural detail. At the same time, it is emphatically theological, expressed from first to last in the author's distinctive idiom. So powerful is the Johannine style that it might appear that he has entirely drowned out the voice of the One whose words he claims to present. Yet, on closer inspection we discover that the content and even the form of these words may be closer to Jesus' own words than we thought at the beginning.

This brings us to the all-important question whether John's Christ is true to the historical figure *as he was back then* or to the figure he had become in the minds of his disciples once the Paraclete had come and glorified him in their hearts.

When we begin to investigate John's presentation of Jesus as the Christ and as the Son his Father sent into the world, we feel some sense of surprise. John's portrayal of Christ's *own view of himself* proves to be somewhat understated and rather closer to the synoptics' presentation than we may have assumed. Here we must distinguish between Jesus' own words about himself in John and the writer's persistent use of narrative devices to keep our attention riveted on his Subject whom he so highly exalts.

Jesus' own references to himself as the Christ are few indeed, limited to the conversation he had with the woman of Samaria (4:25-26; cf. 1:41, 49; 11:27). When in the company of the unsympathetic, Jesus is as reticent to declare his messiahship as he is in Mark's account (John 7:26-42; 10:24; cf. 9:22).

John's account of Jesus' declared divine Sonship is likewise restricted. He makes the claim obliquely in defending his act of healing the invalid on the Sabbath (5:19-20). Similarly, it is only when pressed at the Feast of Dedication whether he is the Christ that he asserts that he is the Son of his Father based on the miracle works (10:22-38). Yet these incidents are scarcely dominant in the Gospel of John. Contrary to our expectations, Jesus does not appear on every page explicitly claiming to be the Christ or the Son of God.[79] The facts are otherwise and quite similar to Jesus' oblique and indirect assertions about himself in the synoptics.

What, then, of the Son of Man's self-references that are so prominent in Mark? Here we note three points of similarity with Mark in John's usage of the "Son of Man":[80] (a) only Jesus uses the term in the Gospel of John, as also in Mark; (b) it is always *the* Son of Man; and (c) it is mostly in an eschatological reference (as it mostly also is in Mark). The similarity to Mark of John's attribution to Jesus of the Son of Man references is noteworthy.

In Mark, Jesus the Son of Man is the proclaimer and bearer of the kingdom of God, and there are many references. By contrast, John records only two occasions where Jesus speaks about the kingdom of God (3:3, 5; cf. "my kingdom" — 18:36). Nonetheless, few though they be, they appear in the important conversation with Nicodemus.

---

79. So, too, M. M. Thompson, "The Historical Jesus and the Historical Christ," in *Exploring the Gospel of John*, 29-31.

80. John 1:51; 3:13, 14; 5:27; 6:27, 53, 62; 8:28; 9:35; 12:23, 34; 13:31.

Conclusion

In this chapter I have argued that the idiomatic and idiosyncratic Gospel of John has a serious attitude to overall global sequence (despite its omissions from and additions to Mark's outline), to historical and other detail, and to the teachings of Jesus. Accordingly, it merits respect as a source of information about the historical Christ. While John writes about Jesus through the eyes of one who has been blessed by the Paraclete, he soberly manages to allow Jesus to portray himself as he was *back then* as the Christ and the Son the Father sent. Yet he does this in surprisingly understated ways that are recognizable when set alongside Mark and the synoptics.

EIGHT

Christ in Paul's Letters

I count everything as loss because of the surpassing worth of knowing Christ Jesus my Lord.

Philippians 3:8

Even when used on its own, the title "the Jesus of history" implies a balancing category like "the Christ of faith." Too easily this implies that he was not "the Christ" beforehand, and not the object of "faith" beforehand.[1]

According to Luke-Acts, the crucified but now exalted *Kyrios* and *Christos* was the Jesus the disciples *earlier* confessed to be the Christ (Luke 9:18-20; Acts 2:36). This contradicts those who say the historical "Jesus" hit an impenetrable wall at crucifixion so that he was dead and was buried and existed no more and that the early Christians (i.e., Paul) invented the "Christ of faith" as an idealized Memory, whose spirit lived on as ruler of the church and savior of souls.[2]

Historically it was not like that. Jesus was the Christ pre-Easter, and his followers expressed "faith" in him pre-Easter.[3] Accordingly, the resurrection did not create Christology. On the contrary, the resurrection confirmed him to be the Christ whom the disciples had already recognized.

1. As observed by J. D. G. Dunn, "Messianic Ideas and Their Influence on the Jesus of History," in *The Messiah*, ed. J. H. Charlesworth (Minneapolis: Fortress, 1992), 365-81.

2. See, e.g., the reconstruction of D. H. Akenson in his *Saint Saul* discussed in Barnett, *Birth of Christianity*, 5-7.

3. So Dunn, "Messianic Ideas," 365-81.

Preaching Christ Crucified

Before Paul came to Corinth around 49, he had decided to "know" only one message "among [them]," and that was "Jesus Christ . . . crucified" (*estaurōmenon* — 1 Cor 2:2). Perhaps he had contemplated attempting to convince the Corinthians by another message delivered with "the wisdom of speech" (*sophia logou* — 1:17), but he rejected that option. He summarized his message to them in these few words: "We preach Christ crucified" (*Christon estaurōmenon* — 1:23).

Nor is this a rhetorical flourish for the Corinthians. He writes similarly to the Galatians, reminding them of his mission preaching: "Foolish Galatians! Who has bewitched you, before whose eyes Jesus Christ was publicly portrayed as crucified?" (*proegraphē estaurōmenon* — Gal 3:1). It is evident that the message "Christ crucified" was fundamental to Paul's kerygma.

What is implied here? It does not matter whether we translate "Christ crucified" or "a crucified Christ," the point is the same. He was "Christ" when they crucified him. He did not become Christ post-crucifixion. The crucified One was *already* the Christ.[4]

Paul makes the same point in another of his main titles, the Son of God. "We were reconciled to God by the death of his Son" (Rom 5:10). "[God] did not spare *his own Son* but gave him up for us all" (Rom 8:32; cf. Gal 2:20).

The One the Father "did not spare" was *already* "his *own* Son" (*tou idiou huiou*). True, his resurrection "designated" him "Son of God *in power*," that is, "Jesus Christ our *Kyrios*." Paul is identifying the resurrected *in-power-Son* as the exalted *Kyrios*. Yet prior to his resurrection he was already "his Son, who was descended from David" (Rom 1:3-4), that is, the anointed one who was also God's "own Son," whom the Father "did not spare."

What about Paul's other main title, *Kyrios?* Several times Paul refers to the pre-Easter Jesus as *Kyrios,* especially in various teachings and instructions "of the Lord" (e.g., 1 Thess 4:2, 15; 1 Cor 7:10, 12; 11:23; cf. Rom

---

4. We find a similar perspective in the kerygmatic passage in Heb 5:5, 7. "So also [the] Christ *did not exalt himself* to be made a high priest. . . . *In the days of his flesh,* Jesus offered up prayers and supplications, with loud cries and tears, to him who was able to save him from death, and he was heard for his godly fear." He was the Christ "in the days of his flesh," i.e., preexaltation, as high priest in the order of Melchizedek.

14:14). He can even say that "the rulers of this age . . . crucified *the Lord of glory*" (1 Cor 2:8; cf. Rev 11:8).[5]

Our conclusion is that Paul speaks of his three main post-Easter christological categories — the Christ, the Son, and the Lord — in pre-Easter terms.

Paul recoils in horror as he refers to God not sparing *his own* Son (Rom 8:32). Nonetheless, it is the other impossible juxtaposition that he most frequently refers to: "[the] Christ crucified." For centuries Jewish hopes had been directed to the Anointed One who would be a *victor*, stained with the blood of defeated enemies.

> How beautiful is the king Messiah,
> who will arise from those who are of the house of Judah.
> He goes forth and orders the battle array against his enemies
> and slays kings along with their overlords,
> and no king or overlord can stand before him;
> he reddens the mountains with the blood of the slain,
> his clothing is dipped in blood like a winepress. (*Palestinian Targum,*
> Gen 49:10)

It is likely that Paul's initial hostility against the disciples in Jerusalem was their assertion that the *crucified* Jesus was the Christ. Ironically, after the Damascus event the anger the persecutor directed at the disciples came to be directed at him, as he preached a message that was a *skandalon* to Jews (1 Cor 1:20).

Accordingly, the "Jesus of history"/"Christ of faith" dichotomy is historically unhelpful and should be abandoned. With Paul as our guide we should portray him rather as the "forsaken Son," the "crucified *Christos*," and the crucified *Kyrios* (pre-Easter) who is now the exalted *Kyrios* (Phil 2:9-10) to whom the churches sing (Eph 5:19) and pray (1 Cor 16:22). This exactly corresponds with Pliny's version of the lapsed Christians' testimony in Bithynia circa 110, that they invoked (the executed) Christ "*as if* a god."[6]

---

5. The *confession* of the crucified, exalted *Kyrios* is from a post-Easter perspective (Rom 10:9; 1 Cor 12:3), likely influenced by Paul's experience of the intervention of the ascended *Kyrios* near Damascus (1 Cor 9:1; 15:8; 2 Cor 3:16, 18; 4:1, 5, 6).

6. See above, chapter 3.

"Christ Crucified" in the Tradition

The evidence chronologically closest to Jesus the Christ is the letters of Paul. His letters written from and to Corinth are not in dispute regarding authorship,[7] dating, or textual integrity. Paul wrote 1 Thessalonians fewer than twenty years after the crucifixion, and Romans only seven years after that.

These letters are rich in preformulated material that predates the writing of these texts and brings us even closer to the historical Christ. Let us move from the latest to the earliest of these texts. We begin with Romans, written circa 57.

Romans 1:1-4

Paul's choice of words at the head of his letter seems calculated to establish his apostolic credentials.

> the gospel of God
> which he promised beforehand through his prophets in the holy scriptures
> concerning his Son
> > who came from the seed of David
> > > according to the flesh
> > who was set apart as the Son of God in power
> > > according to the Spirit of holiness
> > > by his resurrection from the dead
> > Jesus Christ our Lord.

Various elements betray an original underlying credo or catechesis, as many have recognized: (i) the symmetrical "shape" of the text following "his Son," with two legs each introduced by a participial phrase ("who came . . ."; "who was . . ."); (ii) each of which is balanced by the antithetical "according to the flesh" and "according to the Spirit"; (iii) the archaic-sounding "Spirit of holiness" (words not appearing elsewhere in the NT).

This tradition points to the Son's successive modes of existence. In the first, the Son "came" *(genomenou)* from *(ek)* the messianic line of David. This mode was "according to the flesh," that is, subject to human circumstances and observation. In the second mode the Son is "the Son of

---

7. Some doubt that Paul wrote 2 Thessalonians.

God in power" (= *Kyrios*) following his resurrection. This mode is "according to the Spirit of holiness," that is, by the Spirit's witness to him from heaven, beginning at Pentecost (cf. 5:5 — "God's love has been poured into our hearts through the Holy Spirit which has been given to us").

These two modes appear consistently throughout Paul's letters and within other NT letters. It is sufficient here to emphasize that the tradition points to the Son of God as "from the seed of David," that is, as the Christ/Messiah *before the resurrection.*

Romans 6:3-4, 17

These passages occurring in the one chapter are clearly connected.

> Do you not know that all of us who have been baptized into Christ Jesus were baptized into his death? We were buried therefore with him by baptism into death, so that as Christ was raised from the dead by the glory of the Father, we too might walk in newness of life. (Rom 6:3-4)

> But thanks be to God, that you who were once slaves of sin have become obedient from the heart to the standard of teaching to which you were committed. (Rom 6:17)

Both texts speak of the readers' radical change of life's direction, one (said to be) following baptism and the other (said to be) following "obedience" to the "standard of teaching." The change of life followed catechetical instruction at baptism, as signaled by Paul's formulaic appeal (v. 3 — "do you not know?"). They were "committed to" that "standard of teaching" at the time of their baptism that spelled the end of the old life and the beginning of the new.

Their "obedience" to the "standard of teaching" to which they were "committed" or "handed over" (*hypēkousate de ek kardias eis hon paredothēte typon didachēs* — v. 17) must be read alongside the later reference to "the doctrine which you have been taught" (*tēn didachēn . . . emathete* — 16:17). This "rabbinic" language ("standard of teaching," "handed over," "learned," "obeyed") points to the instruction at the time of baptism that *was as likely true for Paul* as it had been for his readers ("*all of us* who have

180

been baptized" — v. 3). Whether from within his mission or from outside it, Paul can appeal to a (more or less) universal practice of baptismal instruction based on Christ, his death/burial and resurrection.

What was the content of that "standard of teaching"? While Paul has written his own powerful appeal into the *typon didachēs,* there can be little doubt as to its main "teaching." It is christological, focused on Christ Jesus who died and was buried and was raised. The word order — Christ Jesus — is close to and consistent with Christ as a title: Messiah Jesus. The prebaptismal instruction was centered on Christ, and the act of baptism (down into, and up from, the water) portrayed his death and his burial and his resurrection.

As with Romans 1:1-4, the most natural way of reading this text is to see Christ Jesus as *already* the Messiah at the time of his crucifixion.

Traditions Given to Churches in Macedonia and Achaia (ca. 48-50)

Moving backward chronologically from the writing of Romans to Paul's arrival in Corinth circa 50, we hear echoes of Paul's initial proclamation of Christ there at that time: "I delivered to you . . . what I also received, that *Christ* died for our sins . . . , that he was buried, that he was raised on the third day . . . , that he appeared to Cephas . . ." (1 Cor 15:3-5). The critical question is: When, where, and from whom did Paul "receive" this tradition? Paul could have learned this teaching on three possible occasions: in Damascus circa 34, in Jerusalem circa 36/37, or in Antioch-on-the-Orontes circa 45. The first is the most likely.[8]

This view is based on various statements in the book of Acts. In Damascus following the Christophany outside the city, Ananias instructed him, "You will be a witness for [the just one] to all men of what you have seen and heard" (Acts 22:15), whereupon "Saul . . . confounded the Jews

---

8. We may agree with F. F. Bruce, *Paul, Apostle of the Free Spirit* (Exeter: Paternoster, 1977), 86-93, that the tradition (1 Cor 15:3-7) Paul quotes has a Palestinian, therefore, a Jerusalem, provenance (and I would add, originated with Cephas). Whereas Bruce argues that Paul "received" that tradition in Jerusalem, our opinion is that Damascus is more likely. 1 Cor 15:3-7 specifies a catechesis "handed over" to Paul that he "received." This sits better with a baptismal setting than the likely awkward circumstance of Paul as a guest in the house of Cephas in Jerusalem. Paul had been proclaiming the Son of God in his own right since the Damascus "call" for up to three years before his first return visit to Jerusalem.

who lived in Damascus by proving that *Jesus was the Christ*" (Acts 9:22). The author of Acts means us to understand that Paul "immediately" began preaching "the Christ" in the synagogues in Damascus (Acts 9:20).

Furthermore, it is clear that Paul had also been baptized by Ananias, who instructed him, "Rise and be baptized, and wash away your sins, calling on his name" (Acts 22:16). Since Paul preached *the Christ,* and had had his *sins* washed away, we reasonably assume that Paul had been instructed in terms of or along the lines of the tradition he quotes in 1 Corinthians 15:3 that refers to *Christ* and his death for *sins.* If this is correct, it means that the christological tradition Paul "received" in Damascus had been formulated beforehand, within the very short period between the first Easter and the conversion/call of Paul.

In the months before Paul came to Corinth in 49/50 he had preached in the cities of Macedonia, including in Thessalonica. Our supposition that he also preached "Christ crucified" there, as he would weeks later in Corinth, is well supported by his reminder to the Thessalonians of the message he brought to them.

> God . . . destined us . . . to obtain salvation through our Lord Jesus *Christ, who died for us.* (1 Thess 5:9-10; cf. 1:9-10)

> It was necessary for *the Christ to suffer* and to rise from the dead. (Acts 17:3)

Our contention is that the words "Christ died for our sins"/"Christ died for us"/"it was necessary for the Christ to suffer" are variants of the one basic early tradition that Paul "received" in Damascus from Ananias in about 34. It is fundamental to this tradition that the *preresurrection* Christ died for sins.

If Paul "received" this tradition (from Ananias), someone else must have formulated it beforehand. We are interested to know when, where, and by whom the tradition was created.

In my view all fingers point to the earliest Jerusalem-based apostolate, led by Peter (and John), as the formulators of the tradition that would become the basis of the Pauline Christology.

i. Through Paul's eyes we see the impressive authority of Cephas/Peter as the leading apostle in Jerusalem. God gave Cephas the "apostolate" to the circumcised (in the land of Israel) for the first decade or so (Gal 2:7-8).

Naturally it was to Cephas that the newly converted Paul must come in his first return visit to the Holy City (Gal 1:18). The imprimatur of the Jerusalem "pillars" was critical for Paul's apostolate to the Gentiles (Gal 2:2, 9).

ii. According to Paul's own words in Galatians, he the persecutor had previously attempted to "destroy" both "the church of God" (Gal 1:13) and "the faith" (Gal 1:23). "The church of God" and "the faith" are closely connected. Cephas and the Jerusalem apostles were the leaders of "the church of God" in Jerusalem, who formulated "the faith."

iii. We must not overstate the role of the Hellenists in the formulation of "the faith."[9] True, their numbers likely became greater than the Galilean "Hebrew" apostles and disciples. Their influx appears to have come from the Greek-speaking synagogues. Yet Paul does not mention them in his letters, and the book of Acts makes clear that the *apostles'* teaching was foundational.[10] The apostles (who had been the disciples of the preresurrection Christ) must be seen as the ones who formulated the christological "faith."

iv. The prior influence of Peter may be seen in part in his preaching in the house of Cornelius, where there is an important point of contact with the tradition Paul cites in 1 Corinthians 15:3. When we place this "received" tradition alongside Peter's preaching in Acts, we see a number of parallels, as we will note later.[11]

Conclusion: "Christ Crucified" in the Letters of Paul

From Romans and 1 Corinthians we identify traditions that most likely were preformulated, originating in the apostolic leadership in Jerusalem,

9. Contra M. Hengel, *Between Jesus and Paul* (London: SCM, 1983), 30-47, who generally attributes a greater role to the Hellenists in the formulation of Christology than is warranted. Yet it is conceivable that the Jerusalem-based Hellenists assisted in converting the Aramaic traditions into the Greek forms, as we encounter them in Paul's letters (e.g., 1 Cor 11:23-26; 15:3-7).

10. The prominence in Acts of the Hellenists and of Antioch may be attributable to the author's own interests and background as an Antiochene and a Godfearer. J. A. Fitzmyer, *The Gospel according to Luke: Introduction, Translation, and Notes I-IX* (Garden City, N.Y.: Doubleday, 1981), 45ff., argues that Luke's background was in Antioch. The author's opening dedication of his two-volume work to "Theophilus" and his frequent reference to Godfearers in the book of Acts point to a special interest in Gentile Godfearers.

11. See chapter 9.

and that came into Paul's possession in Damascus (at baptism) and upon which he depended for his christological preaching. These brief traditions indicate that the *Kyrios* whom the churches confessed was, *preresurrection,* the Christ whom men crucified, God's *own Son* whom he did not spare.

Paul's Knowledge of the Preresurrection Christ

Our argument is that the traditional material embedded in Paul's letters shows that he thought of the preresurrected One as the Christ and as the Son. But how much *else* did he know?

Paul's relative lack of detailed reference to the historical Christ is usually explained in one of two ways: either Paul knew only that there was such a man but knew (or cared to know) little more (so Bultmann),[12] or he knew quite a lot but didn't need to elaborate this in his letters beyond what his readers already knew (so Hengel).[13]

Paul's Access to Knowledge about Christ

Paul had considerable opportunity to learn about Jesus of Nazareth. If, as seems likely, Paul settled in Jerusalem circa 17 as a scholar in Gamaliel's rabbinic academy, he would have heard about the charismatic rabbi from Galilee who emerged there as a public figure circa 29. Otherwise we must conclude that Paul was not living in Jerusalem at that time, something we have no reason to assume. It is, therefore, more likely than not that Paul had at least heard about Jesus and his execution.

Furthermore, since I date Paul's conversion/call at Damascus to 34, that is, to within a year or so of the crucifixion, it follows that his persecutions in Jerusalem occurred over a very brief period. We reasonably conclude that Paul the persecutor heard something about Jesus from Stephen and from others who had been arrested.

Again, Paul would have learned about Jesus at his baptism and from the disciples in Damascus. The Hellenists who had fled from Jerusalem to

---

12. See Barnett, *Paul,* chapter 2.

13. M. Hengel, *The Four Gospels and the One Gospel of Jesus Christ* (London: SCM, 2000), 152.

Damascus would have had at least some information about Jesus from their involvement with the apostles in Jerusalem.

Paul's words "even if we knew Christ according to the flesh *(kata sarka),* we know him so no more" (2 Cor 5:16) mean that his pre-Damascus knowledge of Christ was superficial and erroneous, as compared with his present knowledge. Nonetheless, because he later regarded it as superficial and wrong allows us to infer that he did have some knowledge about the preresurrection Christ.

It is likely that for the first several years Paul was a man "in Christ," his knowledge of the historical Christ was relatively fragmentary and incomplete. All that changed, however, when Paul made his first return visit to Jerusalem in 36/37 when he stayed with Cephas for fifteen days and also met James the brother of the Lord (Gal 1:18-19). This visit, which appears to have been irenic, provided Paul with the opportunity to learn firsthand about the ministry and teaching of Jesus (from Cephas) and about Jesus' early life in Nazareth (from James). This is Paul's own account; it does not come via, e.g., the filter of the book of Acts. We must treat Paul's words as factual and beyond doubt or dispute, and that should settle forever the question about Paul's knowledge of the preresurrected Jesus. Within three years of his conversion/call Paul had access to comprehensive knowledge about Jesus of Nazareth.

Evidence of Paul's Knowledge

We are able to classify Paul's scattered references[14] to the historical Christ under three aspects: his life, his teachings, and his character.

As to his *life,* he was a descendant of Abraham and a direct descendant of David who was "born of a woman" (a reference to virginal conception?), raised as an observant Jew, and lived in relative poverty. He had a brother named James and other brothers who are not named. Since Peter was a leader in Jerusalem after the resurrection, we reasonably believe he had been a disciple and a leader before the crucifixion. Jesus' ministry was primarily directed to Jews. On the night of his betrayal he instituted a memorial meal. He was killed by Roman crucifixion at the instigation of the Jews, buried in a tomb, raised alive on the third day, and seen by many witnesses, some of them named.

---

14. See Barnett, *Paul,* chapters 2, 8–9, for a comprehensive list of references.

Are there aspects of Paul's life that are by his choice in "material agreement"[15] with Christ's life and that point to a "historical continuity" between Christ and Paul? Here are four such "agreements":

i. Paul's *willingness to suffer deprivation,* as reflected in Paul's *peristaseis* (listed in 1 Cor 4:11-12; 2 Cor 6:9-10; 11:23-27), possibly mirrors (for example) "the Son of man has nowhere to lay his dead" (Luke 9:58).

ii. Paul's *renunciation of marriage* as a charisma for serving Christ (1 Cor 7:6-7, 32-35) seems in continuity with Jesus' self-reference as one who had renounced marriage because of the kingdom of heaven (Matt 19:10).

iii. Paul's *studied humility* in lowering himself to exalt others (2 Cor 11:7; cf. 6:10) is in line with another self-reference by Jesus, "Whoever would be first among you must be slave of all" (Mark 10:44; cf. Luke 9:48; 14:11; 18:14; 22:26).

iv. Paul's *contempt for persecution* (e.g., 2 Cor 12:10) and his sense of participation in the sufferings of Christ (2 Cor 1:5; Phil 3:10; cf. Gal 6:17) are consistent with Jesus' words that the Son of Man must suffer many things (Mark 8:31; cf. Matt 5:10).

These examples of parallel conduct do not exhibit explicit verbal echoes of the Jesus tradition, so certainty of direct influence is not attainable. Nonetheless, this is not a fatal objection since each of these four aspects of behavior is uncharacteristic of the Pharisaic values that the pre-Christian Paul would have held. It is more likely than not that Paul deliberately chose these behaviors for only one reason, because the historical Christ was his practical template in all things.

Scholars debate the frequency of Paul's echoes of Jesus' *teaching,* but few doubt that Paul's letters reflect various "instructions" of the Lord.[16] The task of identifying these "words" is not straightforward since Paul depended on sources that were only later consolidated in the gospels. Most likely these sources were already in Greek written form.[17] Furthermore, Paul often echoes Jesus' words back to the churches as reminders of teachings already given and already adapted or readapted by Paul to a specific pastoral situation (e.g., 1 Cor 7:10).

15. See G. F. Wessels, "The Historical Christ and the Letters of Paul: Revisiting Bernard C. Lategan's Thesis," in *The New Testament Interpreted,* ed. C. Breytenbach et al. (Leiden: Brill, 2006), 43-46.

16. See Barnett, *Birth of Christianity,* 120-26.

17. See chapter 6.

The *Character* of the Christ[18]

Paul often makes the moral *character* of Christ the basis for his appeals for ethical behavior by members of the churches of his mission. As it happens, these texts about Christ relate to (a) his incarnation, (b) his manner of behavior, and (c) his death.

The Incarnation

2 Corinthians 8:9

It is evident from this letter that the relationship between Paul and the Corinthians had been stretched to the breaking point. His poor showing recently in Corinth over a disciplinary matter, and his failure to return as promised but his dispatching instead a harsh letter (borne by Titus), left the members of this church significantly alienated from their founding apostle (2 Cor 1:12–2:4; 6:11-13; 7:5-12). A symptom of this broken confidence was their declining interest in the "collection" for the saints of Judea that Paul had established a year or so earlier. A major reason for writing this letter may be discerned in chapters 8 and 9 where Paul appeals to them to revive their contributions to the "collection."

Paul begins by shaming them with the example of the poor Macedonians who, by contrast with the reluctant Corinthians, had by their own initiative pleaded to contribute to the collection (8:1-8). He then points by contrast to the "rich" Christ who made himself "poor" for them.

For you know the grace of our Lord Jesus Christ,

	he was	rich *(plousios ōn)*
that though		
yet for your sake	he became	poor *(eptōcheusen)*
	so that by his	poverty
	you might become	rich.

The preexistent *(ōn)* Christ himself is subject of the action *he* took in impoverishing himself *(eptōcheusen)* to make others rich. Paul is appealing to the Corinthians' knowledge of Christ's character as expressed by this

18. See further G. N. Stanton, *Jesus of Nazareth in New Testament Preaching*, SNTSMS 27 (Cambridge: Cambridge University Press, 1974), 99-110.

act, that is, his voluntary embrace of poverty in birth and life and humiliation in death (implied by "[God] *made him to be sin . . ."* — 5:21). In the broad, Paul is speaking about the generosity of Christ in every aspect of life and death as a template for the Corinthians to copy in their generosity toward the poor saints in Judea.

Philippians 2:5-8

The commonsense and traditional view is that Paul wrote (or quoted) this passage to correct the Philippians' pride, self-interest, and divisions.[19] Rather, let the Philippians "adopt towards one another the same attitude which (was) also (found) in Christ Jesus."[20]

> Christ Jesus, who, though he was *(hyparchōn)* in the form of God *(morphē theou)*, did not count equality with God a thing to be grasped *(harpagmon hēgēsato)*, but emptied himself *(heauton ekenōsen)*, taking the form of a slave *(morphēn doulou)*, being born in the likeness of men. And being found in human form he humbled himself *(etapeinōsen heauton)* and became obedient unto death, even death on a cross.

In this much-discussed passage we need only note the actions Christ took to express what was in his "mind" (way of thinking). The emphasis is on the mind of Christ and the actions *he* took. Without going into the exegetical complexities of this remarkable passage,[21] we are able to say that Christ *deliberately chose* the downward course he took. From being "in the form of God" (as to his mode of being) and "equal with God" (as to his status), he took a succession of steps down from that lofty height that took him ever lower, first as a man and finally as a crucified felon. The exegetical-pastoral application is clear: let the Philippians choose the way of humility in their relationships with one another.

For our purposes we need to note that Paul has given us a character sketch of the incarnate Christ who was to be exalted as the glorified *Kyrios.*

---

19. So Stanton, *Jesus of Nazareth,* 100-102.

20. C. F. D. Moule, "Further Reflexions on Philippians 2:5-11," in *Apostolic History and the Gospel,* ed. W. W. Gasque and R. P. Martin (Exeter: Paternoster, 1970), 264.

21. See, e.g., P. T. O'Brien, *Commentary on Philippians,* NIGTC (Grand Rapids: Eerdmans, 1991), 186-271.

Although the text is permeated with theological nuances, the historical thread is unmistakable, that is, Christ's self-chosen humility in life that culminated in his humiliation in death.

Christ's Manner of Behavior

In 2 Corinthians 10 Paul begins to prepare the Corinthians for his impending third and final visit. The second visit had been a defeat for Paul in his attempt to discipline the leader of an opposing faction. Worse still, Paul had not returned directly, as he had undertaken to do, but had sent the stern letter demanding repentance from the leading offender. On his return to Paul in Macedonia, Titus brought the mixed report of the offender's repentance but also of the Corinthians' dissatisfaction with the apostle: "they say, 'His letters are weighty and strong, but his bodily presence is weak, and his speech of no account'" (2 Cor 10:10). They complain that he is "humble when face to face" but "bold . . . when . . . away" (10:1b). Paul assures them that he will exercise discipline (excommunication) when he comes unless the disaffected party is reconciled to him (10:2-6, 11; 12:20–13:4). Nonetheless, Paul's more typical approach is different, based on Christ's manner.

2 Corinthians 10:1

> I, Paul, myself entreat you, by *(dia)* the meekness *(prautētos)* and gentleness *(epieikeias)* of Christ — I who am humble *(tapeinos)* when face to face with you. . . .

Paul's heartfelt appeal is noteworthy. First, this is an extraordinarily strong appeal. It commences with the emphatic "myself" followed by the rare "I, Paul," who expresses himself by his "appeal" made "through" *(dia)* no less than Christ himself.

Second, Paul appeals without further explanation to characteristics of the historical Christ as a defense of his own ministry (which [some of] the Corinthians despise). His entreaty only makes sense if he knew that the Corinthians were able to recall Paul's teachings that Christ was *like this*. We reasonably assume that Paul in his initial ministry typically gave instruction about various aspects of Christ's life and manner.

Third, Paul actually specifies elements of Christ's manner that connect with Jesus' own self-disclosure in the gospel tradition, that (i) he was "gentle and humble *(praus . . . kai tapeinos)* of heart" (Matt 11:29), (ii) he pronounced the blessing of God on the "meek" (Matt 5:5), and (iii) promised the exaltation of the "humble" (Luke 18:14; cf. Matt 18:4). Notwithstanding his kingly status (Matt 21:5), Christ's own "meek" servanthood is recorded in several passages in the gospel (Mark 9:33-37 par.; John 13:14-17).

Romans 15:7-9

This text follows directly from Romans 14:1–15:6 in which Paul seeks to bring unity between "the strong" and "the weak" among the Roman believers (see below, Romans 15:1-3, under the heading "Christ's Death").

> Welcome one another, therefore, as Christ has welcomed you, for the glory of God. For I tell you that Christ became a servant to the circumcised to show God's truthfulness, in order to confirm the promises given to the patriarchs, and in order that the Gentiles might glorify God for his mercy.

Paul is evoking memories of the historical Christ, though it is uncertain to what degree Paul may have been confident in this among believers he had not previously instructed. His words "I tell you" imply that his information about Christ may have been new to (some of) them. Whatever the situation, Paul is here appealing to several aspects of the manner of the historical Christ.

First, "as Christ has welcomed you"[22] evokes memories of Christ's "welcome" to various among the people of Israel, in particular the "sinners."[23] Jesus was known as "a friend of tax collectors and sinners" (Matt 11:19). The scathing denunciation of the Pharisees and scribes, "This man *receives* sinners and eats with them" (Luke 15:1-2; cf. 19:7), is illustrated by various stories of that "friendship" across the gospel stories (e.g., Mark 2:15-17 par.; Luke 7:36-49; 19:1-10). Christ's "welcome" of the "sinners" and the "lost sheep" in Israel anticipated his postexaltation welcome of the Gentiles (through the mission of Paul — Rom 15:15-19).

22. It is likely that the "you" here means believers from Israel and Gentiles.

23. See B. F. Meyer, *The Aims of Jesus* (London: SCM, 1979), 158-62; J. Jeremias, *New Testament Theology* 1 (London: SCM, 1971), 108-13.

Second, Paul's observation "Christ became a servant *(diakonos)* to the circumcised" likely picks up Jesus' disclosure "the Son of man . . . came . . . to serve *(diakonēsai)*" and provided a model for Paul and his co-missionaries as "servants *(diakonoi)* of God" (2 Cor 6:4). It is possible that Christ's servanthood to the "circumcised" is meant to refer not to Jews in general but to irascible (legalistic) Pharisees,[24] thus setting the example to "the strong" in Rome to "welcome/bear with the (legalistic) weak" (Rom 14:1; 15:1).

1 Corinthians 10:33–11:1[25]

In Gentile Corinth there were "gods many and lords many," and everyday food was routinely offered to the gods in the temples, creating social issues for the new believers. The Corinthians themselves sent a series of practical questions to Paul, including one about *eidōlothyton/*"*idol-sacrificed meat*" *(see 8:1), to which he responds in 1 Corinthians 8:1–11:1. In a final summation he appeals to the example of Christ.*

> Just as I try to please all men in everything I do, not seeking my own advantage *(to emautou symphoron),* but that of many *(to tōn pollōn),* that they may be saved. Be imitators of me, as I am of Christ.

These words complete the *inclusio* that began in verse 24, "Let no one seek his own good *(to heautou),* but that of the other *(to tou heterou).*" Paul does not seek "his own good"/"his own advantage" but that of "his neighbor"/"the many," and he exhorts the Corinthians to "be imitators *(mimētai)*" of him, as he is "of Christ."

Paul is addressing the Corinthian attitude that took unqualified "freedom" as its starting point ("all things are lawful" — 10:23), specifically to eat "idol-sacrificed" food in any and every situation. That was a false premise (8:7-13) regarding eating in the presence of the "brother" whose "conscience"/"consciousness" *(syneidēsis)* is "weak" *(asthenēs),* but it is equally defective in the presence of an "unbeliever" (10:27). Paul is imagining a setting where the unbeliever invites a believer to a meal (whether in a

---

24. So C. K. Barrett, *Commentary on the Epistle to the Romans* (London: Black, 1957), *ad loc.*

25. See J. Dickson, *Mission-Commitment in Ancient Judaism and the Pauline Communities,* WUNT 159 (Tübingen: Mohr Siebeck, 2003), 254.

private home or, e.g., a temple — the context is unclear) where someone observes that the food "has been offered in sacrifice *(hierothyton)*."

If nothing is said, the believer should eat saying nothing, but once the food has been declared "idol sacrificed," then the believer should not eat. Here the believer's "freedom" is qualified and overruled by a higher principle, the "good" of "the other," who in this context is an unbeliever, whether the host or a fellow guest. The believer should not want his theoretical "freedom" to eat to appear to endorse the worship of idols, which he would do by eating once the religious history of the food had been made an issue. Rather, says Paul, by refusing to eat, and explaining why you are not eating, you are seeking the "good" of "the other."

Let the Corinthians understand that in his mission Paul lives by this same principle. He is constantly putting the "good" of others before his own freedom (9:19-23), and in this he is the "imitator . . . of Christ" *(mimētēs . . . tou Christou)*. One thing that is clear is that Paul was aware of the character and manner of the historical Christ, who put the needs of others before his own, which Paul says he imitates and which he exhorts the readers also to imitate in their social relationships with unbelievers.[26]

Christ's Death

Romans 15:1-3

Paul repeats several items from passages we discussed earlier: (1) Paul's concern "to please all men in everything I do" based on the example of Christ (e.g., 1 Cor 10:33–11:1) is repeated in Romans 15:1, 2, 3; (2) the prior-

---

26. There is a further possibility signaled by Paul's words, that he is "*seeking (zētōn)* the advantage . . . of the many, that they may be *saved*" *(sōthōsin)*. That is to say, that the "good" *(symphoron)* of the many that Paul "seeks" is their salvation. Here we may hear the echo of the word of Christ that "the Son of man came to seek and to save *(zētēsai kai sōsai)* the lost" (Luke 19:10). Reference to "lost" Zacchaeus, a "son of Abraham" (Luke 19:9), is evocative of the mission of the Shepherd-Christ to "*lost* sheep of the house of Israel" (Matt 10:6; 15:24) as expressed in his parable of the lost sheep, and its adjunct parables of the lost coin and the lost son (where vocabulary of "lost" occurs frequently — Luke 15:4/Matt 18:12, 14; Luke 15:6, 24, 32). Paul appears to know the tradition(s) stemming from the words of Christ in his self-forgetting mission seeking to save "lost" Israelites. Paul appears to be adapting Christ's mission words to Israel pastorally to his mission among the Gentile Corinthians.

ity to "edify" the "other" (1 Cor 10:23-24) is repeated in Romans 15:2 by Paul's appeal to each of "the strong" in Rome to "edify . . . his neighbor" (where "the other" and "neighbor" are synonymous).

> We who are strong ought to bear with the failings of the weak, and not to *please* ourselves; let each of us *please* his *neighbor* for his good, to *edify* him. For even *(kai gar)* the Christ did not *please* himself; but, as it is written, "The reproaches of those who reproached thee fell on me."

Once more Paul is qualifying a theoretical freedom by a higher principle. In the setting of Roman Christianity, "the strong" wanted the liberty to eat anything, notwithstanding the scruples of the "weak." Paul calls this theoretical freedom of the strong "their good" (Rom 14:16), but he appeals to them to concede it for the sake of "mutual upbuilding" *(tēs oikodomēs tēs eis allēlous)* in the community of faith. Paul readily acknowledges that "everything is . . . clean" *(katharos)* but adds immediately, "it is wrong for any one to make others fall by what he eats" (14:20), since that would not be "to walk in love" (14:15). In effect, Paul is appealing to "the strong" to accommodate to "the weak" when eating with them, so as not to "*dis*-edify" them by a display of freedom.

Paul appeals to the example of the historic Christ *(ho Christos)*, "for even" *(kai gar)* he "did not please himself." On the contrary, as the substantiating citation from LXX Psalm 68:9 illustrates, the hostility men feel toward God was directed to his Son (on the cross). Paul is appealing to the Romans' awareness of the historical fact that, at great cost to himself, Christ died an untimely death. Christ could have taken another course but "did not please himself," and chose rather to embrace a manner of death that was deeply humiliating, for the sake of others. Once again, Paul is alluding to an aspect of the character of the precrucifixion Christ that he expected his readers to know.

Ephesians 5:2

Again Paul bases an ethical appeal ("walk in love") on the example of Christ.

> And walk in love, as Christ loved us and gave himself up for *(hyper)* us, a fragrant offering and sacrifice to God *(tō theō)*.

Paul is portraying the crucifixion as "a fragrant offering and sacrifice." This is "Levitical" language to indicate a true sacrifice, acceptable to God (see, e.g., Lev 1:9). Christ died not as a martyr or as an exemplar; his death was a true sacrifice since it was offered "to God" and it was "for *(hyper)* us."

As well, Christ "handed himself over" *(paredōken heauton)* as a voluntary act (cf. the similar Gal 2:20 — "the Son of God . . . *loved* me and *gave himself* [*paradontos heauton*] *for* [*hyper*] me"). The verb "hand over" *(paradontos)* echoes the gospel narrative, where it is directly employed for those who betrayed, arrested, and executed Christ (Mark 9:31; 10:33; 14:1–15:15 passim). In Ephesians 5:2, however, *Christ* "hands over *himself* to God," evoking the sense of *his* ultimate control even in this setting of ultimate vulnerability. This detail strongly hints that Paul was aware of Christ's initiative in coming to Jerusalem and the fatal danger he anticipated there.

2 Corinthians 11:1–12:13 and 2:14-15

2 Corinthians is notable as Paul's apologia for a ministry that was in many aspects *inglorious,* whether regarding his ignominious forced departure from Ephesus, his undeserved bad reputation, or his chronic unremoved "thorn"/*skolops* (2 Cor 1:8; 6:8; 12:7-10). How was it that one who heralded the "glorified Christ" was himself such a failure? The arrival of "super-apostles" *(hyperlian apostoloi* — 11:5; 12:11) whose signal word was *hyper,* to indicate their "superiority" to Paul, only served to remind the believers in "successful" Corinth how truly *inferior (hyster-)* he was (cf. 11:5; 12:11).

In the latter part of the letter his "fool's speech" (11:1–12:13) is an apologetic daringly cast in antitriumphalist terms. His catalogue of successes — astonishingly — is a catalogue of "weaknesses" or missionary sufferings that culminated in the unremoved "thorn" (11:21b–12:13). It would be incorrect to regard this "speech" as a perverse if clever piece of rhetoric to win the patient sympathy of the Corinthians for "poor Paul" (cf. 11:1). Rather, the "speech" is implicitly christological since by his succession of missionary sufferings ("weaknesses") Paul identifies himself with the *suffering* Christ (1:5; cf. Phil 3:10) and thereby validates himself as a "better"/*hyper* "servant *(diakonos)* of Christ" (2 Cor 11:23) while labeling the triumphalist opponents as truly the "inferior" ones. Clearly, the Christ Paul "served" was the Christ who *suffered.*

Paul made a similar point near the beginning of the letter (2:14-15).

> But thanks be to God, who in Christ always leads us in triumph, and through us spreads the fragrance of the knowledge of him everywhere. For we are the aroma of Christ to God among those who are being saved and among those who are perishing.

Despite considerable discussion about the cultural background of the passage, the traditional view that it portrays a Roman triumphal victory procession remains the most likely. It depicts prisoners of war being led in humiliation through the streets of Rome in a military parade. It is, therefore, strikingly antitriumphalist regarding Paul, whom God is leading along as his captive on his way to execution.

Reference to "aroma" evokes Levitical sacrifices acceptable in the nostrils of God (e.g., Lev 1:9). Just as Christ's sacrifice was an aroma pleasing to God, Paul's sacrifice as a man "in Christ" is similarly pleasing to God. In other words, Paul is asserting that as he preaches Christ crucified he also replicates Christ crucified in the various missionary sufferings (1:3-11; 4:7-12; 6:3-10; 11:23–12:10). That is to say, Paul validates his ministry by contending that his missionary sufferings identify him as a faithful minister and proxy of the suffering Christ. For this reason he is not inglorious *before God* since the true glory of God was seen in the Crucified One. Accordingly the "success"-based triumphalism of the opponents is the opposite of the true glory of God.

Paul's apologetic in these two passages establishes that he and, to some extent, his readers were familiar with the historic sufferings of Christ, including his crucifixion.

The Character of Christ: Summary

We conclude that Paul had ample opportunity to know about the historical Christ, especially from Cephas and James. Paul's letters display awareness of various biographical details that, however, he does not amplify at length; they are passing references. The reasons for this are twofold. It was not in the nature of letter writing (Paul's or anybody else's in the NT) to give detailed biographical information about Christ; letters were for exhortation and encouragement. Furthermore, it is more likely than not that Paul supplied adequate information about the historical Christ at the early stages of his ministry in various places.

Paul also reveals knowledge of the historical Christ in various hortatory passages. These touch on the broad outlines of the historical Christ — his lowering of himself in incarnation, his servant ministry, and his sacrificial death.

It is evident that Paul used these critical elements of the "story" of Christ's incarnation, ministry, and death as a template for his own life and for the lives of believers in the churches of his mission.[27]

Conclusion: The Character of Christ

The foregoing discussion allows us to draw important conclusions about Paul's knowledge of the precrucifixion Christ.

i. Paul had extensive access to information about the historical figure Jesus of Nazareth. His lengthy stay with Cephas and his meeting with James three years after the Damascus event provided this opportunity (Gal 1:18-19). Yet Paul must have had considerable knowledge of Christ beforehand, as we have noted.

ii. Paul's summary message "Christ crucified" implies that he was *already* Messiah/Christ when crucified. Furthermore, the tradition he cites in 1 Corinthians 15:3-8 establishes the *continuity* of the Christ's personhood through death and burial to resurrection and exaltation as the one who "appeared also" to Paul.

Another tradition echoed in Romans 1:2-4 points to the two modes of existence of the Son of God: as the son of David in his historical persona, and his heavenly persona as the resurrected, Spirit-giving Son of God in power (i.e., the *Kyrios*).

iii. There are reasonable grounds to believe that Paul received these traditions in Damascus, indicating thereby their early formulation soon

---

27. Osama bin Laden, founder of the Al-Qaeda movement, who declared jihad against the United States, overtly based himself on the Prophet he serves. His austere appearance as of a prophet, with flowing robes, and his voluntary exile in a cave in anticipation of his coming military triumph all seem deliberately based biographically on the known story of Muhammad. Bin Laden apparently finds a template for his life in the Prophet's life story. Paul's "imitation of Christ," however, though similar in principle, was radically different. Paul showed no interest in replicating the specifics of Christ's appearance, clothing, or geographical movements. For Paul, Christ's "story" in incarnation, death, and resurrection was the *typos*/pattern for the ideal moral and spiritual life based on the ideal moral and spiritual life of the one he served.

after the first Easter. Cephas and the college of the apostles likely created these traditions in Jerusalem.

iv. As well as the specific biographical details, Paul alludes in a number of key passages to the character of Christ — reflected in his incarnation, his ministry, and his death — as the basis for the radical ethical life-direction of believers. Through Paul we have the impression of Christ himself directing his actions and movements. Paul was seized by Christ's generosity and humility in lowering himself in incarnation (2 Cor 8:9; Phil 2:5-8); his "meekness and gentleness" in the "servant" ministry as he both "received" and "sought for" the "lost" (2 Cor 10:1; Rom 15:6-8; 1 Cor 10:33–11:1); and that in death he "did not please himself" but "gave himself" in "love" as a "sacrifice for" others (Rom 15:3; Eph 5:2).

Paul based his life on the example of Christ's revealed character and appealed to his readers to do the same.

Christ's Radical Influence on Paul

It is possible to identify the influence of Christ on Paul's thinking. The briefly explored elements that follow, however, are only illustrative of the impact of the Christ on this man "in Christ," Paul. We merely seek to establish in principle that the ex-Pharisee Paul was radically influenced by the teachings of Christ. Many monographs would be needed to explore this comprehensively.[28]

These traces are just that — traces; we are not always able to identify them specifically. This is, in part, because Paul's references are not usually exact quotations but are his already adapted and applied versions of Christ's teachings. In any case, we do not have the traditions upon which this depends, which were incorporated in the gospels sometime later. Nonetheless, it can be demonstrated at many points that Paul, the former leading Pharisee, underwent a massive change in his worldview and teachings under the impulse of Christ.

---

28. I have taken as my guides at a number of points Jeremias, *New Testament Theology 1*, and D. Wenham, *Paul: Follower of Jesus or Founder of Christianity?* (Grand Rapids: Eerdmans, 1995).

Kingdom Eschatology Actualized in (the) Christ

Christ, Paul, and the Pharisees were devout monotheists who shared a fundamental love for the Tanak whose worldview and piety permeate their teachings. The difference between Christ/Paul and the Pharisees is their radically different interpretations of the Law and the Prophets. Christ articulated an *actualized eschatology* that was centered on *him.*

> "But if it is by the finger/Spirit of God that I cast out demons, then the kingdom of God *has come* upon you." (Luke 11:20)

> "The kingdom of God is not coming with signs to be observed; nor will they say, 'Lo, here it is!' or 'There!' for behold, the kingdom of God *is in the midst of you.*" (Luke 17:20-21)

At many points this radical reinterpretation has left its mark in Paul's writings.

> Now these things happened to them as a warning, but they were written down for our instruction, upon whom the end of the ages *(ta telē tōn aiōnōn) has come.* (1 Cor 10:11)

> Christ Jesus, whom God *made* our wisdom, our righteousness and sanctification and redemption. (1 Cor 1:30)

> Then comes the end, when he hands over the kingdom to God the Father. . . . For he *must reign* until he has put all his enemies under his feet. (1 Cor 15:24-25)

The eschatology of the Pharisee (reflected, e.g., in the "Nineteen Benedictions"/*Shemoneh 'Esreh*) was focused on the future, whereas the eschatology of Jesus, followed by Paul, was actualized in the Messiah who already *had* come.

Children of Abba in His Kingdom

While the fundamental teachings about God in the Tanak as the all-wise, omnipotent, sovereign King and judge remain in the teaching of Jesus, they are no longer at the center. For Christ and his disciples — through his teaching and example — the God of Israel was first and foremost *Abba,* "dear Father." "At that time Jesus declared, 'I thank thee, *Father,* Lord of heaven and earth'" (Matt 11:25).

For Paul, as for Christ, the *Father* was now central truth about God, as to both theology and relationship. This is evident throughout Paul's letters, including his "benediction" of the Father near the beginning of 2 Corinthians. "Grace to you and peace from God *our Father* and the Lord Jesus Christ. Blessed be the God and *Father* of our Lord Jesus Christ, the *Father* of mercies and God of all comfort, who comforts us in all our affliction" (2 Cor 1:2-4).

The "God and Father of our Lord Jesus Christ" is "our Father."

Life of the Disciple/Believer

A condition of entry to the kingdom of *Abba* God was to become "like a child" (Matt 18:3). Once one was in that kingdom and a child of *Abba,* it was as if the Day of Salvation had *already* come. Everything for the children of *Abba* in the fallen world ruled by Satan is now changed.

> "*Fear not,* little flock, for it is your Father's good pleasure to give you the kingdom." (Luke 12:32)

> "*Do not be anxious* about tomorrow, for tomorrow will be anxious for itself. Let the day's own trouble be sufficient for the day." (Matt 6:34)

> "*Ask, and it will be given to you;* seek, and you will find; knock, and it will be opened to you. . . . If you then, who are evil, know how to give good gifts to your children, how much more will your Father who is in heaven give good gifts to those who ask him!" (Matt 7:7, 11)

> "I *thank* thee, Father, Lord of heaven and earth." (Matt 11:25)

> "Do *[not] think* that these Galileans [on whom the tower fell] were worse sinners." (Luke 13:2)

These logia of Jesus teach the child of the kingdom not to fear; not to be anxious; to "ask . . . your Father who is in heaven" for his "good gifts"; to be active in giving thanks to God; and not to regard *sufferings* as personal punishment.

J. Jeremias, an expert in rabbinic teaching, illustrates how radical were these teachings.[29] In Jesus' day God was seen as remote; prayer was formalistic, discouraged for small matters and seen to attract merit (salvation without merit was inconceivable); and suffering was to be viewed as punishment for sins.

It is not difficult to point to ways in which the ex-Pharisee Paul's views had been affected by the radical teaching of his Lord regarding *fear, anxiety, thanksgiving,* and *suffering.*

> You did not receive the spirit of slavery to fall back into *fear,* but you have received the spirit of sonship. When we cry, "Abba! Father!" it is the Spirit himself bearing witness with our spirit that we are children of God. (Rom 8:15-16)

> Have no *anxiety* about anything, but in everything by prayer and supplication . . . let your requests be made known to God. (Phil 4:6)

> You also must help us by prayer, so that many will give *thanks* on our behalf for the blessing granted us in answer to many prayers. (2 Cor 1:11; cf. 1 Thess 5:18)

> I consider that the *sufferings* of this present time are not worth comparing with the glory that is to be revealed to us. (Rom 8:18)

The Messiah's Death Hyper/"for" Others

Paul's repeated assertion that Christ died *hyper/*"for" sins (e.g., 1 Thess 5:10) depended on preformulated "traditions" he "received" regarding the gospel message (1 Cor 15:3) and the institution of the Eucharist (1 Cor 11:23-26/Luke 22:19-20). It is noteworthy that the Servant in Isaiah's fourth Servant Song does not die *hyper/*"for" sins in LXX Isaiah 52:13–53:12 (where prepositions *dia* and *peri* are used). Paul's connection of Christ's death *hyper/*"for" sins departing from the LXX calls for explanation, the most plausible of which is that it originated with Christ's own interpretation of his death (cf. Mark 10:45).

---

29. Jeremias, *New Testament Theology 1,* 178-203.

Liberty and Love in the Kingdom

Christ identified with "sinners," sitting at table with them against the scruples of the Pharisees (Mark 2:16). Furthermore, he deliberately broke the halacha about Sabbath-keeping (Mark 2:23) and the purification of hands (Mark 7:1-5), and gave alternative halacha befitting the kingdom. "The sabbath was made for man, not man for the sabbath" (Mark 2:27).

The Mishnah tractate *Shabbat* indicates a detailed casuistry prohibiting numerous and complex actions on the Sabbath. According to the rabbis, man "is delivered over to the Sabbath," that is, made a slave of the Sabbath,[30] a teaching Christ exactly reversed.

Second Temple Judaism was preoccupied with purity and the avoidance of defilement. The sixth division of the Mishnah tractate *Teharot* is devoted to "Cleannesses." The issue of purity is evident in the gospels (Mark 7:1-5 par.; John 2:6) and a matter of dispute with Jesus, who said, "There is *nothing outside a man* which by going into him can defile *(koinōsai)* him" (Mark 7:15 par.). The setting of this logion is Christ's accusation of casuistry whereby the corban formula was invoked to avoid care of parents (Mark 7:6-13).

It is clear, then, that Christ opposed the casuistic halacha of the Pharisees regarding table fellowship with moral outcasts, Sabbath legalism, and the supposed efficacy of ritual washing. His alternative halacha, the halacha of the kingdom, was that loving one's neighbor was the greatest commandment after loving God. His word "the sabbath was made for man" is an expression of the loving intent of God that had been distorted by casuistry. Love to neighbor is to be expressed in generosity to beggar and borrower (Matt 5:42), willingness to serve others (Mark 10:42-45; cf. 9:35), and above all, willingness to forgive others (e.g., Mark 11:25). The love Christ taught was not bounded by social, economic, religious, or racial boundaries (Matt 5:43-48). He daringly portrayed the despised "half-breed" Samaritan demonstrating practical love that the religious elite Jewish priest and Levite failed absolutely to show (Luke 10:25-37).

Paul's letters reveal his struggles with the Jerusalem-based countermissionaries whose circle included "believers who belonged to the party of the Pharisees" (Acts 15:5). These countermissionaries sought to impose aspects of the halacha on Gentiles (notably male circumcision)

---

30. Jeremias, *New Testament Theology 1*, 208.

and to reimpose this and other matters on those Jewish believers who had come to regard such practices as *adiaphora* (Acts 21:21). It appears that the Pharisaic opposition to the Christ over halacha continued in the opposition to Paul, apostle to the Gentiles.[31]

Like Christ before him, Paul established "love of neighbor"/"the other" as the central duty of the believer. "Owe no one anything, except to love one another; for he who *loves* his neighbor has fulfilled the law" (Rom 13:8). Pointedly Paul, the ex-Pharisee (Pharisees were noted for *hypocrisy*) and a man "in Christ," writes: "Let *love* be unhypocritical *(anypokritos)*" (Rom 12:9). This "love" is expressed in hospitality, in humility, and in forgiveness of enemy.

> "Contribute to the needs of the saints, practice hospitality" (Rom 12:13).
>
> "Do not be haughty, but associate with the lowly" (Rom 12:16).
>
> "Bless those who persecute you" (Rom 12:14).
>
> "Repay no one evil for evil" (Rom 12:17).

It appears, though, that members of Paul's mission congregations were aware of Christ's assault on ritual practices signaled by the repeated challenge "it is not lawful" (cf. Mark 2:18, 24; 3:4; 7:2). Some of the Corinthians were insisting as "lawful" their "right" to engage in various sexual practices (1 Cor 6:12) and to eat whatever they chose regardless of the social consequences for others (1 Cor 10:23). This, however, was a perversion of Jesus' assertion of freedom from the yoke of Jewish legalism.

Furthermore, Christ's verdict on "defilement" and "purification" (Mark 7:15) appears to have been known in Rome since "the strong" used it to act as they liked in relationship with "the weak" (Rom 14:14, 20). Paul applies the dominical higher principle, "walk in love," against the selfish demands of "the strong" (Rom 14:15). He urges that "the strong" accommodate to the scruples of "the weak" for their edification and for the unity of the church.

Paul sums it up in words that echo those of Christ: "The kingdom of God is not food and drink but righteousness and peace and joy in the Holy Spirit; he who thus serves Christ is acceptable to God and approved by men" (Rom 14:17-18; cf. Matt 6:33).

31. See Barnett, *Paul,* 193-96.

Paul, as a leading younger Pharisee, would not have written like that under the impulse of his master teacher, Gamaliel. These love-based principles are derived from the true master teacher, Jesus the Messiah.

Christ took special interest in the "lost sheep," the "sinners," and the "little" (e.g., Luke 19:10; Mark 2:17; 9:42). Paul, his servant, likewise consistently fought for the have-nots and "the weak" among the churches of his mission (e.g., Rom 14:1; 15:1; 1 Cor 8:7-13; 11:17-22, 33-34; 12:22-26). "Who is weak, and I am not weak? Who is made to fall, and I am not indignant?" (2 Cor 11:29).

Wives and Women Generally

In the Judaism of the NT era husbands one-sidedly had the right to discharge their wives, based on the decree of Moses in the Torah: "When a man takes a wife and marries her, if then she finds no favor in his eyes because he has found some *'erwat dābār* in her, . . . he writes her a bill of divorce and puts it in her hand and sends her out of his house" (Deut 24:1).

The rabbis debated the meaning of *'erwat dābār*.[32] The School of Shammai said it meant "unchastity" whereas for the School of Hillel it was "even if she spoiled a dish for him." Rabbi Akiba said, "Even if he found another fairer than she . . ." What is not in dispute is the ease with which a man could dismiss his wife (also, if she was barren).[33] She, however, could not divorce him nor voluntarily leave him.[34]

When the Pharisees ask Jesus, "Is it lawful for a man to divorce his wife?" (Mark 10:2), they appear to be challenging his well-known attitude. But to articulate that viewpoint spelled danger for Jesus: for contradicting Moses (as in Deut 24:1), but also for implicitly condemning Herod Antipas's "constructive" dismissal of his wife, the Nabatean princess.[35]

Christ did not engage the rabbis in debate but directly abrogated Moses' original instruction, asserting instead: "What therefore God has joined together, let not man put asunder" (Mark 10:9; cf. Gen 1:27; 2:24). God joins a wedded couple together forever. By this single utterance and

---

32. *m. Gittin* 9:10.

33. *m. Gittin* 4:8.

34. See A. C. Thiselton, *The First Epistle to the Corinthians*, NIGTC (Grand Rapids: Eerdmans, 2000), 522.

35. Josephus, *Ant* 18.113-119.

its accompanying prohibition of remarriage Christ secured a revolutionary protection for vulnerable wives from husbands who selfishly invoked Moses' decree and who potentially forced them into destitution.

It is evident from his words to the Corinthians about marriage that the teaching of Jesus had significantly influenced the ex-Pharisee Paul. Paul is responding to two pastoral issues in Corinth. The first arose from an ascetic view that sought Paul's endorsement of marriage without sexual intercourse ("it is well for a man not to touch a woman" — 1 Cor 7:1); apparently the questioners thought sexual activity was "unholy." The second viewpoint was that married believers should separate from spouses who were unbelievers (1 Cor 7:12-13), presumably for fear of moral defilement through sexual intercourse.[36]

Paul's response to the first issue was to assert an equality of sexual mutuality between husband and wife, each serving the other in the marriage bed (1 Cor 7:2-6). This is radically different from the male Jewish attitude that regarded "the woman [as] in all things inferior to the man."[37]

For the second matter Paul invokes the "instruction" of the Lord: "To the married I instruct *(parangellō)*, not I but the Lord, that the wife should not separate *(chōristhēnai)* from her husband . . . and the husband should not divorce *(aphienai)* his wife" (1 Cor 7:10-11).

Most likely Paul is not citing the Lord exactly but incorporating his own gloss in these words. He is appealing to the dominical logion that declared the will of the Creator for marriage to be lifelong and exclusive (Mark 10:9, as above). The effect of Paul's incorporated gloss is that a woman should not leave her husband (voluntarily) or be sent off by him (involuntarily). To this logion Paul adds his own word, that neither husband nor wife should divorce *(aphienai)* the other merely because the spouse was an unbeliever (1 Cor 7:12-13). In the Greco-Roman world (unlike among the Jews) both husband and wife could initiate divorce (and did so with considerable frequency).

In short, Paul the ex-Pharisee knew of and pastorally applied Christ's concern for the protection of women from the one-sided privileges that men had in Jewish society.

---

36. Most likely both concerns arose from Jewish believers in Corinth: (1) Jews did not believe in sexual intercourse apart from the purpose of procreation (Josephus, *Against Apion* 198), and (2) their religion prohibited mixed marriages.

37. Josephus, *Against Apion* 201.

Alongside Christ's protection of wives was his recognition of women socially. Under Judaism female children were not educated, as boys were; in the temple precincts women were denied access beyond the Court of Women; their appearance was effectively obscured by plaited coiffure; generally speaking they were confined to the home and did not converse with men apart from family members; it was assumed that they did not act as witnesses in court hearings.[38] Jesus, however, instructed a woman (Luke 10:38-42; 11:27-28), conversed alone with a woman (John 4:27), was accompanied and supported by women (Mark 15:40-41 par.; Luke 8:1-3), and entrusted a woman to carry the message of his resurrection to men (John 20:11-18).

Paul followed Christ's radical affirmation of women. He accepted the hospitality and patronage of women (Acts 16:15; Rom 16:2) and assumed without comment the rightness of women to be engaged in evangelism alongside him (Phil 4:3) and to pray or prophesy in the assembly (1 Cor 11:5). He entrusted the carriage of the letter to the Romans to Phoebe the *diakonos,* and in his list of proven mission coworkers and supporters in Rome he mentions Prisca (first), Mary, Junia (an apostle), Tryphena, Tryphosa, Persis, and the mother of Rufus (also Paul's "mother"). Once again, we see Paul the former strict Pharisee having radically changed his attitudes, and the changes most likely stem from Christ himself.

Rejection of Theocracy

The temple authorities accused Jesus of doing what he had strenuously opposed, prohibiting the payment of the poll tax tribute to the Romans (Luke 23:1-2). Ironically this was the very crime for which the Romans had executed his fellow Galilean Judas two decades earlier. In his famous reply to the Pharisees' and Herodians' entrapment question, Jesus said, "Render *(apodote)* to Caesar the things that are Caesar's" (Mark 12:17 par.). In this single logion Christ's injunction to pay the tax effectively rejected altogether the zealots' theocratic ideal and program for Israel.[39]

---

38. According to Josephus, "From women let no evidence be accepted, because of the levity and temerity of their sex" (*Ant* 4.219). Cf. *m. Rosh HaShanah* 1:8; generally the tractates *Sanhedrin* ("the Sanhedrin") and *Eduyyot* ("Testimonies").

39. I employ the word "zealot" broadly; the Zealot faction did not arise until circa 67.

There is strong evidence of an early catechesis in relation to disciples and the state that emerges from Romans 13:1-7 and 1 Peter 2:13-17.

In Romans 13:1 Paul advocates being "subject *(hypotassesthō)* to the governing authorities," and in 1 Peter 2:13 Peter says, "Be subject *(hypotagēte)* . . . to every human institution." The similarity is clear. In Romans 13:3 Paul observes that "rulers are not a terror to good *(tō agathō)* conduct, but to bad *(tō kakō),*" and in 1 Peter 2:14 Peter states that kings and governors are sent "to punish those who do wrong *(kakopoiōn)* and to praise those who do right *(agathopoiōn)*." Again the similarity is evident. In Romans 13:7 Paul encourages giving "honor *(timē)* to whom honor is due," and in 1 Peter 2:17 Peter urges his readers to "honor *(timēsate)* all." Once more the similarity is clear. Nonetheless, these texts from Paul and Peter are not identical.

The similarities point to some connection between the texts, but the dissimilarities imply that they are depending on a common source rather than one upon the other. In other words, a catechetical source had been created in the few decades between Jesus and the writing of these texts that called for a distinctive ethical attitude to the Roman state. That source did not arise from within Judaism since anti-Roman feeling ran high among the Jews at that time. On the contrary, this tradition sprang from Jesus' distinctive attitudes; on one hand he spoke against zealotry, and on the other he recognized the role of Caesar, Gentile though he was.

Significantly, there are further connections between these two state-related passages. I refer to the almost identical demands of these respective letters — Romans and 1 Peter — for nonretributive behavior against official persecution.

In the passage in Romans immediately preceding his injunctions regarding the state, Paul writes, "Repay no one evil for evil *(mēdeni kakon anti kakou apodidontes)*" (Rom 12:17), whereas Peter writes, "Do not return evil for evil *(mē apodidontes kakon anti kakou)*" (1 Pet 3:9). The words are strikingly similar yet not identical. Once again the juxtaposition between similarities and dissimilarities points to an earlier independent common catechetical source that was formulated soon after Jesus (cf. 1 Thess 5:15 — *horate mē tis kakon anti kakou tini apodō* — "See that none of you repays evil for evil").

In addition to the injunction to "not return evil for evil" *(mēdeni kakon anti kakou apodidontes* — Rom 12:17), Paul also exhorts, "Bless those who persecute you; bless and do not curse them" *(eulogeite tous diōkontas, eulogeite kai mē katarasthe* — Rom 12:14). Clearly this nonretributive behavior urged by Paul springs from the teaching of Jesus in the gospel tradition (Matt 5:38-39; Luke 6:29, 35 for Rom 12:17, and Matt 5:44; Luke 6:27 for Rom 12:14).

Payment of Workers

Paul explicitly attributes to "the Lord" the "command" that "those who proclaim the gospel should get their living by the gospel" (1 Cor 9:14; cf. Gal 6:6; 1 Tim 5:18).

Paul is evidently referring to Jesus' instructions to the Twelve for their mission to the villages of Galilee: "Take no gold, nor silver, nor copper in your belts . . . for the laborer deserves his food" (Matt 10:9-10); "Remain in the same house, eating and drinking what they provide, for the laborer deserves his wages" (Luke 10:7).

In Paul's hands the Lord's words have been restated for the new missionary setting. Nonetheless, the influence at least in principle is clear.

Stumbling Blocks

Jesus spoke scathingly about causing "little ones," meaning children, to "stumble" (e.g., Mark 9:42-43). His disciples bear great responsibility to behave so that they do not deflect these "little ones" from the blessings of the kingdom of God. Paul uses the same vocabulary admonishing believers in the churches along similar lines (Rom 14:13, 21; 1 Cor 8:13; 2 Cor 11:29). Paul, like the Christ, was concerned lest the behavior of the mature be a negative influence on the little.

Conclusion: The Radical Influence of Christ

Neither Christ nor his apostle Paul established a systematic law code that was in any way comparable with the codes embedded within the Pentateuch or that emerged during the Second Temple era, as codified in the Mishnah. Rather, Christ proclaimed the coming kingdom that was actualized in *himself* and in which God was now to be known as *Abba*. Within this kingdom sins were already forgiven and disciples freed from the yoke of ritual legalism (including Sabbath keeping).

The ethical and moral outworkings for disciples, however, were curiously incomplete but were dominated by the demand to love neighbor as oneself. Three very noticeable elements of Jesus' teaching that differed from Judaism, however, were (a) his abolition of one-sided husband's rights to discharge a wife, (b) his rejection of the "zealot" theocratic ideal and program (replaced by "love of enemy" and the "render to Caesar" principle), and (c) the elimination of purity and dietary restrictions.

These are among the areas where the teachings of Christ can be seen to profoundly affect the former Pharisee Paul. Clearly, therefore, while Paul's was a "religious" conversion, it changed his attitudes *ethically* from beginning to end, radically and dramatically. Nonetheless, Paul exercised significant freedom adapting and applying "Christ" in a non-Semitic setting of his mission. When to these various specific teachings we add aspects of Christ's character that Paul imitates (noted above), we have some idea of the impact and influence of the *historical* Christ on the former rising star among the Pharisees.

Concluding Reflection: Christ in the Letters of Paul

Our argument is that the "Jesus of history" reference is unhelpful when set symmetrically alongside the "Christ of faith" since it implies that Jesus of Nazareth only became "the Christ" for "faith" *after* his resurrection. The evidence from Paul, our earliest source of evidence, is that Jesus was *already* regarded as the Christ when he was crucified. This is to be inferred from Paul's insistence that he preached "*Christ* crucified." This is consistent with the uniform assertion of the gospels that Jesus was crucified precisely because (of the claim that) he *was* the Christ.

Paul's core proclamation of the crucified One is connected seamlessly with the very early tradition that *Christ* died for sins, was buried, was raised on the third day, and was seen alive by many witnesses. He was the Christ *already* at his death. Ananias delivered this tradition to Paul at his baptism in Damascus, though it originated in Jerusalem from the college of the apostles led by Peter. It is possible that the Hellenist disciples translated it from Aramaic to the Greek forms we encounter embedded in Paul's first letter to the Corinthians.

Moreover, Paul's letters exhibit numerous echoes of Christ's teaching, his life, and his moral character. Paul makes extensive appeal to Christ's decisive actions in his incarnation, life, and death to be imitated by Paul himself and by the believers in the churches. The point is that Paul knows about the *historical* Christ in order to speak of him as the *typos* to be imitated.

Finally, we are able to see dotted throughout Paul's letters evidences of radical liberality that we would not have expected from one who was "as to the law, a Pharisee." The authorities Jeremias and Wenham have demonstrated that many of these radical new attitudes in Paul are attributable to Christ and indeed are difficult to explain otherwise. Paul's dependence on the word of the Lord for pastoral advice regarding marriage matters in Corinth, for example, indicates that he did not look for direction from the exalted Christ, as mediated by a prophet, but depended on verbal traditions that originated from the preresurrected Christ.

NINE

Glimpses of Jesus in Galilee: Criteria and Context

From the beginning the Christian faith has been a confession of events in human history.

B. F. Meyer[1]

Since the advent of the critical era, scholars and nonscholars alike have been concerned with the historical reliability of the gospels. No question related to Christianity has so completely occupied the imagination as this. Although the word "gospel" remains a popular metaphor for truth, the same cannot be said for the general opinion about the truthfulness of gospel documents. For many years the skepticism of scholars has filtered down into the popular media and eroded the confidence former generations had in the gospels.

In this chapter we will concentrate on Jesus' activities in Galilee and regions to the north and east and accordingly direct our attention to our chief source, the Gospel of Mark. Our underlying concern is whether Mark is a reliable guide for our studies. Here we must recognize Mark's limitations. Modern studies of Galilee are compendious, complex, and multifaceted, examining the likely economic structures and demography of various regions, even to the point of analyzing human remains to ascertain the absence or otherwise of a pork-free diet of the local people.[2] Mark, however,

---

1. B. F. Meyer, *The Aims of Jesus* (London: SCM, 1979), 95.
2. See, e.g., M. H. Jensen, "Herod Antipas in Galilee: Friend or Foe of the Historical Jesus?" *JSHJ* 5, no. 1 (2007): 7-32.

is an ancient document, relatively brief and with a simple focus on the activities of Jesus. Those who evaluate the usefulness of this gospel need to do so with a degree of understanding and humble appreciation.

Gospel Story and Gospel Sayings

In addressing this issue we need to distinguish between the gospel overview and the gospel sayings. On the former, it is straightforward to argue for a "broad brush" accuracy of the story of Jesus in the gospels. Only the most skeptical would question that Nazareth was his home, that he preached around Lake Tiberias, and that he was crucified in Jerusalem where his followers claimed he had been resurrected. Despite their differences, the traditions in the synoptics and John agree with this broad overview. Let us assume this global account is true.

This assumption, however, takes us only a short distance and does not reach other matters like the authenticity of particular incidents reported in the gospels or the specific teachings of Jesus recorded in the gospels.

Let us defer for the moment the historicity of the incidents, and concentrate on the individual "words" of Jesus.

The Authority of the Lord's Words

The place to begin is in the earliest years of the early church, that is to say, with the letters in the New Testament. Reflecting on these letters, we make three observations:

a. The words Jesus spoke were regarded as authoritative and final.
b. Consequently the leaders in early Christianity did not invent sayings of the Lord.
c. Yet they reinterpreted those words in varying pastoral situations.

Observations a. and c. are well illustrated by Paul's response to the Corinthians' question about betrothed daughters. "Now concerning the betrothed, I have no command *(epitagē)* from the Lord, but I give my judgment *(gnōmē)* as one who is trustworthy" (1 Cor 7:25).

Paul is appealing to his knowledge of teachings of the preresurrection Lord on the subject of a father's betrothal of a daughter. He must give his own "judgment" on this matter, however, since he has no word of the Lord about this. Yet it is clear that had there been a teaching of Jesus on betrothed daughters, Paul would have appealed to it as definitive and final.

Observation c. is also well illustrated from 1 Corinthians 7. Earlier in the chapter Paul addresses a matter that implied the questioners' ascetic attitude: "Now concerning the matters about which you wrote, that it is good for a man not to touch a woman . . ."[3] (1 Cor 7:1, author's translation).

That ascetic attitude (from some) toward sexual intimacy apparently extended to their desire to abandon altogether marriages with unbelieving spouses (7:10-11). How will Paul respond to this important pastoral situation in Corinth? He was fortunate in having at hand two (related) teachings of the preresurrection Lord.

Paul	Jesus
"The wife should not separate — *mē chōristhēnai* — from her husband" (1 Cor 7:10)	"What therefore God has joined together, let not man put asunder *(mē chōrizetō)*" (Mark 10:9)
"The husband should not divorce his wife; she should not divorce *(mē aphietō)* him" (1 Cor 7:11, 13)	"Whoever divorces *(apolysē)* his wife and marries another, commits adultery; and if she divorces *(apolysasa)* her husband and marries another, she commits adultery" (Mark 10:11-12)

Here Paul is appealing to different (but related) traditions of Jesus on marriage: first, against "separation" of spouses *(mē chōrizetō),* and second, against a husband/wife who "sends away" a spouse *(ho apolyōn).*

Another pastoral issue Paul must address is table fellowship between Jewish and Gentile believers in Rome. Once more Paul appeals to a teaching of Jesus.

---

3. Following A. Thiselton, *The First Epistle to the Corinthians,* NIGTC (Grand Rapids: Eerdmans, 2000), 498-501.

Paul	*Jesus*
"I know and am persuaded in the Lord Jesus that nothing is unclean *(koinon)* in itself. . . . Everything is indeed clean *(kathara)*" (Rom 14:14, 20)	"Whatever goes into a man from outside cannot defile *(koinōsai)* him. . . . (Thus he declared all foods clean [*katharizōn*])" (Mark 7:18-19)

The situation Paul addresses in Rome (encouraging "weak" believers to eat with the "strong") is different from the context of Jesus' word spoken in Galilee (Levitical purity based on washings). Yet Paul applies that word authoritatively ("I know and am persuaded in the Lord") to the Roman setting.

The teachings of Jesus also appear in the letters of Peter and James, with this difference. Whereas Paul usually hints that the teaching originated with the Lord, Peter and James merely echo a dominical teaching without acknowledging its source. Many examples could be given, but several will be sufficient to establish the point that the words of Jesus were definitive but able to be applied in differing settings.

1 Peter	*Jesus*
"Maintain good conduct among the Gentiles, so that in case they speak against you as wrongdoers, they may see your good works *(ergōn)* and glorify God on the day of visitation" (1 Pet 2:12)	"Let your light so shine before men, that they may see your good works *(erga)* and give glory to your Father who is in heaven" (Matt 5:16)
"If you are reproached *(oneidizesthe)* for the name of Christ, you are blessed *(makarioi)*" (1 Pet 4:14)	"Blessed *(makarioi)* are you when men revile *(oneidisōsin)* you" (Matt 5:11)

James	*Jesus*
"Count it all *joy* . . . when you meet various trials" (James 1:2) "*Blessed* is the man who endures trial" (James 1:12)	"Blessed are you when men . . . persecute you. . . . *Rejoice* and be glad" (Matt 5:11-12)

Peter and James drew upon traditions of Jesus that were in circulation and would later become embedded in the gospels. As noted, Peter and

James do not attribute these words to the Lord in the way Paul does. Yet the Lord's words have profoundly influenced the shaping of their respective epistles. It does not take great imagination to see Jesus silhouetted behind their texts and to hear his voice speaking to the churches.

Our initial observations about postresurrection attitudes to Jesus' preresurrection words, therefore, are correct. For Paul (at least), these are the words of "the Lord" and therefore authoritative. True, Paul adapts and reinterprets them for the pastoral circumstances of the churches, as Peter and James have done. Yet this freedom would not have extended to creating teachings and attributing them to the Lord. Such an idea would have been unthinkable, given their respect for the Lord.

The implication of these observations from the letters is considerable. It is that the respect Paul (and inferentially Peter and James) displayed for the words of the Lord would have also been shown by the gospel writers Matthew, Mark, Luke, and John. Accordingly, as apostolic leaders in early Christianity, the gospel writers would have shared the same three attitudes toward the teachings of Jesus as the letter writers, with one additional element: *they did not omit any saying of the Lord.*[4] Clearly, if the early Christians would not invent a saying of the Lord, it follows that they would not omit a saying of the Lord.

For the gospel writers, then, we infer:

1. The words Jesus spoke were authoritative and final.
2. Consequently the leaders in early Christianity
   a. did not invent sayings of the Lord, and
   b. *did not omit any saying of the Lord.*
3. They reinterpreted those words in varying pastoral situations.

Observation 3 likely warrants further comment.[5]

---

4. For example, Jesus' words (italicized) in the last two verses of Mark 9 appear to have been included despite having no connection with their predecessors. "And if your eye causes you to sin, pluck it out; it is better for you to enter the kingdom of God with one eye than with two eyes to be thrown into hell, where their worm does not die, and the fire is not quenched. *For every one will be salted with fire. Salt is good; but if the salt has lost its saltness, how will you season it? Have salt in yourselves, and be at peace with one another*" (Mark 9:47-50).

5. See the words of Jesus in Matthew and Luke.

Are Jesus' Words Correctly Located in the Synoptics?

Here we face a difficulty. That is, while we are generally able to work out the church situations Paul addresses in his letters, it is otherwise for the situations the gospel writers address. These authors are anonymous and we cannot be sure when they wrote or the circumstances of their readers (hearers).

True, we can assume the rough time frame in which these writers penned their gospels, that is, circa A.D. 60-80. Furthermore, Luke identifies himself as the companion of Paul, and there are credible traditions from the second century connecting Mark with Peter (suggesting a Roman provenance for the second gospel) and identifying the beloved disciple with John Zebedee (stating that he issued his gospel from Ephesus). Apart from these scattered bits of information, we are unable to say much about the *Sitz im Leben* of the gospel audiences, despite the confidence of many scholars. Consequently, unlike Paul's letters to his mission churches, we are unable to establish if or how the gospel writers may have applied Jesus' words to the pastoral needs of the churches. We simply do not know.

The Reported Words of Jesus in the Gospel of Mark

There is, however, a striking characteristic about the sayings of Jesus in the Gospel of Mark. It is that the majority of Jesus' words fit precisely into their narrative situation.[6] In almost all cases Jesus' recorded teachings respond to the specific setting in which they are given. This observation holds true despite not knowing the *Sitz im Leben* of the Gospel of Mark, whether it was specific to a particular church or general for all the churches.[7]

---

6. Contra E. P. Sanders, *Jesus and Judaism* (London: SCM, 1985), 10-22, who argues that the precise locations of the sayings of Jesus are for the most part lost. Less extreme is C. A. Evans, "Authenticating the Activities of Jesus," in *Authenticating the Activities of Jesus,* ed. B. Chilton and C. A. Evans (Leiden: Brill, 1999), 4, who states, "what we can recover is a more or less general context, not the *specific* contexts of *specific* sayings" (emphasis in original).

7. R. Bauckham, "For Whom Were the Gospels Written?" in *The Gospel for All Christians: Rethinking the Gospel Audiences*, ed. R. Bauckham (Grand Rapids: Eerdmans, 1998), 9-48, challenged the widely held view that the gospels were to be understood from the provenance.

A quick survey of the *sayings of Jesus* in their respective *settings* in Mark will establish the point.

	Setting	Saying
1:14	Galilee beginning	"The time is fulfilled . . ."
1:16	Calling Simon and Andrew	"Follow me."
1:21	To the unclean spirit (Capernaum)	"Be silent, and come out."
1:40	To a leper who said, "If you will . . ."	"I will; be clean."
2:5	To the paralytic (Capernaum)	"My son, your sins are forgiven."
2:7	To the scribes	"Why do you question thus in your hearts?"
2:14	To Levi the tax collector	"Follow me."
2:16	To the scribes	"Those who are well have no need of a physician."
2:18	To people who asked, "Why do John's disciples . . . fast?"	"Can the wedding guests fast . . . ?" Parables of the unshrunk cloth and of the new wine
2:24	Pharisees' question about reaping on the Sabbath	"The Sabbath was made for man."
3:2	Pharisees' question about healing on the Sabbath	"Is it lawful on the Sabbath to do good . . . ?"
3:22	Scribes' accusation, "He is possessed by Beelzebul."	Parables of divided kingdom and of strongman's house
3:31	Regarding his mother and brothers	"Who is my mother . . . ?"

In chapter 4 we encounter a cluster of four parables that Jesus delivered from a boat to a crowd seated on the shore (the four soils; the lamp under a basket; the secretly growing seed; the mustard seed). The setting is sufficiently imaginable to be regarded as authentic, and there is no good reason to doubt it. Even so, does it necessarily follow that Jesus gave *these* parables on that occasion? Here we cannot be quite so confident. On one hand, he may have spoken these parables because they are consistent with the early stages of Jesus' "kingdom" preaching. On the other hand, however, it is possible that Mark has located them here for the sake of convenience and because *he does not wish to omit any known teaching of Jesus.*

Jesus' words are central in the remaining pericopes of this gospel.

	Setting	*Saying*
4:35-41	Jesus calms the storm	"Peace! Be still!" "Why are you afraid?" "Have you no faith?"
5:1-20	Jesus heals "Legion"	"What is your name?" "Go home to your friends, and tell them . . ."
5:22-34	Jesus heals a woman	"Daughter, your faith has made you well."
5:35-43	Jesus raises Jairus's daughter	*"Talitha cumi."*
6:1-6	Jesus in Nazareth	"A prophet is not without honor . . ."
6:7-13	Jesus sends out the Twelve	"Where you enter a house . . ."
6:30-44	The feeding of the five thousand	"Come away by yourselves . . ." "How many loaves have you?"
6:45-52	Jesus walks on the lake	"Take heart; it is I; have no fear."
7:1-13	Dispute over purity	"You leave the commandment of God, and hold fast the tradition of men."
7:14-22	Private instruction on purity	"The things which come out of a man . . . defile him."
7:24-29	Faith of Syro-Phoenician woman	"Let the children first be fed . . ."
7:31-37	Jesus heals a deaf man	*"Ephphatha."*
8:1-10	Jesus feeds four thousand	"I have compassion on the crowd."
8:11-13	Pharisees demand a sign	"Why does this generation seek a sign?"
8:14-21	Leaven of the Pharisees	"Take heed, beware of the leaven of the Pharisees and the leaven of Herod."
8:22-26	Jesus heals a blind man	"Do you see anything?"
8:27-30	Jesus at Caesarea Philippi	"Who do men say that I am?" "Who do you say that I am?"
8:31-33	Jesus to Peter	"Get behind me, Satan!"
8:34–9:1	Jesus' challenge to follow him	"If any man would come after me . . ."
9:2-13	Following the transfiguration	"Elijah does come first to restore all things."

9:14-29	Boy with unclean spirit	"O faithless generation, how long am I to be with you?"
9:30-32	Passing through Galilee	"The Son of Man will be delivered into the hands of men, and they will kill him."
9:33-37	In Capernaum	"If any one would be first, he must be last of all."
9:38-50	Someone else casting out demons in Jesus' name	"Do not forbid him."
10:1-11	Question about divorce	"What did Moses command you?"
10:13-16	Children brought to Jesus	"Let the children come to me."
10:17-31	The rich man's question	"Why do you call me good?"
10:32-34	On the road to Jerusalem	"Behold, we are going up to Jerusalem."
10:35-45	Request of James and John	"You do not know what you are asking."
10:46-52	Jesus heals blind Bartimaeus	"What do you want me to do for you?"
11:1-11	Jesus rides up to Jerusalem	"Go into the village opposite . . ."
11:12-14	Jesus curses the fig tree	"May no one ever eat fruit from you again."
11:15-19	Jesus clears the temple	"Is it not written, 'My house shall be called a house of prayer . . . '?"
11:20-26	The withered fig tree	"Have faith in God."
11:27-33	By what authority?	"I will ask you a question . . ."
12:1-12	Allegory of vineyard	"A man planted a vineyard . . ."
12:13-17	Question about tax	"Why put me to the test?"
12:18-27	Question about resurrection	"You know neither the scriptures nor the power of God."
12:28-34	Question about the great commandment	"'Hear, O Israel: The Lord our God . . . is one.'"
12:35-40	Question about the Christ	"How can the scribes say . . . ?"
12:41-44	The widow's offering	"This poor widow has put in more . . ."
13:1-37	On the Mount of Olives	"Do you see these great buildings?"
14:1-9	The anointing at Bethany	"Let her alone."

14:10-21	Passover arrangements	"A man carrying a jar of water will meet you."
14:22-25	The Last Supper	"Take; this is my body."
14:26-31	Peter will deny	"You will all fall away."
14:32-42	Prayer in Gethsemane	"Sit here, while I pray."
14:43-52	Arrest of Jesus	"Have you come out as against a robber . . . ?"
14:53-65	Jesus before the Council	"I am; and you will see the Son of man seated at the right hand of Power."
14:66-72	Peter's denial	"Before the cock crows twice . . ."
15:1-5	Jesus before Pilate	"You have said so."
15:33-41	The death of Jesus	*"Eloi, Eloi, lama sabachthani?"*

As one surveys the words of Jesus in their successive settings in Mark's gospel, several things become clear. The first is that the *words* of Jesus are the most important part of the respective pericopes. Jesus' words are the focal point of each passage. His authority is repeatedly heard in the wisdom, weightiness, and finality of his utterances. His words are irresistible and absolute. Secondly, as noted above, one has the impression that his words exactly match their settings passage by passage. It is difficult to identify passages where this is not so.

These observations, however, do not necessarily establish as true the precise sequence of pericopes in this gospel. While the overall sequence is most likely a fair representation of real history, it is possible that Mark has located a number of incidents for dramatic (and theological) effect. Thus Mark may have grouped together various conflict episodes (2:1–3:6), parables (4:1-34), and miracles in and around the lake (4:35–5:43) as a counterfoil to the unbelief Jesus faced in Nazareth (6:1-6). The healings of the deaf and the blind (7:31-37 and 8:22-26) occur prior to the disciples' (eventual) identification of Jesus as the Christ and may point to their spiritual "hearing" and "sight" at Caesarea Philippi (8:27-29). The various questionings of Jesus in Jerusalem (11:27–12:40) may have occurred over a longer period than Mark implies. Nonetheless, the observations about (i) the centrality and (ii) the unerring applicability of Jesus' words in their settings remain true, even if the precise sequence at all points is uncertain.

How do we account for these two remarkable features about the words of Jesus in the Gospel of Mark? There are two main options. One is that Mark was a remarkably gifted storyteller who, episode by episode, created situations for Jesus to utter defining and authoritative oracles. Alternatively, Mark (somehow) reproduced (and to a degree rearranged) episodes that were previously part of oral and written kerygmatic traditions[8] that had their origin in the actual events focused on Jesus and words spoken by him. The former alternative identifies Mark as the genius who created his gospel as a literary text. The latter regards *the events and words themselves* as the source of Mark's episodes, without denying to him due recognition for the literary and dramatic artistry evident in this gospel. Which of these alternatives is the more likely? Essentially, the choice is between regarding the Gospel of Mark as primarily a work of literature and regarding it as primarily a work of history.

In my view, the latter explanation is more satisfactory. Mark is writing his text for church reading and has a single goal, to direct his hearers to loyal allegiance to Christ. This he achieves through his portrayal of events and words centered on Christ. Every syllable of Mark's text is crafted to that end. Consider the alternative. The numerous miracles in this gospel would identify it as *nonhistorical,* as essentially *mythical.* The myth genre, however, generally lacks the plethora of credible geographical and historical detail we find in Mark. Furthermore, Mark's narrative is expressed in down-to-earth language, not in bizarre or overblown terms as in various mythologies.[9] We sense that Mark's medium for his pastoral care of his readers is history-based, the narration of actual events and words, not fiction (i.e., myth).

The Words of Jesus in Matthew and Luke

Most likely one of the reasons Matthew and Luke decided to write their gospels was to record words of Jesus that had not appeared in the Gospel of Mark. Between them, Matthew and Luke had access to many extra words of Jesus in the special Matthew source (M), the special Luke source (L), and the common source (Q). True, each writer had his own theologi-

8. See chapter 6.

9. As, e.g., in earlier works like Plutarch, *Parallel Lives* (*Alexander* 2.1–3.2, recounting the birth of Alexander), Diodorus Siculus, *Library of History* 4.9.1-10 (recounting the birth of Herakles), or later Christian works the *Infancy Gospel of Thomas* (ca. A.D. 125) and the *Gospel of Peter* (ca. A.D. 175).

cal viewpoint that needed a gospel, the vehicle at hand, to express it. Yet one of their motives appears to have been the desire to find a permanent home for words of Jesus that existed in mere collections of texts without developed narrative structures.

Remarkably each writer chose to use Mark as the skeletal frame for his gospel, thereby endorsing and confirming the efficacy of that gospel. Each writer followed Mark's sequence and replicated (but abbreviated) much of his text, including the words of the Lord. This is an implicit recognition that the eyewitness Peter was the ultimate source of the gospel Mark wrote, based on his memory of Peter's teachings.[10]

Where Matthew and Luke follow Mark, they tend to locate Jesus' words in the same settings, often in shortened form. Here, once more, we note the respect Matthew and Luke hold for Mark.

Yet the sources noted above (M, L, and Q) have many more words of the Lord to be incorporated in Matthew and Luke. Matthew inserts lengthy blocks of sayings material into his gospel, whether the Sermon on the Mount, the mission instructions, the collected parables, the woes for the scribes, or the end-time Olivet Discourse (chapters 5–7; 10; 13; 23; 24–25). Luke briefly notes some of Jesus' activities in Galilee (chapters 4–8) before narrating his journey to Jerusalem (9–19). Where Matthew and Luke depend on non-Markan sayings sources, they do not locate the words of Jesus with the contextual exactitude of the one on whom they rely elsewhere, Mark. True, each in his own way follows Mark in the broad, yet when they incorporate material from non-Markan sources they do so without the precise applicability of the weighty words of Jesus in their respective settings that is so much a feature of Mark's gospel.

Like the Gospel of Mark, but unlike the letters of Paul, the situations for which Matthew and Luke write are veiled to us. Yet we are right to assume that each gospel writer was broadly conscious of the pastoral needs of his intended audience, so that the location of the words of the Lord would have been influenced by each author's sense of his readers' circumstances. But we do not know, and indeed there is no scientific way to know, what were the pastoral circumstances of the audiences Matthew and Luke were addressing.

We understand, therefore, that the same word of the Lord might appear in Matthew and Luke with a different nuance, as in the following quotation from Jesus.

10. See chapter 3.

Matthew 11:12: "From the days of John the Baptist until now the kingdom of heaven has suffered violence *(biazetai)*, and men of violence *(biastai)* take it by force *(harpazousin)*."

Luke 16:16: "The law and the prophets were until John; since then the good news of the kingdom of God is preached *(euangelizetai)*, and every one enters it violently *(biazetai)*."

Matthew's version of the Q text is a historical window into recent critical religio-political activities and is most likely close to the authentic word of Jesus. We will refer later to this text. In Luke's hand, however, this logion becomes a salvation history midpoint. The dispensation of law and prophets ended with John and has been superseded by the dispensation of the kingdom of God as "evangelized" by Jesus and later by "servants of the word." Metaphorically speaking, "everyone" (i.e., sinners) has been "entering it violently" (cf. Luke 4:43; 8:1; 15:1-2).

Of course, it would be easy to criticize Matthew and Luke for their inexact location of and adaptation of (some of) Jesus' (non-Markan) words. Yet it is worth reflecting that the sources they employ (M, L, Q) were collections of sayings that lacked so precise a biographical framework as Mark's. It was not possible for them always to know when, where, to whom, and under which circumstances Jesus' words were spoken. To their credit, they remained faithful to the Markan biographical outline. Furthermore, they went to great lengths in writing their gospels to preserve the teachings of the Lord that they embedded in the matrixes of their gospels. Furthermore, nothing was to be omitted.

Criteria for the Words of Jesus

Our argument is that it is unlikely that the gospel writers either created or omitted words of the Lord. This, however, is not a universally held view. Scholars have developed criteria by which to evaluate or reject the authenticity of a saying of Jesus.[11] Several of these have been found deficient, for example:

11. For survey and discussion see Meyer, *The Aims of Jesus*, 23-110; R. H. Stein, "The 'Criteria' for Authenticity," in *Gospel Perspectives*, vol. 1, ed. R. T. France and D. Wenham (Sheffield: JSOT Press, 1980), 225-63; J. P. Meier, *A Marginal Jew: Rethinking the Historical Je-*

i. The "criterion of dissimilarity" is said to apply where a gospel tradition is dissimilar to Jewish teaching and practice, on one hand, and early church teaching and practice, on the other. Where the account of Jesus' teaching is dissimilar to both, it points to authenticity. Many rightly point out, however, that Jesus was a Jew and the founder of Christianity and this criterion demands that he be neither a Jew nor the founder of the faith. This criterion is quite limited in usefulness.

ii. The "retroversion" criterion is based on the translation backward from Jesus' words in the Greek of the gospels to a supposed Aramaic original. But there is little agreement among scholars that original Aramaic versions of Jesus' words can be recovered. In any case, the early church used Aramaic for a period, so the words "retroverted" may have come from the early church rather than from Jesus himself.

Other criteria, however, have found wider acceptance.

iii. The "criterion of multiple attestation" identifies a saying of Jesus that is found across two or more of the independent primary sources Mark, Q, L, M, and John. If so, it has a claim to authenticity. This is an appropriately objective criterion.

iv. The "criterion of inclusion" points to the likelihood of authenticity based on the simple reality that a saying included in the canonical gospel is more likely than not to be authentic.[12] This is close to my earlier argument based on the assumption that the leaders of early Christianity were unlikely either to falsify a saying of the Lord or to omit a saying of the Lord from their permanent record.

v. The "criterion of embarrassment" identifies damaging sayings of Jesus that are unlikely to have been invented. Examples within the Gospel of Mark include Jesus' association with people of ill repute (2:14-16); the accusation of demon possession (3:22-27); the appearance of failure in his hometown, Nazareth (6:4), that his healing was not always immediate (8:22-26); and his apparent petulance toward the fruitless fig tree (11:12-14). This criterion is cogent and applicable.

vi. The "criterion of similarity *and* dissimilarity" helpfully recognizes

---

sus, vol. 1, *The Roots of the Problem and the Person*, ABRL (New York: Doubleday, 1991), 167-95; S. E. Porter, *Criteria for Authenticity in Historical Jesus Research: Previous Discussion and New Proposals* (Sheffield: Sheffield Academic, 2000); G. Theissen and A. Merz, *The Historical Jesus: A Comprehensive Guide* (London: SCM, 1998), 115-18.

12. See N. T. Wright, *The New Testament and the People of God* (London: SPCK, 1992), 104-7.

that as a Jew many of Jesus' words are "similar" to Jewish thought while also observing that Jesus' radicalism will often subvert or overturn Jewish thought.[13] Again, this is a helpful criterion.

Several parables from the rabbis of that era have a story line that Jesus also used.[14] Jesus' use of but radical adaptation of these parables illustrates the criterion of similarity and dissimilarity.

The Lost Coin (R. Phineas b. Jair, ca. 200)

R. Phineas b. Jair opened his exposition with the text "If thou shalt seek her as silver": etc. (Prov 2:4). If you seek after the words of Torah as after hidden treasures, the Holy One, blessed be He, will not withhold your reward.

A parable. It is like a man [who] if he loses a sela [half a shekel] or an obol [a valuable coin] in his house, he lights lamp after lamp, wick after wick, until he finds it.

But behold, if for these things that are only ephemeral and of this world a man will light so many lamps and lights till he finds where they are hidden, how much more ought you search for the words of the Torah, which are the life both of this world and the next world, as for hidden treasure? Hence, "If you seek her as silver . . ." etc.

In Jesus' parable of the lost coin (Luke 15:8-10), it is *Jesus* (representing his Father) who, in his eating with sinners (15:1-2), is seeking the lost. Jesus' implied rejection of the Torah as the appropriate object to search for and his implicit identification of himself with God searching for the lost were likely outrageous and offensive.

The Wayward Son (R. Meir; ca. 150; *Deuteronomy Rabbah* 2:24)

Another explanation: "Thou wilt return to the Lord thy God" (Deut 4:30).

R. Samuel Pargrita said in the name of R. Meir: Unto what is the matter like? It is like a son of a king who took to evil ways. The king sent a tutor to him, saying: Repent, my son. But the son sent him back

---

13. See N. T. Wright, *Jesus and the Victory of God* (Minneapolis: Fortress, 1996), 132-33.

14. These parables are to be found in H. K. McArthur and R. M. Johnston, *They Also Taught in Parables: Rabbinic Parables from the First Centuries of the Christian Era* (Grand Rapids: Academie Books, 1990).

to his father [with a message], How can I have the effrontery to return? I am ashamed to come before you. Thereupon the father sent back word: my son, is a son ever ashamed to return to his father? And is it not to your father that you will be returning?

Even so the Holy One, blessed be He, sent Jeremiah to Israel when they sinned, and said to him: Go, say to my children: Return. Whence is this? For it is said: "Go and proclaim these words" etc. (Jer 3:12). Israel asked Jeremiah: How can we have the effrontery to return to God? Whence do we know this? For it is said: "Let us lie down in our shame and let our confusion cover us" etc. (v. 25). But God sent back word to them: My children, if you return, will you not be returning to your Father? Whence is this? "For I am become a father to Israel" etc. (Jer 31:9).

In Rabbi Meir's parable the wayward son of the king (= God) was Israel; he was too ashamed to "return" to God. By contrast, in Jesus' parable (Luke 15:11-32) there are *two* sons.[15] The historical setting of the parable (Luke 15:1-2) identifies the two sons: the "lost" son representing the "sinners" Jesus was welcoming and with whom he was eating, and the judgmental brother representing the Pharisees who condemned Jesus for eating with sinners. Again, Jesus' implicit identification of himself with the Father (God) welcoming the lost son (by eating with sinners — 15:1-2) and admonishing his brother (representing the Pharisees) was likely also outrageous and offensive.

The Industrious Labourer (*y. Berakhot* 5c, chapter 2, halacha 8)

To what may R. Bun bar Chiya be compared? To a king who hired many labourers. One of them was extremely industrious in his work. What did the king do? He took him and walked with him the length and width [of the vineyard]. In the evening the labourers came to take their wages. But [the king] gave a full wage to [the man with whom he had walked]. The labourers murmured and complained, "We have worked all day long, but [the king] has given this one who only worked two hours a full wage like us." The king answered them, "He has done more in two hours than what you did for the entire day!"

---

15. For extensive argument supporting the historicity of Jesus' parable, see C. A. Evans, "Reconstructing Jesus' Teaching," in *Jesus in Context: Temple, Purity, and Restoration*, ed. C. A. Evans and B. Chilton (Leiden: Brill, 1997), 153-63.

Thus though R. Bun laboured in Torah only twenty-eight years, he studied more than a mature scholar could have studied in a hundred.

Although the parable pointed to Rabbi Bun's superior diligence as a scholar, it implies God's greater reward for harder work. By contrast Jesus' parable (Matt 20:1-16) calculatedly points to God's sovereign generosity (grace), a shocking assertion in the light of the Pharisees' synergistic view of good works attracting God's cooperation.[16]

Wisdom and Works (Mishnah, *Pirqe 'Aboth* 3:18)

Whosesoever wisdom is in excess of his works, to what is he like? To a tree whose branches are abundant, and its roots scanty; and the wind comes, and uproots it and overturns it.

And whosesoever works are in excess of its wisdom, to what is he like?

To a tree whose branches are scanty, and its roots abundant; though all the winds come upon it, they stir it not from its place.

According to *Pirqe 'Aboth*, a life rooted in works will survive the heavy winds. By deliberate (and challenging) contrast, Jesus' parable of the two builders, coming at the end of the Sermon on the Mount (Matt 7:24-27), makes the hearing and doing of *Jesus'* words the unshakable foundation in the last day.

The Unworthy Tenants (anonymous; *Sifre on Deuteronomy* 312)

"For the Lord's portion is His people" (Deut 32:9).

A parable. It is like a king who owned a field and who gave it to the renters. They took it but robbed the owner. Then he took it away from them and gave it to their children, but they turned out to be even worse than the others. Then a son was born to the king, and he said to them: Get out of my possession. You can no longer remain there; give me back my portion.

Even so when our father Abraham was alive, he brought forth evil: Ishmael and the sons of Keturah. Then when our father Isaac was alive, he brought forth evil: Esau, the ruler of Edom, who was worse than the

---

16. Josephus, *War* 2.163 — "The Pharisees . . . hold that to act rightly or otherwise rests with men, but that in each action Fate [providence] cooperates."

others. But when Jacob was alive, he did not bring forth evil, but all his sons were honest, as he himself was. Whom did God call his portion? Was it not Jacob, for it says: "And Jacob was a quiet man, dwelling in his tents" (Gen 25:27). Whereupon God obtained his portion from Jacob, as it is said: "The Lord's portion is His people, and Jacob his allotted heritage" (Deut 32:9); and it says: "For the Lord has chosen Jacob for himself" (Ps 135:4).

In the *Sifre* the son "born to the king" is Jacob, whom the Lord "has chosen . . . for himself." Again, provocatively, Jesus identifies himself to the temple hierarchy as the last of the prophets who had come to Israel's leaders and been mistreated (Mark 12:1-11). Jesus is not only a prophet, however, *he* is the beloved Son of the Father, who will give the vineyard to others.

These parables illustrate well the "criterion of similarity *and* dissimilarity." These rabbinic parables share with Jesus' parables a common stock of social and biblical referents. This is to be expected in a rabbinic, biblically based but agrarian society. What is unexpected is the radical degree to which Jesus alters the story lines of these parables. In each of the examples above Jesus makes *himself* central, to the exclusion of Torah, Israel, and Jacob. Furthermore, the way of Jesus is the way of grace, not works of righteousness.

We summarize our discussion about the words of the Lord in the gospels.

i. The New Testament letter writers reveal such a reverent attitude to the words of the preresurrection Lord that they are unlikely to have invented or substantially altered those words, though they applied them creatively to differing pastoral settings.

ii. We assume that the gospel writers shared the same respect for the words of the Lord, and that they did not omit from their gospels any word of the Lord.

iii. In the Gospel of Mark the words of Jesus are the climactic points in the pericopes and are universally applicable and final in the matrixes of those pericopes.

iv. Where Matthew and Luke follow Mark's text, they faithfully reproduce sayings of the Lord within Mark's pericopes, though often in shortened forms.

v. Where Matthew and Luke are embodying Jesus' words from sayings sources (Q, M, L), they are not able to do so with the same contextual exactitude as Mark.

vi. The most useful criteria applicable to the sayings of Jesus are the criterion of multiple attestation, the criterion of inclusion, the criterion of embarrassment, and the double criterion of similarity and dissimilarity (which is especially useful in analysis of several of the parables of Jesus when considered alongside some rabbinic parables).

Historical Contexts for the Gospels' Narratives in Galilee

Space does not allow a comprehensive survey of Jesus' political and religious context in Galilee. We must limit ourselves to several "windows" through which we can glimpse the landscape for Jesus' activities in Galilee.

Historical Markers

In a statement of remarkable precision Luke names six historically notable persons who form the historical and jurisdictional setting for Jesus' public ministry. "In the fifteenth year of the reign of Tiberius Caesar, *Pontius Pilate* being governor of Judea, and *Herod* being tetrarch of Galilee, and his brother *Philip* tetrarch of the region of Ituraea and Trachonitis, and *Lysanias* tetrarch of Abilene, in the high-priesthood of *Annas* and *Caiaphas,* the word of God came to John the son of Zechariah in the wilderness" (Luke 3:1-2).

The political jurisdictions of King Herod's former realm were quite complex, yet Luke (or his source) has them exactly right. In Tiberius's *fifteenth* year (i.e., 28/29) Herod's kingdom existed in three principalities — Judea, Galilee (with Perea), and Ituraea-Trachonitis,[17] governed respectively by Pontius Pilate, Herod Antipas, and Herod Philip. Judea, the Roman province, encompassed three subsidiary jurisdictions, Idumea, lesser Judea, and Samaria, each with its own governing council. Lesser Judea was a sacral state centered on its holy city Jerusalem, whose Sanhedrin was ruled by the high priest and his relatives. Annas was high priest A.D. 6-15, but his dynastic influence continued throughout the pontificate of his son-in-law Caiaphas (18-37).

---

17. At the time Abilene was an independent region to the northwest of Damascus, which Josephus confirms was ruled by Lysanias (*War* 2.215; *Ant* 19.275). There is no record of Jesus visiting Abilene.

Divisions after Herod (Luke 3:1-2)

The gospels innocently reflect the complexities of these jurisdictions as they narrate the activities of Jesus in Galilee, Ituraea-Trachonitis, and lesser Judea as well as within the borders of Tyre, Sidon, and the Decapolis. This is the more impressive since later emperors Gaius, Claudius, and Nero in turn altered the administrations in these regions. Consider, for example, the changing fortunes of Galilee. Under Gaius (Caligula) Galilee ceased being a tetrarchy in 39 and became part of the kingdom of Agrippa I. Under Claudius, following Agrippa's death in 44, Galilee with Judea was placed under direct Roman provincial administration. Under Nero, in 54 Galilee reverted once more to Herodian rule, now under King Agrippa II.[18]

In other words, the jurisdictions the gospels portray remained only for a few years after the life span of Jesus, after which they were repeatedly altered. The point to make is that the gospels accurately set Jesus *in the real historical* contexts of his time, and not as they would be several decades later when the gospels were written.

The synoptics and John have differing but credible jurisdictional perspectives on Jesus' activities. The synoptic tradition (Mark in particular) mainly concentrates on Galilee,[19] and John on Jerusalem-Judea. The synoptics' narratives include various people associated with the tetrarch Antipas who became followers of Jesus, for example, the tax collector Levi from Capernaum and Joanna wife of Chuza from Tiberias, who was the tetrarch's estate manager[20] (Mark 2:13-14; Luke 8:3); John also mentions a "royal official" from Capernaum (John 4:46).

Mark hints at the inner workings of Antipas's tetrarchy in his account of Antipas's birthday banquet where John was beheaded (Mark 6:21).[21] Present were the three elite groups of his establishment: chief officials *(megistanes)*, army commanders *(chiliarchoi)*, and first men

---

18. Josephus, *War* 2.253; *Ant* 20.159.

19. For further information about Galilee, see S. Freyne, *Galilee from Alexander the Great to Hadrian: A Study of Second Temple Judaism* (Wilmington, Del.: Glazier, 1980); L. I. Levine, ed., *The Galilee in Late Antiquity* (Jerusalem: Jewish Theological Seminary, 1992); R. A. Horsley, *Galilee* (Valley Forge, Pa.: Trinity, 1995); J. L. Reed, *Archeology of the Galilean Jesus: A Re-Examination of Evidence* (Harrisburg, Pa.: Trinity, 2000); S. Freyne, "Galilee and Judea," in *The Face of New Testament Studies,* ed. S. McKnight and G. R. Osborne (Grand Rapids: Baker, 2004), 22-35.

20. Greek: *epitropos.* Alternatively, he may have been foreman of an estate or estates (cf. Josephus, *Ant* 18.194).

21. Freyne, "Galilee and Judea," 28-29.

(prōtoi).[22] The elite groups present at Antipas's birthday banquet, when considered together, most likely approximated the mysterious group Mark calls the "Herodians" (Mark 3:6; 12:13). They were dependent upon his patronage, he upon their support.

Following the politically provocative mission of the Twelve in Galilee and the feeding of the five thousand, Jesus' withdrawals from Antipas's jurisdiction are entirely understandable (Mark 7:24–9:30). Antipas had killed one prophet and would not hesitate to kill another.

For his part, John is interested in Nicodemus, a well-known Jerusalem leader (John 3:1-15; 7:50-52; 19:39). He mentions numerous times the great festivals in the temple city (2:23; 5:1; 6:4; 7:2-37 passim; 10:22; 11:56; 12:12, 20; 13:1, 29) and the frequent exchanges between the Galilean Jesus and the chief priests and Pharisees (7:32, 45; 11:47, 57; 12:10; 18:3, 35; 19:6, 15, 21). This gospel reaches its climax with Jesus' arrest by Roman soldiers and temple officials and his appearance in turn before Annas, Caiaphas, and Pilate (18:1–19:22).

This is not to imply that the gospel writers' aim was primarily to write precisely about the jurisdictions and their leaders. The writers' horizons are filled with Jesus the Christ; they make only passing reference to those leaders who were the historical context for his words and works. Yet those references are so generally correct that they enhance the historical credibility of their portrayal of their main subject, Jesus of Nazareth.

We must not fail to mention John the Baptist, who is mentioned almost ninety times in the gospels.[23] By our reckoning John preached and baptized for approximately a year.[24] He began in Tiberius's "fifteenth year," that is, in 28/29, and was imprisoned soon after Jesus' first Passover in Jerusalem (John 3:24; 4:43; cf. Mark 1:14), in 29/30.

22. In regard to "chief men," Josephus mentions a faction in Tiberias composed of "respectable citizens," included among whom were several named "Herod," who were evidently members of the royal house (*Life* 33). Josephus also refers to the ten "chief men" (*prōtoi* — the same term used in Mark 6:21), who were the executive committee of the city council *(boulē)* of Tiberias (*Life* 296, 67, 313, 381). Evidently the "chief men" were the wealthy landowners who dominated the civic/political life in Tiberias and other large towns and who formed Antipas's court.

23. See also chapter 2 above; D. C. Allison, "The Continuity between John and Jesus," *JSHJ* 1, no. 1 (2003): 6-27.

24. P. L. Maier, "The Date of the Nativity and the Chronology of Jesus' Life," in *Chronos, Kairos, Christos,* ed. J. Vardaman and E. Yamauchi (Winona Lake, Ind.: Eisenbrauns, 1989), 120, estimates the duration of John's public activities as from six to nine months.

Based on the gospels we observe the following: (i) John baptized large numbers of Jews in the Jordan River, so far as we can see, on the eastern or Perean side, within Antipas's jurisdiction, possibly to avoid trouble with the Romans, who now controlled Judea.[25] (ii) John was popularly believed to be a prophet (Mark 11:32). His baptizing was in the context of his preaching to the people who came out to him in the wilderness (Matt 3:1-10; Luke 3:7-14). It is specifically noted that John "did no sign" (John 10:41). (iii) John was imprisoned by the tetrarch of Galilee/Perea, and at the request of his wife Herodias, was beheaded (Mark 6:21-29).[26]

Like Pilate, Antipas, Philip, Annas, and Caiaphas, John the Baptist also finds a place in the record of Josephus, who, like Mark, attributes his death to Herod Antipas (Mark 6:14-26). In the following passage Josephus refers to two of the chief figures who formed such a large part of Jesus' political and religious landscape, Herod Antipas and John the Baptist.

To some of the Jews the destruction of Herod's army seemed to be divine vengeance . . . for his treatment of John, surnamed the Baptist. For Herod [Antipas] had put him to death, though he was a good man and had exhorted the Jews to live righteous lives, to practice justice towards their fellows and piety towards God, and so doing to join in baptism. In his view this was a necessary preliminary if baptism was to be acceptable to God. They must not do it to obtain pardon for whatever sins they had committed, but as a consecration of the body implying that the soul was already thoroughly cleansed by right behaviour.

When others too joined the crowds about him, because they were aroused to the highest degree by his sermons, Herod became alarmed. Eloquence that had so great an effect on mankind might lead to some form of sedition, for it looked as if they might be guided by John in everything that they did. Herod decided therefore that it would be much better to strike first and to be rid of him before his work led to an uprising, than to wait for an upheaval, get involved in a difficult situation

25. John 1:28; 10:40. There is ample evidence from Josephus that the Roman authorities were concerned about charismatic prophetic figures. See further P. W. Barnett, "The Jewish Sign Prophets AD 40-70: Their Intention and Origin," NTS 27 (1980): 679-97. For the argument that John's baptizing activities also occurred in Batanaea, see R. Riesner, "Bethany Beyond the Jordan (John 1:28): Topography, Theology and History in the Fourth Gospel," TynBul 38 (1987): 29-63.

26. John is silent about John's death; Luke does not attribute it to Herodias's influence.

and see his mistake. Though John, because of Herod's suspicions, was brought in chains to Machaerus . . . and there put to death.[27]

Generally speaking, the three details noted above in the gospels about John are also to be found in Josephus. There are differences, however. (i) Josephus does not specify the Jordan River as the location for John's baptizing. (ii) Josephus supplies the name of the prison as Machaerus, located in Perea overlooking the Dead Sea. (iii) Whereas the gospels[28] attribute John's arrest and execution to his rebuke of the tetrarch for his marriage to the wife of a living brother, Josephus states that it was due to Antipas's fear of John's popularity and the possibility of an uprising led by him.[29] (iv) Most significant of all, however, is the synoptic gospels' apocalyptic mode of description of John, as opposed to Josephus's nonapocalyptic language. This is typical of Josephus, who regularly translates such elements within Judaism into political or philosophical ones, as for example, his portrayal of the Pharisees, the Sadducees, the Essenes, and the Revolutionaries as "four *philosophies.*" Thus, whereas in Matthew John preached "repentance" in the face of the approaching "kingdom of heaven," in Josephus John exhorted the people "to live righteous lives, to practice justice towards their fellows and piety towards God." There can be no question, however, but that the gospels have the correct emphasis. Josephus's preacher of morality must be made to fit in with the gospels' truer picture of the prophet of Yahweh's impending kingdom and judgment.[30]

These four differences are not contradictions, however, but variations of emphasis and detail arising from the writers' respective viewpoints and interests. When the synoptic gospels and Josephus are looked at together, they provide a coherent account of the public ministry of John the Baptist.[31]

27. Josephus, *Ant* 18.117-119 LCL.

28. While the Gospel of John gives no reason for John's arrest, a degree of hostility toward him from the religious establishment in Jerusalem is suggested by their interrogation of him (John 1:19-29; 4:1).

29. Nonetheless, Josephus knows about Antipas's divorce of his Nabatean wife and his remarriage to Herodias (*Ant* 18.103, 113).

30. Matthew's account of John's ministry (3:1-12) is likely to be historically accurate. The failure of a fiery apocalyptic fulfillment of his words is itself evidence of their veracity.

31. It is noted, however, that the synoptics and John give different impressions of Jesus' involvement with the Baptizer. The synoptics imply that Jesus' ministry began only when John was imprisoned, that is, their ministries were "back to back." John's more expan-

We have now reviewed six political and religious leaders, mentioned with others in Luke 3:1-2, who were important in the historical landscape and who provide the context for the public ministry of Jesus of Nazareth. These men, as mentioned in other historical sources (Josephus mainly), enable us to establish a reasonably complete historical context and setting for the brief public ministry of Jesus of Nazareth (ca. 29-33). He is a believable historical figure within the setting these men provide for him.

Beyond that, however, Jesus as presented in the gospels was *connected* with these people in various ways, whether John the Baptist, Herod the tetrarch, Annas, Caiaphas, or Pontius Pilate. He intersects with them. But the gospels' accounts of these intersections, for the most part, are given only in passing, enhancing their historicity.

End-Time Expectations: Forcing the Kingdom of God

An unusual saying of Jesus allows us to imagine the contemporary eschatological excitement of the people of Galilee. These revelatory words, which are from the Q tradition, represent Jesus' negative commentary[32] on recent events (see earlier in this chapter). "From the days of John the Baptist until now the kingdom of heaven has suffered violence *(biazetai)*, and men of violence *(biastai)* take it by force *(harpazousin)*" (Matt 11:12).

Who are the "men of violence," and what is meant by "the kingdom of heaven has suffered[33] violence"? Many scholars have admitted failure to understand this logion or to answer these questions,[34] and others have called it "unintelligible," "incomprehensible," and in one case "a *Trümmerfeld,* a heap of ruins."[35]

---

sive account suggests that the ministries of the two men overlapped for a period (see Mark 1:14; Matt 4:12-13; Luke 3:18-23; cf. John 3:22-24; 4:1-2).

32. So W. E. Moore, "*Biazō, Harpazō* and Cognates in Josephus," *NTS* 21 (1974): 541; cf. P. Barnett, "Who Were the *Biastai?*" *RTR* 36, no. 3 (1977): 65-70.

33. Although the verb *biazetai* could be middle, it is usually considered to be passive, "suffered violence" (RSV) or "acquired by force."

34. For review of the use of the verb *biazein* and the possible meanings of this text, see S. R. Llewelyn, *New Documents Illustrating Early Christianity* (Sydney: Macquarie University, 1994), 130-62. Various suggestions include: the sufferings of the persecuted Q community (Hoffmann); violent zealotic Pharisees (Moore); the "present wicked generation in Israel" (Schulz); opposition to Jesus and the kingdom (Kosch); and the holy war at Qumran (Betz).

35. D. Daube, *The New Testament and Rabbinic Judaism* (London: Athlone Press, 1956), 130.

We note that the logion refers to a brief time span, "from the days of John the Baptist" (28/29) "until now" (31/32). It is, therefore, Jesus' comment on a *recent* historical phenomenon. Are there any hints within the gospels themselves to help us identify these *biastai?*

One possible clue is found in John 6:14-15. "When the people saw the sign which [Jesus] had done, they said, 'This is indeed the prophet who is to come into the world!' Perceiving then that they were about to come and force *(harpazein)* him to be king, Jesus withdrew again to the mountain by himself."

The immediately preceding events were the mission of the Twelve in Galilee and the feeding of the five thousand, both of which were deeply eschatological. In reporting that the Twelve *cast out demons* and preached that people must *repent,* Mark implies that the disciples of Jesus proclaimed the imminent nearness of the kingdom of God (Mark 6:12), as their master had done beforehand (1:14-15, 21-28). The Twelve were replicating but enlarging Jesus' end-time preaching with its accompanying sign, the casting out of demons. We are not surprised, therefore, that "many . . . ran together from every town" for a hoped-for eschatological rendezvous with their leader, the Son of Man (6:31-33).

At that meeting place on the eastern side of the lake, Jesus fed the hungry crowd in the manner of a Moses providing manna from heaven, another deeply eschatological action. The excited crowd immediately construed this wilderness *sēmeion* performed at Passover as evidence that Jesus was the long-awaited Prophet-like-Moses (Deut 18:15, 18), whereupon they attempted to impose kingship upon him.[36]

This incident critically reveals two aspects of the eschatological mind-set of the people of Galilee. One was their prominent hope for the appearing of the revelatory Moses-Prophet (also mentioned in John 1:21; 7:40). Closely connected, apparently, was the mechanistic idea that the appearance of an eschatological figure would somehow act as a trigger to activate the hand of God to inaugurate the Coming Age.

This latter notion is well attested within Second Temple Judaism. In the *Assumption of Moses* the martyrdom of faithful Taxo will *cause* God's kingdom to "appear through all his creation" (9:7–10:7). The succession of "sign prophets" who arose in Israel circa A.D. 45-70 and who in the manner of Moses or Joshua attempted various exodus-conquest

---

36. H. W. Montefiore, "Revolt in the Wilderness?" *NTS* 8 (1962): 135-41.

miracles[37] likewise seems to view their "signs" as levers to *activate* the hand of God to deliver his people, as in times of old. According to D. Daube, several rabbinic texts specifically use the language of *"forcing the end,"* for example, Joshua ben Levi (mid–third century) explained Isaiah 35:4 as admonishing the "hasty" who attempted to "force the coming of the end." Daube argues that this third-century text preserves a tradition from the previous century,[38] nearer to the NT era.

Several factors intensified this ultra-eschatological fervor: the tetrarch's wickedness in imprisoning John the Baptist, the compromised worldliness of the Annas high priesthood, and the occupying presence of the Romans in Judea. The appearance on the scene of Jesus, a prophet of the end time, followed by the mission of his disciples prophesying the end time and Jesus' feeding *sēmeion* at Passover led the Galileans to hail him as the Mosaic Prophet-King.[39] By so doing they expected to "force" the kingdom of God to appear immediately.

In short, their action (John 6:14-15) and Jesus' logion (Matt 11:12) provide windows into the highly excitable eschatological world to which Jesus came in the Galilee of his day. His logion implies that the preaching and baptizing of John precipitated a series of attempts by "men of violence" *(biastai)* to "force" *(harpazein)* the appearance of the kingdom. These *biastai* remain nameless, yet we can scarcely doubt their attempts to precipitate the arrival of the kingdom of God.

It is clear, however, that Jesus strenuously opposed this attitude. His response to the attempt to "force" the kingship upon him was to dismiss the crowd, to compel the disciples to cross the lake, and to withdraw alone to the mountain (Mark 6:45-46). The logion from the Q tradition (Matt 11:12) also clearly reveals his opposition to these eschatological expectations and actions.

37. Josephus, *Ant* 20.97-99, 167-172; 20.188; Acts 21:38. Barnett, "Jewish Sign Prophets," 679-97; cf. R. Bauckham, "Messianism according to the Gospel of John," in *Challenging Perspectives in the Gospel of John*, ed. J. Lierman, WUNT 219 (Tübingen: Mohr Siebeck, 2006), 34-68 (here 49-50), who interprets their signs as *authenticating* themselves as the prophet like Moses.

38. Daube, *Rabbinic Judaism*, 289-92.

39. For information about the Moses-Prophet, see H. M. Teeple, *The Mosaic Eschatological Prophet* (Philadelphia: Fortress, 1957).

Three Towns: Chorazin, Bethsaida, and Capernaum

In this Q saying (Luke 10:13-15/Matt 11:20-24) Jesus pronounced his eschatological woes (opposite to his "blessed are . . ." sayings, as in the Beatitudes) on three "cities" *(poleis)*,[40] Chorazin, Bethsaida, and Capernaum, where most of his mighty works had been done.

This is historically credible. In Galilee the Jewish people were concentrated in the northwest quadrant of the lake. The southwest quadrant was dominated by Tiberias, the tetrarch's capital built circa 17 near burial grounds and therefore ritually offensive to Jews. The southeast quadrant belonged to the Decapolis and was a predominantly Gentile region. The northeast, although ruled by Philip, a Herodian prince, was significantly Hellenized with a somewhat lesser Jewish representation than in the northwest. Archaeology reveals a concentration of synagogues in the northwestern quadrant and a smaller component in the northeastern quadrant, but significantly fewer in the other two.[41]

The saying is also geographically credible. Chorazin was only a few kilometers north of Capernaum and Bethsaida was a few kilometers east, across the Jordan within Trachonitis-Ituraea. Although we do not know the exact location of Bethsaida, its name ("House of Fishermen") demands that it be close to the lake.

Furthermore, Jesus' word is consistent with his declared priority for "the lost sheep of the house of Israel" (Matt 10:5-6). Accordingly, as in Mark's narrative, Jesus began to preach in synagogues in Capernaum and the immediate vicinity like Chorazin and Bethsaida but was forced further afield by the opposition of the local religious leaders and the menace of the tetrarch. Ultimately this meant travel beyond Antipas's jurisdiction into the regions of Tyre, Sidon, Trachonitis-Ituraea, and the Decapolis. In other words, the Q saying represents a genuine oracle from the earlier period of Jesus' ministry to three adjacent settlements, Chorazin, Bethsaida, and in particular, Capernaum.

40. Strictly speaking, Sepphoris and Tiberias were the only cities in Galilee; Chorazin and Capernaum were smaller (*kōmai* in Josephus's classification). Bethsaida was in Trachonitis-Ituraea, which Josephus calls a "city" (*War* 2.168); its location remains in dispute.

41. E. M. Meyers and J. F. Strange, *Archeology, the Rabbis, and Early Christianity* (London: SCM, 1981), figure 7; J. J. Rouseau and R. Arav, *Jesus and His World* (Minneapolis: Fortress, 1995), 271.

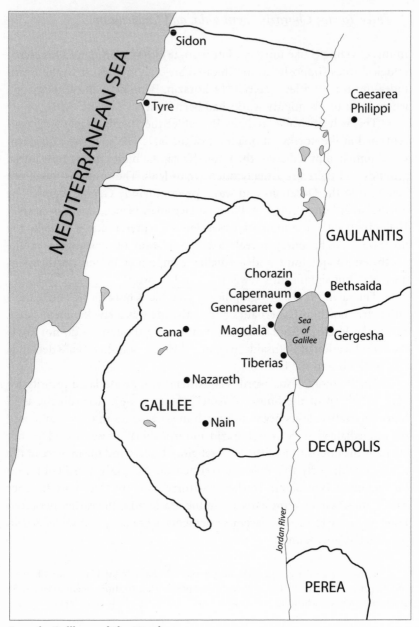

Jesus in Galilee and the North

Jesus' Mighty Works

"Jews seek signs," wrote Paul in commentary on his nation's interest in the bizarre and inexplicable (1 Cor 1:22). Jesus is likewise on record warning about his generation's preoccupation with "signs" (*sēmeia* — Mark 8:11-12). Contemporary Jewish attitudes are evident in Josephus's fascination with portents *(terata)* at many points, for example, in overnight storms, weird phenomena in the heavens, and mysterious happenings in the temple.[42] Though an intelligent man and an observant Jew, Josephus was deeply influenced by portents and signs.

Paul, Jesus, and Josephus are referring to superstitious interpretations of natural phenomena that were in some way unexpected or unusual. Contrary to our expectations (based on the claims of the "history of religions" school), however, actual references to "miraculous events" and "miracle cures" among the Jews in the NT era are relatively infrequent in the surviving records.

Some of the more prominent miracle-workers from the era of Jesus are:

  i. The holy rabbi Honi the Circle-Drawer, also known as Onias[43] (first century B.C.), who was said to have successfully prayed for rain, not merely for a downpour or a drizzle but "a rain of grace" (*m. Ta'anit* 3:8).

 ii. John the disciple drew Jesus' attention to a man casting out demons in Jesus' name (Mark 9:38). It was not the fact of the exorcisms but their execution in Jesus' name that caused the comment. Josephus reports witnessing a Jewish exorcist named Eleazar drawing a demon through a man's nostrils and consigning it to a basin of water (*Ant* 8.46-49). Evidently, exorcisms were not unheard of or exceptional.

iii. Rabbi Gamaliel, the teacher of Saul of Tarsus, once prayed during a storm at sea, whereupon the sea subsided (*b. Bava Metzi'a* 59b).

 iv. In the A.D. 70s the devout rabbi Hanina ben Dosa prayed for the dangerously ill son of his teacher, Yohanan ben Zakkai, and the boy lived (*b. Berakhot* 34b).

---

42. Josephus, *War* 4.287; 6.288-300; and 6.292, respectively.
43. Josephus, *Ant* 14.22.

In the gospels the *sheer number and variety* of Jesus' miracles strike us as extraordinary. Mark reports no fewer than eighteen miracles, the majority of which are reproduced in Matthew and Luke. Found only in the Q source are two miracles, in M there are three, in L there are seven, and in John there are six.[44] Miracles represented a critical aspect of Jesus' ministry.

In the synoptic gospels the miracles of Jesus are evidence of his true identity as the messianic bearer of the kingdom of God.

> "But that you may know that the Son of man has authority on earth to forgive sins . . . I say to you, rise, take up your pallet [bed] and go home." (Mark 2:10-11)

> "If it is by the Spirit ['finger,' Luke] of God that I cast out demons, then the kingdom of God has come upon you." (Matt 12:28/Luke 11:20)

The miracles of Jesus were always within the bounds of nature and not "contrary" to nature's patterns, that is, freakish or bizarre like the "signs" and "portents" that the Jews sought. His miracles were restrained, done for the good of those in need and not as spectacles in the manner of magicians. They served to point to Jesus as at one with the Creator in achieving his beneficent, end-time purposes on earth. In the miracles of Jesus the kingdom of God was present among them as the Son of Man went about doing good.

Should the miracles of Jesus as the gospels record them be regarded as historical? Several considerations give us grounds for confidence. First, there is some evidence from the non-Christian sources, Josephus and the Talmud. Josephus, writing in the 90s, clearly intends us to understand that Jesus performed miracles when he states that "Jesus . . . wrought surprising feats" (*paradoxōn ergōn* — *Ant* 18.63). The Talmud, written much later, says that "they hanged Yeshu" because "he practised sorcery" (*b. Sanhedrin* 43a),[45] a probable reference to exorcism by the power of the devil, something Jesus was accused of in the gospel account (Mark 3:22).

---

44. For a list of miracles see R. H. Fuller, *Interpreting the Miracles* (London: SCM, 1963), 126-27.

45. For further (late) Jewish references to Jesus' miracles, see B. Blackburn, "The Miracles of Jesus," in *Studying the Historical Jesus,* ed. C. A. Evans and B. Chilton (Leiden: Brill, 1994), 353-94 (here 361).

Second, the apostle Peter refers to the miracles of Jesus in his two major speeches recorded in the Acts of the Apostles.

"Jesus of Nazareth, a man attested to you by God with *mighty works and wonders* and signs which God did through him in your midst, as you yourselves know." (Acts 2:22)

"God anointed Jesus of Nazareth with the Holy Spirit and with power; how *he went about doing good and healing all who were oppressed by the devil.*" (Acts 10:38)

Like the crowds in Jerusalem, Cornelius knew of these remarkable deeds of Jesus (Acts 10:37).

Third, some scholars find the *sayings* of Jesus about miracles particularly significant, especially those able to be retroverted into Aramaic. Consider, for example, Jesus' reply to the messengers from John the Baptist in prison. "Go and tell John what you have seen and heard: the blind receive their sight, the lame walk, lepers are cleansed, and the deaf hear, the dead are raised up, the poor have good news preached to them" (Luke 7:22/Matt 11:4-5).

J. Jeremias, an authority on Aramaic language, argued that these words originally occurred in a speech rhythm that was characteristic of the way Jesus spoke.[46] In what is certainly a logion of Jesus, Jesus is appealing to what has been seen and heard in respect to miracles of healing the blind, the lame, the lepers, the deaf, and raising the dead.

Again, in another passage common to Matthew and Luke (Q), Jesus said: "Woe to you, Chorazin! woe to you, Bethsaida! for if the mighty works done in you had been done in Tyre and Sidon, they would have repented long ago. . . . And you, Capernaum . . ." (Luke 10:13-15/Matt 11:21, 23). Once more, in a logion that appears to be historical, Jesus appeals to miraculous events that, by common agreement, had happened in Chorazin, Bethsaida, and Capernaum. It is difficult to account for these various miracle sayings unless they corresponded in some way with Jesus' actions.

Fourth, there are examples of multiple attestation to exorcism, nature miracles, healings, and the raising of the dead across the primary gospel sources Mark, John, Q, L, and M, as the following table demonstrates.

46. J. Jeremias, *New Testament Theology 1* (London: SCM, 1971), 21.

EXORCISM

Mark	John	Q	L	M
Capernaum demoniac (1:21-28)				The dumb demoniac (9:32-34; cf. 10:5-8)
Gerasene demoniac (5:1-20)				

NATURE MIRACLES

Mark	John	Q	L	M
Stilling the storm (4:35-41)				
Feeding the five thousand (6:30-44)	Feeding the five thousand (6:1-13)		Draft of fishes (5:1-11)	
Walking on water (6:45-52)	Walking on water (6:16-21)			

HEALING

Mark	John	Q	L	M
Withered hand (3:1-6)	Official's son (4:46-54)	Centurion's boy (Matt 8:5-13)	Bent woman (13:10-17)	
Blind Bartimaeus (10:46-52)	Man born blind (9:1-34)			

RESURRECTION

Mark	John	Q	L	M
Daughter of Jairus (5:21-43)	Lazarus (11:1-44)		Widow's son (7:11-17)	

A wide range of miracle types is thus attested independently. According to B. Blackburn, "the miracle-working activity of Jesus — at least exorcisms and healings — easily passes the criterion of multiple attestation."[47] J. P. Meier devoted five hundred pages to reviewing Jesus' miracles and declared their multiple attestation to be "massive."[48]

Scholars are divided over the historicity of Jesus' miracles as reported in the gospels.[49] Among those who doubt their truth is N. Perrin, who asserted that we cannot "accept the necessary authenticity of any single story as it stands at present in the synoptic tradition; the legendary overlay and the influence of parallel stories from Hellenism and Judaism on the tradition are too strong for that."[50] More positively, Jeremias observed that "even when strict critical standards have been applied to the miracle stories, a demonstrably historical nucleus remains. Jesus performed healings that astonished his contemporaries."[51] Based on his extensive review of scholars' opinions, Blackburn concluded that the view that "Jesus acted as an exorcist and healer can easily be described as *the consensus* of the modern period."[52]

Jesus' Unlawful Actions[53]

Many incidents occur in the first half of the Gospel of Mark where Jesus and his disciples behave in ways contrary to the halacha of the Pharisees. Their criticism is expressed twice as an outright accusation of unlawful behavior ("It is not lawful . . ."/*ouk exestin* — Mark 2:24; 3:4). On both occasions the Pharisees accuse Jesus and his disciples of behaving *unlawfully* in

47. Blackburn, "The Miracles of Jesus," 356.

48. J. P. Meier, *A Marginal Jew: Rethinking the Historical Jesus,* vol. 2 (New York: Doubleday, 1994), 631.

49. For a review of those who doubt the truth of the miracles, see Blackburn, "The Miracles of Jesus," 363-68.

50. N. Perrin, *Rediscovering the Teaching of Jesus* (New York: Harper and Row, 1967), 136; also B. Mack, *A Myth of Innocence: Mark and Christian Origins* (Philadelphia: Fortress, 1988), 75-77, 91-93, 215-24.

51. Jeremias, *New Testament Theology 1,* 92.

52. Blackburn, "The Miracles of Jesus," 362 (emphasis added). Even R. Bultmann, *Jesus and the Word* (New York: Scribner, 1934), observed, "undoubtedly [Jesus] healed the sick and cast out demons" (173).

53. See above, chapter 8.

breaking the Sabbath. On other occasions they express their opposition indirectly, through their questions.

2:16   "Why does he eat with tax collectors and sinners?"

2:18   "Why do . . . your disciples . . . not fast?"

7:5   "Why do your disciples not live according to the tradition of the elders, but eat with hands defiled?"

Thus we are able to identify the various expressions of halacha that Jesus and his disciples did not observe and over which disputes occurred. How historically consistent are these unlawful acts? Here we depend mainly on later Jewish collections of regulations like the Mishnah (ca. 200). Scholars generally accept that the laws and practices in the Mishnah are a true reflection of earlier periods, including the era of the NT.

Two Breaches of Sabbath Keeping (Mark 2:24; 3:4)

In the first incident Jesus and his disciples were plucking grain on the Sabbath. That there was a restriction against doing this is intimated by the Mishnah tractate *Shabbat* 7:2: "The main classes of [prohibited] work are forty less one: sowing, ploughing, *reaping*, binding sheaves . . ." The Mishnah distinguished between "forgetful" acts and "mindful" (deliberate) breaches. Most likely, the Pharisees regarded Jesus' acts as "mindful."

In the second, Jesus healed a man's withered hand on the Sabbath and did so deliberately (provocatively?). Again, there is clear instruction, from the Mishnah tractate *Shabbat* 22:6: "[T]hey may not . . . set a broken limb. If man's hand or foot is dislocated he may not pour cold water over it."

Mark's account of the Pharisees' protests at Jesus' breaches of the Sabbath is consistent with our knowledge of their strictness in observing the Sabbath.

Eating with Tax Collectors and Sinners (Mark 2:16)

In Second Temple Judaism a distinction was made between "the righteous" and "the sinners," a distinction Jesus signally failed to observe.[54] Not only

---

54. Meyer, *The Aims of Jesus*, 158-62.

did he fraternize with those who were designated "sinners," but worse, he sat at table with them (cf. Matt 11:19; Luke 15:1-2). Since one ate in the presence of the Lord and in anticipation of the messianic banquet, this eating together was especially offensive to the Pharisees, the guardians of righteousness. Again, the Mishnah is the chief source for prevailing attitudes in the NT period.

> He that undertakes to be trustworthy (i.e., a Pharisee) may not be the guest of one of the people of the land (i.e., a "sinner"). (*m. Demai* 2:2)

> He who undertakes to be an associate (i.e., a disciple) . . . may not be a guest of one of the people of the land nor may he receive him as a guest. (*m. Demai* 3:3)

The Mishnah passages confirm Mark's narrative, that the Pharisees rebuked Jesus for sitting at table with sinners.

Failure to Fast (Mark 2:18)

According to the OT, the only day fasting was mandatory was the Day of Atonement (Exod 20:10; Lev 16:1-24). By NT times, however, it had become customary (though not obligatory) to fast twice in the week (Luke 18:12; *Did* 8.1). The Mishnah enjoins fasting where rain had not fallen, to secure the breaking of drought (*m. Ta'anit* 1:4-5).

Most likely, the incident Mark narrates was consistent with the growing practice of fasting, which by New Testament times was becoming de facto a requirement of the righteous.

Failure to Purify Themselves Ritually (Mark 7:5)

The Mishnah tractate *Kelim* ("Vessels") reveals the extent to which Jews had become obsessed with purity. While it is possible that these views had intensified by the era of the Mishnah, it is nonetheless likely that tactile purity was very important in the era of the New Testament, and in particular in the time of Jesus. So concerned were they for purity that even the airspace enclosed within an oven or a jar was unclean if an unclean person or object had been nearby. Carefully prescribed washing of the hands and arms from water in stone vessels, therefore, was obligatory prior to entering the house and eating food.

A codified version of this appeared later in the Babylonian Talmud, which said "the ablution of the hands before eating profane things is practiced up to the (elbow) joint" (*b. Hullin* 106a).

In short, our brief survey of Mark's version of Jesus' "lawless" acts in Galilee is broadly confirmed by later instructions found in the Mishnah and other Jewish literature. An indication of the problem Jesus was to the local Pharisees can be seen in Mark's references to scribes from Jerusalem who came down to Galilee (3:22; 7:1). Furthermore, to be rid of Jesus the local Pharisees united their efforts with their natural enemies, the Herodians in Tiberias (3:6), despite their likely view of them as "unrighteous." Tiberias was built near a graveyard and was characterized by Gentile practices.

Summary

It is customary today for scholars to write comprehensive, multifaceted works about Galilee in the NT era. Writers offer extensive analyses of politics, geography, climate, socioeconomics, religion, etc.[55] Mark, whose gospel narrates Jesus' activities in Galilee, does not write in such a compendious manner. Rather Mark writes a gospel, a kerygmatic biography. This does not mean, however, that he is altogether silent about various facets of Galilean life. In the course of our brief and selective survey we catch glimpses of John the Baptist baptizing, Herod Antipas ruling, the high priest presiding, and Pontius Pilate governing. Because Jesus is so much the center of his narrative, Mark mentions these prominent people only in passing. Nor are his references perfect; there are some minor examples of untidiness. Herod was not a king but a tetrarch (6:14), and there is some doubt whether Herodias was his brother Philip's wife (6:17-18).

Apart from these possible blemishes, Mark's incidental references to political rulers, John the Baptist, eschatological expectations, centers of Jesus' activities, mighty works, and unlawful actions generally are consonant with other sources. Since these aspects of the gospel narrative are coherent and credible, there are good grounds for taking Mark's account of Jesus' words and works seriously.

55. See n. 19 above.

Conclusion

Provided that we accept the limitations inherent in the Gospel of Mark, in its brevity and single focus, we have good reason to believe it provides a historically credible account of Jesus' activities in Galilee, the regions of Tyre and Sidon, Ituraea-Trachonitis, and the Decapolis. The words of Jesus, which are weighty and wise, are singularly applicable to the pericopes in which they occur. The parables in Mark as well as in Matthew and Luke are arguably authentic, based (in particular) on the cogent double criteria of similarity and dissimilarity. In any case, we argue that the gospel writers would neither invent nor omit a word of the Lord, though they felt free to adapt a word appropriately.

The narrative of Mark and the synoptics is set within the complex jurisdictions of the thirties, but not those as they would be altered in the decades following. As the narratives unfold we note the inconspicuous ways in which Jesus' movements cohere with the political realities of those times. Furthermore, Jesus' own path crossed the paths of the notables of that time, whether John the Baptist, the tetrarch Antipas, the high priests Annas and Caiaphas, or the Roman prefect, Pontius Pilate. In the course of the narratives we encounter those who were eschatologically excited ("the men of violence") as well as the "sinners" with whom Jesus aligned himself as a lawbreaker. Furthermore, we see Jesus as the worker of mighty deeds, including in those towns where most of his mighty works were done.

In brief, we have in Mark a gospel that is a useful source of information about Jesus' words and actions in Galilee and adjacent regions in the north.

APPENDIX: A NOTE ON GOSPEL GENRE

In attempting to identify the gospels in terms of existing literary genres, it is not always recognized, as it should be, that Mark alone calls his book by that name. Furthermore, the four canonical gospels differ from each other in both character and intention. Mark wrote his text to be read aloud in church meetings (Mark 13:14) to demonstrate that Jesus was the awesome Son of Man who disappeared as mysteriously as he had appeared. Luke wrote his two-volume "narrative" to confirm catechumens like Theophilus in the truth in which he had been instructed (Luke 1:1-4). Matthew wrote his gospel as a manual for the instruction of disciples, based on the collected teachings of the Christ (Matt 28:19). John wrote his book with special interest in Jesus' miracle signs and lengthy pastoral and polemical discourse. The character and intention of each gospel are different. Luke and Matthew felt that Mark's gospel was inadequate, so they adapted it and added other material to suit their purposes. John wrote his "book" to reassure his Christian hearers that Jesus was truly the Christ, the Son of God (John 20:30-31).

Clearly each gospel is biographical in character and bears some similarities to the Greco-Roman *bioi* of that general era, e.g., Suetonius's *Twelve Caesars* or Plutarch's *Parallel Lives*.[56] Nonetheless, the gospels are unusual if not unique because their intended readership and purpose are so exclusively defined. Whereas the contemporary biographers and histo-

---

56. So R. Burridge, *What Are the Gospels?* (Cambridge: Cambridge University Press, 1992).

rians wrote to inform everyone in general and no one in particular, the gospelers wrote their texts narrowly and specifically for Christians for "in-house" use. Accordingly, attempts to classify the gospels according to this genre or that should be regarded as secondary. The primary observation should be to recognize their unique intended audience as *church-directed* and their *function* as ecclesial-liturgical (Mark), polemical-apologetic (John), and instructional (Matthew, Luke-Acts).[57]

Mark is a special case. The writer's explicit direction to the lector to explain the meaning of an obscure text (Mark 13:14) and the many implied side comments to those present (e.g., 7:11, 19; 13:37; 15:21) identify this text as designed to be *read aloud* in a church meeting. Mark must be classified alongside the letters of Paul and the Apocalypse as a text the author specifically wrote for an aural purpose in a liturgical, ecclesial setting.[58] That was also likely true of Matthew, Luke-Acts, and John.

The gospels claim another dimension as well, the supranatural. That is to say, the gospels are *existentially* the word of the risen and ascended *Kyrios* that are read aloud to his assembled people (cf. Mark 13:14 — "Let the lector explain"). Mark's opening words indicate that what follows is "the gospel of (i.e., *from*) Jesus Christ, the Son of God," that is to say, *his* word to his hearers in the churches. The man Mark is merely the human cipher through whom the words of the risen Lord come to his people. Using different language, John asserts that the "book" he writes is a "true . . . witness" to Christ's "signs" for his hearers to safely "believe" for immediate entry to "eternal life" (John 20:30-31; 19:35; cf. 21:24).

Does the supranatural character of Mark suggest that his gospel is ahistorical, in fact mythical in character? No. Mark roots his narrative in the soil of geography (e.g., Nazareth, Capernaum, Gennesaret, Bethsaida, Tyre, Sidon, the Decapolis, Caesarea Philippi, Jerusalem) and (as noted) in the context of John the Baptist and of known political leaders (Herod the king [actually, tetrarch], the high priest, Pontius Pilate). Jesus' movements as fugitive from the ruler of Galilee (chapters 6–9) are consistent with one avoiding the borders of Herod Antipas's jurisdiction. Mark's gospel is the word of the living Christ to the churches and a work that is both historical and geographical.

---

57. See P. R. Eddy and G. A. Boyd, *The Jesus Legend* (Grand Rapids: Baker, 2007), 309-61, for a critical review of the various theories about the genre of the gospels.

58. E.g., 1 Cor 14:37; Col 4:16; Rev 1:3; 22:18.

We offer two observations about the genre of the gospels. First, their special readership (church groups) and purpose (liturgical/polemical/apologetic/instructional) make it difficult to classify them alongside other contemporary texts. Second, insofar as they are able to be classified, they belong to the broad group of biographies *(bioi)*. In short, they are ecclesial documents that are biographical and historical in character.

For both Mark and John their words are supranaturally true. Yet at the same time they must also be *historically* true. If they are not historically true, they cannot be supranaturally true.

The Christ We Find

A certain geographical order was . . . understood from the start: Jesus came from Nazareth, his public career was itinerant, and he died in Jerusalem.

B. F. Meyer[1]

This book is the last in a short series called *After Jesus*. It takes a retrospective approach based on the view that everything we know about Jesus was written after his life span. *Immediately* after Jesus there were oral traditions and most likely written ones as well (30-50), most of which would have been incorporated later in the letters and the gospels.[2] The *next* phase was the letters of Paul and likely James and perhaps Hebrews (ca. 48-64). *Overlapping* and succeeding that phase came the gospels, written circa 60-80. *Finally,* the Apocalypse was written circa 95.

Such was the impact of Christ on his contemporaries that it was transmitted immediately and directly in the oral traditions and through them to the NT literature. One subject dominates these traditions and this literature, Jesus Christ. The measure of the man was the impact he made.

---

1. B. F. Meyer, *The Aims of Jesus* (London: SCM, 1979), 71.
2. See chapter 4 above.

After Jesus: His Impact

The impact of Jesus' teaching and activities can be traced in the aftermath of his death and resurrection.[3] This is the more remarkable given the brevity of his public ministry, a mere three to four years. Let us consider four aspects of early Christian belief that can be explained only by the radical influence of Jesus.

His Followers Called the Preresurrection Jesus "Lord"/Kyrios

Embedded in Paul's Greek letter to Corinth is the Aramaic prayer *Maran atha,* "Lord, come [back]" (1 Cor 16:22). Evidently the Aramaic-speaking believers in Palestine worshiped Jesus as *Mara,* "Lord." There are strong hints that Paul (a monotheistic Jew) identified this Lord/*Kyrios* with YHWH, Israel's covenant God. Paul had just written, "If anyone has no *love* for the Lord, let him be anathema," words that echo the Shema, "You shall love YHWH your God . . ." (Deut 6:5). Earlier in the letter his words "there is . . . one Lord, Jesus Christ" (1 Cor 8:6) also echo the Shema ("Hear O Israel, YHWH our God . . . is one"). Clearly Paul and the early Christians had come to identify and rank Jesus with YHWH. The confession "Jesus is Lord" was the evidence of the inner presence of the eschatological Spirit and the focal point of Christian gatherings (1 Cor 12:3; Rom 10:9; Phil 2:11; Eph 5:19; Col 3:16).

Furthermore, the early Christians regarded the *preresurrection* Jesus as "Lord"/*Kyrios*.[4] He was the "Lord" whose words they treasured and obeyed.

For this we declare to you by the word of the *Lord.* (1 Thess 4:15)

To the married I give charge, not I but the *Lord.* (1 Cor 7:10)

Now concerning the unmarried, I have no command of the *Lord.* (1 Cor 7:25)

The *Lord* commanded that those who proclaim the gospel should get their living by the gospel. (1 Cor 9:14)

3. See chapter 8 above for the impact of Jesus' teaching on the attitudes of Paul.
4. See chapter 8 above.

For I received from the *Lord* what I also delivered to you. (1 Cor 11:23)

I know and am persuaded in the *Lord* Jesus that nothing is unclean in itself. (Rom 14:14)

The attitude to the preresurrection "Lord" reflected in obedience to his words is revelatory. The words exclude any idea of postmortem apotheosis or divinization. The One who *is* Lord now, and who is being invoked to "come back," *was* Lord then. The veneration of the words he spoke *then* is evidence of this.

How are we to explain this *retrospective* honoring of Jesus as Lord in the postresurrection church? The explanation is that the disciples must have been deeply affected by his messianic *acts* (exorcisms, healings, nature miracles), his messianic *wisdom* (evident in his word, including against the authorities), and his messianic *consciousness* (the "I have come to . . ." sayings). But these do not precisely account for the postresurrection identification of him as *Lord*.

Most likely the answer is to be found in Jesus' own provocative question, "How can the scribes say that the Christ is the son of David" when David himself (in Ps 110:1) referred to the Christ as "my Lord" who was seated at the "right hand" of YHWH? Jesus' riddle-question was: How can the descendant of David also be his *Lord* at God's right hand? The answer was not apparent at the time, though it would be when Peter cited Psalm 110:1 following Jesus' resurrection and exaltation, adding, "God has made him both *Lord* and *Christ*, this Jesus whom you crucified" (Acts 2:36).

In fact, reference to Jesus at God's "right hand" (based on Ps 110:1) becomes the OT text that is most echoed in the New Testament, being found in the letters of Paul, Hebrews, 1 Peter, Revelation, and the book of Acts. How are we to account for this proliferation of "right hand of God" references in the postresurrection literature except to say they sprang from Jesus' memorable exegesis of Psalm 110:1 prior to his crucifixion?

It appears, therefore, that Jesus' *messianic* acts, *messianic* wisdom, and *messianic* self-awareness affected profoundly the disciples' convictions that Jesus was *the Christ*, but that his precise anticipation that he would soon be the Christ and Lord at God's right hand together represented the bridge from the preresurrection Jesus to those who would very soon proclaim and worship him as "Lord and Christ."

The God of Israel Was Now Redefined as Abba, "Father"

The NT letters reveal that Greek-speaking Gentiles were addressing the covenant Lord of Israel by means of an Aramaic word that spoke of an almost unheard-of intimacy of relationship with the deity.

> And because you are sons, God has sent the Spirit of his Son into our hearts, crying, "Abba! Father!" (Gal 4:6)

> For you did not receive the spirit of slavery to fall back into fear, but you have received the spirit of sonship. When we cry, "Abba! Father!" it is the Spirit himself bearing witness with our spirit that we are children of God. (Rom 8:15-16)

> You invoke as *Father* him who judges each one impartially. (1 Pet 1:17)

> Grace to you and peace from God our *Father*... the God and *Father* of our Lord Jesus Christ. (2 Cor 1:2-3)

Jesus' own relationship with God as "Abba" and his teaching that God was a Father were a radical departure from Jewish belief and practice. Reference to God as "Father" in a personal sense is rare in the OT, and absent altogether from the Jewish liturgies like the Shema (uttered twice daily by adult males) and the *Shemoneh 'Esreh* (the Nineteen Synagogue *Berakhoth*/Benedictions). By clear contrast, *after Jesus* God was defined as "Father," including in the quasi-liturgical "grace" prayer typically appearing at the head of Paul's letters (e.g., Rom 1:7; 1 Cor 1:3; 2 Cor 1:2; Gal 1:3; etc.).

Access to God through a New Temple

For Jews in the Second Temple period the temple was critical for access to and worship of God. John's record of the words of the woman of Samaria doubtless reflected current thinking about the centrality of the temple. "Our fathers worshiped on this mountain; and you [Jews] say that in Jerusalem is the place where men ought to worship" (John 4:20). This view rested upon a long-held tradition and belief.

But you shall seek the place which the Lord your God will choose out of all your tribes to put his name and make his habitation there; thither you shall go. (Deut 12:5)

Then the Lord appeared to Solomon in the night and said to him: "I have heard your prayer, and have chosen this place for myself as a house of sacrifice." (2 Chron 7:12)

Jesus' connected prophecies that the temple would be destroyed and that he would be raised from the dead came to be understood as a declaration that his resurrected body would be the eschatological temple to replace the former temple (John 2:19-22).[5] The new holy of holies is a dying but resurrected Savior.[6]

After Jesus, therefore, when Jews and Gentiles gathered as believers, they uttered their prayers to God "through" the Son of God, in whose name they spoke the Aramaic *amen*. "For the Son of God, Jesus Christ, whom we preached among you, Silvanus and Timothy and I, was not Yes and No; but in him it is always Yes. For all the promises of God find their Yes in him. That is why we utter the *Amen* through him, to the glory of God" (2 Cor 1:19-20).

The crucified but resurrected and ascended Jesus became the new temple as the end-time meeting place with God, as he intimated beforehand by prophesying his resurrection and the replacement of the earthly temple.

Atonement Was through His Death, Not Temple Sacrifices

Even while the temple was still standing and fully operational, the believers had come to see that Jesus' sacrifice had superseded the sacrifice of animals in the temple. In circa 54 Paul reminded the Corinthians of the traditions he "delivered" to them five years earlier.

For I received from the Lord what I also delivered to you, that the Lord Jesus on the night when he was betrayed took bread, and when he had given thanks, he broke it, and said, "This is my body which is for *(hyper)* you. Do this in remembrance of me." (1 Cor 11:23-24)

5. P. W. L. Walker, *Jesus and the Holy City* (Grand Rapids: Eerdmans, 1996), 8-12.
6. Adapted from Bailey as quoted in Walker, *Holy City,* 12 n. 39.

> I delivered to you as of first importance what I also received, that Christ died for *(hyper)* our sins in accordance with the scriptures. (1 Cor 15:3)

The Last Supper tradition ("This is my body which is for [*hyper*] you") arose from the preresurrection Jesus and the death and resurrection tradition ("Christ died for [*hyper*] our sins") soon afterward. This teaching about atonement represents a fundamental and radical change for Jews like Paul who had been immured in the temple culture of Israel.

After Jesus: The Spread of Christology

Christianity spread rapidly in the six decades after Jesus, that is, during the era in which the NT was written. Throughout those years he was worshiped "*as if* a god" (in Pliny's words)[7] in the countries that ringed the eastern Mediterranean and Italy (e.g., Rom 10:9; Heb 1:7-8; 1 Pet 3:22; Rev 5:12-14). The texts of the New Testament, the mission literature of the movement, were dominated by references to his supernatural identity, to the demands of absolute loyalty to him, but also to the high ethical demands he made of his followers.

How do we explain the centrality of the figure of Christ in the early literature? The logical options are two. One is that Jesus was a *lesser* figure (rabbi, prophet, political subversive, or holy man) and that these "high" views of his identity were superimposed upon him during the postresurrection decades. Alternatively, the preresurrection Jesus was already during his own lifetime a person of "high" identity. Historically speaking, the answer is straightforward based on how early his "high" status was recognized. In the immediate aftermath of his life he was confessed, proclaimed, and worshiped as Messiah, as *Mara/Kyrios*/Lord, and as Son of God. That is to say, the *preresurrection* Jesus must already have been recognized as an eschatological figure, a recognition confirmed and clarified by his resurrection and the coming of the Spirit. Historical logic demands that the pre-Easter Jesus was already recognized by his disciples as a messianic figure and no mere rabbi or prophet.

7. See chapter 3.

The Historical Christ

Jesus of Nazareth was recognized as the Christ during the brief period of his ministry; this did not commence in the postresurrection years. The disciples recognized his messianic identity by physically observing the man Jesus, his words and deeds. Their recognition was contemporary and empirical, made in his physical presence, not retrospective and illusory and made in his absence, susceptible to romantic heightening.[8] Naturally, their appreciation of him was enhanced later through their Spirit-led reflection on the ways he fulfilled the Law and the Prophets (e.g., John 2:22; 12:16; 16:13-15). It was, however, an enhancement that grew naturally from their existing conviction that he was the Christ, the Son of God and the Lord. The post-Easter church did not imaginatively superimpose categories on a man for whom they were never true.

B. F. Meyer states that "the career of Jesus was performatively messianic" and criticizes those who seek to discover the origins of Christology in the "Easter experience" of the disciples. According to Meyer, in their view "the Easter experience of the disciples had been turned into a magic top-hat from which like so many rabbits, there unexpectedly emerged the church itself, the messianic proclamation and its basic soteriology."[9]

Accordingly, the bifurcation between the Jesus of history and the Christ of faith, though superficially attractive, is deceptive and untrue. It is excluded by the logic of history based on available evidence.

What is the evidence? We must consider three loci, Antioch, Jerusalem, and Caesarea Philippi.

Antioch

In Antioch in Syria "the disciples were for the first time called Christians" (*chrēmatisai . . . Christianoi* — Acts 11:26). Luke leaves unanswered the questions: Who gave the disciples that name, and when was it given? Scholars are likely correct in thinking that the name came from Roman administrators.[10] *Christianos* is a Latinism, whose suffix *-ianos* is a Greek

---

8. Contra H. Conzelmann, *Jesus* (Philadelphia: Fortress, 1973), who saw no connecting link between Jesus and Christology "except the Easter experience of the disciples" (10).

9. Meyer, *The Aims of Jesus*, 176-77.

10. D. G. Horrell, "The Label *Christianos:* 1 Peter 4:16 and the Formation of Christian Identity," *JBL* 126, no. 2 (2007): 361-81 (here 362-67).

form of the Latin -*ianus* and indicates a follower of a named leader (e.g., *Hērōdianoi,* "partisans of [a] Herod" — Mark 3:6; 12:13). At this early stage *Christos* was not yet a surname but a title, so that the *Christianoi* were adherents of *the Christos.* Thus it sounds as if *Christianos* was the official term for a member of the new movement in the Syrian capital. Their members belonged to something unheard of, a group where Jews mixed with Gentiles,[11] whose raison d'être was their mutual adherence to the *Christos.*

The dating of the term is logically located within Acts 11:19-26, an *inclusio* passage that begins and ends with reference to "Antioch" and represents a time frame circa 35-45. It might appear from verse 26 that the word "Christian" was coined after Barnabas brought Paul to Antioch, in or after circa 44. It is more likely, however, that the name Christian originated earlier, in the late 30s. The implied inclusion of "Greeks" in the previously exclusive Jewish church membership occurred much earlier than Paul's arrival in Antioch (v. 20) and most likely marks the point when this mixed group were tagged *Christianoi.*

The intriguing question is whether or not the authorities in Antioch placed the movement's roots in Jerusalem. This is by no means unlikely. Judea was subsidiary to Antioch as Rome's chief eastern outpost, whose legions often had to march south in times of trouble. Pilate's execution in Jerusalem of a "king of the Jews" may have come to the attention of his superior, the Roman legate in Antioch. Furthermore, this movement had been launched in Antioch by Jewish émigrés who had arrived from Jerusalem in recent times. The Roman administrators in Antioch are more likely than not to have identified the local *Christianoi* with the one Pilate had crucified as "king of the Jews" in Jerusalem.

Jerusalem

The arrest and trial of Jesus occurred in Jerusalem, which was subject to complex overlapping governance. Jerusalem was at the same time a sacral

---

11. According to Tacitus, "the Jews are extremely loyal towards one another, but always ready to show compassion, but towards every other people they feel only hate and enmity. They sit apart at meals" (*Histories* 5.30; cf. Acts 10:28 — "how unlawful it is for a Jew to associate with or to visit any one of another nation").

city ruled by the high priest and council (Sanhedrin) and part of the Roman province of Judea, subject to the rule of the prefect in Caesarea Maritima. As a Roman province, the *ius gladii,* the authority for capital punishment, resided solely in the one who bore the emperor's imperium, the prefect.[12]

Nothing in the surviving records suggests that Jesus' activities were of concern to the Roman authorities, based in Caesarea. True, he was popularly regarded as a prophet (Mark 8:28 par.), but there is no evidence that the Romans regarded his activities as politically important. By contrast, the Roman procurator reacted violently and immediately a few years later (ca. 44) when the prophet Theudas led a group into the wilderness with the stated intention of miraculously parting the waters of the Jordan and leading his followers back into Judea.[13] Even Jesus' deliberate ride up to Mount Zion in the manner of the king prophesied by Zechariah 9:9 does not seem to have provoked a reaction from the Romans.

For the high priest and his associates, however, Jesus of Nazareth was a "political" threat. Eschatological hopes had been heightened in Judea during the past decades of Roman occupation, especially since the census in A.D. 6 and the imposition of the poll tax (cf. Mark 12:14). Evidence of this tension is seen in the authorities' question to John the Baptist whether he was "the Christ," "Elijah," or "the [Mosaic] Prophet" (John 1:19-21). R. Bauckham has established the historicity of this question in the light of the end-time expectations at that time.[14]

The Jerusalem authorities' concerns about John the Baptist dissipated at his imprisonment and death, only to be revived by the appearance of Jesus of Nazareth, especially when he visited Jerusalem. On those occasions questions about "the Christ" were being asked regarding Jesus, prompting the attempts of the temple authorities to arrest him (John 7:26, 30; 10:24). The Gospel of John is likely correct in saying that the high priest formally issued a warrant for Jesus' execution sometime before his actual arrest.[15]

John says the high priests Annas and Caiaphas in turn interrogated

12. Josephus, *War* 2.117; John 19:31.

13. Josephus, *Ant* 220.95-97.

14. R. Bauckham, "Messianism according to the Gospel of John," in *Challenging Perspectives on the Gospel of John,* ed. J. Lierman, WUNT 219 (Tübingen: Mohr, 2006), 34-68.

15. E. Bammel, "Ex illa atque die consilium fecerunt," in *The Trial of Jesus,* ed. E. Bammel (London: SCM, 1970), 11-40; see earlier, chapter 7.

Jesus, though he doesn't reveal the nature of their inquiries. We reasonably assume that they sought to confirm that Jesus and his followers were making messianic claims. Mark's narrative, however, is quite explicit. Jesus was asked whether he was the Christ, and he replied that he was (Mark 14:61-62). His fate was sealed.

Yet the high priest lacked the authority to execute Jesus, notwithstanding the seriousness of his crime. The high priest, thus, had to translate the Jewish crime of false messiahship into a comparable category of crime under Roman law. Accordingly, the Jewish authorities charged him before the prefect with the crime of treason, that he claimed to be "king of the Jews," as the independent sources John and Mark make clear (John 19:21; Mark 15:2). Overtly, the Romans executed Jesus of Nazareth for the crime of claiming to be "king of the Jews." But this was a mere convenience. His actual crime in the eyes of the high priest was his claim to be the Christ, the Davidic Messiah.

It is difficult to place any other interpretation on these events. No evidence suggests that Jesus was "a person of interest" to Pilate. Arguments that Jesus was a zealot or zealot sympathizer have long since been discredited, if for no other reason than that no attempt was made to round up his disciples. All the evidence points to the Jewish sacral leaders as the ones who wanted to remove Jesus. The gospels' united insistence that it was for the crime of messiahship is cogent and not easy to overturn. What other category of misbehavior was there, apart from messianism, that was so easily translated as "king of the Jews"?

On historical grounds, therefore, we argue that Jesus was regarded as *the Christ* before his arrest, and it was for this "crime," as the high priest saw it, that the Romans crucified him. Paul's laconic "We preach *Christ* crucified" (1 Cor 1:23), therefore, is at once a theological statement and a historical one. The notion that "Christ" was a theological category superimposed after the resurrection upon an *unmessianic* Jesus is untenable.

We contend, therefore, that the *preresurrection* Jesus became widely regarded as the Christ. There was no other reason for the high priest to orchestrate his crucifixion.

This, however, may have been merely the opinion of some based on gossip and rumor in a highly charged environment. Did *Jesus* regard himself and did his disciples regard him as Messiah? The irreducible question is this: Did the historical Jesus of Nazareth claim or accept the claim that he was the Messiah?

Caesarea Philippi

The Journey to Jerusalem

The center point of the Gospel of Mark occurs at Caesarea Philippi where Peter, replying to Jesus on behalf of the disciples, declared, "You are the Christ" (Mark 8:29). So Peter is the focal point at the midpoint of the narrative, as well as at the beginning and the end as the first and the last disciple we meet. Furthermore, as already noted, references to Peter throughout this gospel are disproportionately more numerous than in other gospels.[16] Accordingly, Peter's confession "you are the Christ" at the midpoint of the gospel is critical to the whole gospel.

It was preceded immediately by Jesus giving sight to a blind man in Bethsaida, which set the scene for the disciples and Peter *at last* to recognize the Christ in their midst. It is followed immediately by Jesus' stark words about his rejection and death at the hands of the temple authorities, whereupon he and the disciples set out for the Holy City. On "the way" there he makes two further predictions of the sufferings that await him in Jerusalem (9:30-32; 10:32-34). Finally he arrived in Jerusalem, where he was indeed rejected and killed.

There is, then, some schematization in the narrative. Some elements are omitted for dramatic and theological effect, for example, that the disciples most likely had sensed *beforehand* that Jesus was the Christ. Furthermore, the execution of Jesus may not in fact have occurred so soon after Jesus arrived in Jerusalem as Mark implies (cf. John 7–11). In Mark's hands the narrative is taut and emotionally powerful.

This, however, prompts the question about historicity. Granted that Mark has written a powerful narrative, we must also ask whether and to what degree it corresponds with *what actually happened.* Did they go to Caesarea Philippi and did Peter say those words?

Our sense of history is strengthened by details in Mark's account about what happened next, that is, the journey from Caesarea Philippi in the extreme north to Jerusalem in the south. The otherwise gratuitous time note, "after *six* days," and the reference to a "*high* mountain" (Mount Hermon?) point toward actuality (Mark 9:2). Likewise, the secret passage through Galilee and the return to Capernaum ("in the house") are consis-

---

16. See above, chapter 5.

tent with Jesus avoiding the menace of Antipas following the mission of the Twelve and the feeding of the five thousand (9:30, 33). Likewise cogent is their onward journey "inside the borders *(horia)* of Judea and beyond the Jordan," where the test question about divorce recalled the circumstances of the arrest there of John the Baptist (10:1). Eventually they reach Jericho and then, finally, the villages Bethphage and Bethany on the outskirts of Jerusalem (10:46; 11:1). Upon his arrival in Jerusalem Jesus rode up to the city in calculated fulfillment of prophecy and cleared the vendors from the temple, both of them *messianic* acts. In short, the authenticity of the journey from Caesarea Philippi to Jerusalem and the messianic acts there are historically consistent with Peter's formal acknowledgment that Jesus was "the Christ."

The messianic journey (from Caesarea Philippi to Jerusalem) and the messianic acts in the Holy City are evidence *in themselves* of Jesus' messianic consciousness. Let me give the opinion of the noted authority, M. Hengel: "If Jesus never possessed a messianic consciousness of divine mission, nor spoke of the coming, or present, 'Son of Man,' nor was executed as a messianic pretender — as is maintained by radical criticism untroubled by historical arguments — then the emergence of Christology, indeed the entire early history of primitive Christianity is incomprehensible."[17]

Our contention is that the high priest's concern that a messianic pretender was in Jerusalem (which led to his crucifixion by the Romans as "king of the Jews") imaginably arose at the arrival of Jesus and his followers in the City of David.

Simon the Rock

Deeply controversial is Matthew's insertion of the M passage in his narrative of the events at Caesarea Philippi. I do not refer to the controversies of later centuries over the papacy, but to the questions (a) of the very authenticity of a passage, and (b) if authentic, whether it is correctly located at Caesarea Philippi. The problem, of course, is that it originates from only one source (M) and on that account is doubted by many as to (a) and therefore as to (b).[18]

17. M. Hengel, "Jesus, the Messiah of Israel: The Debate about the 'Messianic Mission' of Jesus," in *Authenticating the Activities of Jesus,* ed. B. Chilton and C. A. Evans (Leiden: Brill, 1999), 323-49 (here 327).

18. Among those who reject the genuineness of this passage as an utterance of Jesus,

Simon Peter replied, "You are the Christ, the Son of the living God." And Jesus answered him, "Blessed are you, Simon Bar-Jona! For flesh and blood has not revealed this to you, but my Father who is in heaven. And I tell you, you are Peter *(petros)*, and on this rock *(petra)* I will build my church, and the powers of death shall not prevail against it. I will give you the keys of the kingdom of heaven, and whatever you bind on earth shall be bound in heaven, and whatever you loose on earth shall be loosed in heaven." (Matt 16:16-19)

In support of its authenticity we note that the passage is structurally a unit with rhetorical elements that are consistent with Jesus' manner of speech (antonyms "flesh and blood," "on earth . . . in heaven"; wordplay *petros . . . petra*). Also, on the a priori grounds of "the criterion of inclusion," whereby words of Jesus were not to be omitted, we contend for the genuineness of this saying. On the other hand, whether or not these words genuinely belonged to the Caesarea Philippi incident is a more open question. A case can be made for both alternatives, though no better context can be imagined than Caesarea Philippi.[19]

One matter, however, is beyond dispute, and that is the historicity of Jesus' renaming of Simon Bar-Jona as *Petros/Kēphas*. The M source quoted above states this, as do the independent authorities Mark (Mark 1:16; 3:16) and John (John 1:42; cf. 21:15, 16, 17). Strikingly, Simon was known by his new name in the postresurrection era where Paul consistently refers to him by the Aramaic name *Kēphas* (1 Cor 1:12; 3:22; 9:5; 15:5; Gal 1:18; 2:9, 11, 14) and calls him *Petros* only in passages where he has already used the name *Kēphas* (Gal 2:7-8). Furthermore, the name *Kēphas* is embedded in the resurrection tradition Paul "received" and "handed over" (1 Cor 15:5). The renaming of Simon as *Kēphas* in the M passage above must be regarded as historical.

Related is the question why Jesus renamed Simon *Petros/Kēphas*. The answer from the M passage is that historically Simon was prominent among the disciples for his recognition of Jesus as "the Christ." Here the

---

see T. W. Manson, *The Sayings of Jesus* (London: SCM, 1961), 202-3. For arguments in favor of it as a dominical saying and which is correctly located at Caesarea Philippi, see Meyer, *The Aims of Jesus*, 185-97.

19. The strength of Markan priority is the barrier to the recognition of Matt 16:16-19 as belonging to Caesarea Philippi. Meyer, however, suggests that the M tradition was older and that Mark is depending on a "truncated form" of the tradition (*The Aims of Jesus*, 189).

M passage is supported by Mark's account of Caesarea Philippi (Mark 8:29), but also tangentially by John 1:41-42 where Andrew told his brother Simon, "We have found the Messiah *(messias)*," whereupon Jesus renamed Simon Bar-Jona *Kēphas.* The Aramaic of the original conversation is evident in Andrew's *messias* and Jesus' name *Kēphas* for Simon *Bar-Jona.* In the Johannine equivalent of discipleship confession to Jesus, it is Simon (called) *Peter* who speaks for them, "We have believed . . . that you are the Holy One of God" (John 6:69). The point is that both independent traditions M and John connect Jesus' name *Kēphas* with recognition of Jesus' messiahship.

Kēphas was the first (male) witness of the risen Christ (1 Cor 15:5) and the leader of the initial mission *(apostolē)* to the uncircumcised (Gal 2:9). The persistent continuity of the new name and his recorded witness to the resurrection of the Messiah (Acts 2–10 passim) are consistent with his preresurrection recognition of Jesus' true identity as "the Christ." In short, Simon's new name *Kēphas,* which was used both before and after the resurrection, is testimony to his confession of Jesus as Messiah before the resurrection.

Summary: Caesarea Philippi, Jerusalem, Antioch

We are reviewing the idea of "the Christ" over a span of about eight years, beginning in Caesarea Philippi circa 32 and ending in Antioch circa 39. Working backward from Antioch circa 39, we identify a mixed group of Jews and Greeks whom the Roman authorities called *Christianoi,* a new term that means "followers of [the] Christ." This is consonant with a group of émigré Jews who had recently come to Antioch from Jerusalem. In Jerusalem, in A.D. 33, the Roman prefect had crucified Jesus, a messianic pretender, for the crime of treason for claiming to be "king of the Jews."

Jesus was so accused, based on widespread rumor that he was — or was said to be — the Christ. Did this belief emanate from Jesus' own circle of followers, or was it merely street talk in Jerusalem? The evidence from Caesarea Philippi and from the renaming of Simon as *Kēphas* supports the contention that even before the resurrection Jesus' followers were convinced that he was the Christ.

Biography of the Christ

E. P. Sanders is noted for asserting in 1985 the historical authenticity of eight activities of the historical Jesus.[20] While regarding Jesus' sayings as problematic, as to both their location and their authenticity,[21] Sanders argued confidently for the following actions of Jesus.

1. Jesus was baptized by John the Baptist.
2. Jesus was a Galilean who preached and healed.
3. Jesus called disciples and spoke of there being twelve.
4. Jesus confined his activity to Israel.
5. Jesus engaged in controversy about the temple.
6. Jesus was crucified outside Jerusalem by the Roman authorities.
7. After his death Jesus' followers continued as an identifiable movement.
8. At least some Jews persecuted at least parts of the new movement.

In 1993, in a more popular work, Sanders added six facts to his list.[22]

1. Jesus was born circa 4 B.C., at the approximate time of the death of Herod the Great.
2. Jesus grew up in Nazareth of Galilee.
3. Jesus taught in small villages and towns and seemed to avoid cities.
4. Jesus ate a final meal with his disciples.
5. Jesus was arrested and interrogated by Jewish authorities, apparently at the orders of the high priest.
6. Although they abandoned Jesus after his arrest, the disciples later "saw" him after his death. This led the disciples to believe that Jesus would return and found the kingdom.

---

20. E. P. Sanders, *Jesus and Judaism* (London: SCM, 1985), 11. In the lists by Sanders and N. T. Wright, I am following C. A. Evans, "Authenticating the Activities of Jesus," in *Authenticating the Activities of Jesus*, 3-5.

21. According to E. P. Sanders and M. Davies, *Studying the Synoptic Gospels* (London: SCM, 1989): "we must be prepared to admit that we *never* know the immediate context . . . the evangelists had individual units and . . . they supplied narrative settings" (339); "Matthew and Luke . . . created sayings material" (116).

22. E. P. Sanders, *The Historical Figure of Jesus* (London: Penguin Books, 1993).

Sanders's addition of extra items is curious and begs the question about method. What had happened between 1985 and 1993 to assist him to find six new activities? Archaeologists had made no dramatic discoveries, nor had new manuscripts been discovered that yielded these additions. This extra information was there all the time, and hardly controversial.

In 1996 N. T. Wright added further facts, including the following.[23]

1. Jesus spoke Aramaic, Hebrew, and probably some Greek.
2. Jesus summoned the people to repent.
3. Jesus made use of parables to announce the kingdom of God.
4. Jesus effected remarkable cures, including exorcisms, as demonstrations of the truth of his proclamation of the kingdom.
5. Jesus shared table fellowship with a socially and religiously diverse group, including those whom many Torah-observant Jews would regard as "sinners."

C. A. Evans adds three further items to the lists of Sanders and Wright.[24]

1. The public viewed Jesus as a prophet.
2. The Romans crucified him as "king of the Jews."
3. That following Easter his followers regarded him as Israel's Messiah.

The list had grown to twenty-two items between 1985 and 1999!

Extra activities could be found without difficulty, as in the following examples.

1. Jesus' public ministry began soon after John the Baptist's began, which was in the fifteenth year of Tiberius's rule.
2. He renamed Simon Bar-Jona *Kēphas*/Peter.
3. Jesus was seen by many as a "rabbi."
4. He engaged in vigorous debate with religious scholars both in Galilee and in Jerusalem.
5. His twelve disciples engaged in a mission to Galilee.

23. N. T. Wright, *Jesus and the Victory of God* (London: SPCK, 1996), 147-50.
24. Evans, "Authenticating the Activities," 5.

6. As a "prophet" of high profile, Jesus would have been vulnerable to the tetrarch of Galilee.
7. Accordingly Jesus often took refuge in neighboring principalities.
8. He was betrayed by one of his disciples, Judas Iscariot.
9. He was denied by the leader of the Twelve, Simon Bar-Jona.

Those who include various activities tend to do so by one or another of the criteria of authenticity. These, however, seem to be rather ad hoc. As I reflect on the nine items I have added, my criterion would be something like "the criterion of inherent probability," or "why would you leave this out?"

There is an element of farce here. On one hand scholars tend to create criteria as they add new items that were always there, prominent in the extant sources. No external data has emerged to identify new activities of Jesus. All that has really happened is that the historians have tacitly admitted that the gospels are the only sources that are available and that, although ancient, they do yield considerable authentic information.

Two elements at least are missing from the lists of activities. One is attention to sequence, which historians have failed seriously to address. Can we improve on the sequence we find in Mark, which is followed by Matthew and Luke, and with which John broadly agrees?

1. Jesus was born in Bethlehem during the reign of Herod the king.
2. He was raised by parents Joseph and Mary in Nazareth.
3. John baptized Jesus in the Jordan, after which he began to teach in the synagogues of Galilee, circa 29/30. Many regarded him as a teacher/rabbi.
4. He moved from Nazareth to Capernaum.
5. He proclaimed that the arrival of the kingdom of God was imminent, for which he taught in parables and pointed to exorcisms as the sign of things to come.
6. He called and was followed by twelve disciples to whom he explained his public teaching.
7. He shared table fellowship with "sinners."
8. Large numbers came to him for healing.
9. He engaged in religious debate with the religious leaders, including

those who came down from Jerusalem, chiefly over halacha relating to the Sabbath, purity, and fasting.

10. His twelve disciples engaged in a mission to the towns of Galilee.

11. Five thousand men converged on him, whom he fed with loaves and fishes.

12. As a fugitive from tetrarch Antipas, Jesus traveled in regions to the north, northeast, and east.

13. At Caesarea Philippi his disciples confirmed their opinion that he was the Messiah, whereas the people at large regarded him as a prophet.

14. Jesus traveled to Jerusalem through Galilee and Perea, arriving at the Feast of Tabernacles but withdrawing several times for his safety.

15. He arrived finally at the Passover.

16. On the evening he was betrayed by Judas he ate a final meal with his disciples, which he charged them to repeat in memory of him.

17. His leading disciple, Simon Bar-Jona, denied any association with him.

18. Jesus was arrested, interrogated by the temple authorities, and handed over to the Romans, who also interrogated him and then crucified him (on a Friday).

19. He was buried in the tomb of Joseph of Arimathea shortly before the onset of the Sabbath.

20. The body of Jesus was not in the tomb when women came on the first day of the week.

21. The risen Jesus appeared to his followers in Jerusalem and Galilee over the next few weeks.

The second element omitted from all our lists — from those of Sanders, Wright, Evans, and myself — is Jesus' *messiahship*. This is the missing piece in the puzzle without which the whole story of Jesus remains incomplete and ultimately unintelligible. His announcement of the kingdom of God is eschatological and points to God's imminent intervention in Israel's affairs. That engagement in *Israel's* affairs, however, implies fulfillment of the Law and the Prophets. The interest of the postresurrection disciples in OT fulfillment logically stems from their preresurrection master's use of the scriptures. This fulfillment principle, in turn, pointed to *someone* about whom the special promises of God clustered, someone *who was expected to come.* John's record of the questions to John the Baptist neatly identified three such persons whose coming was expected, the Christ, Elijah, and the Moses-Prophet (John 1:19-21).[25] Logically, Jesus' announcement of the eschatological kingdom, his exorcisms, his choice of twelve disciples, his authoritative application of OT prophecy to *himself* and to *that time* could mean only one thing — that he was himself the One who was to come, the Christ.

Integrally connected, of course, was their awareness of Jesus' own *messianic consciousness* even if it was largely unspoken.[26] For, to be sure, he chose to present himself as the Son of Man rather than the Christ, and this for reasons so well known as not to need exposition. He must have had a messianic *demeanor* expressive of a messianic awareness for those close to him to confess that messiahship directly to him. Even the unimaginable shock of his arrest and crucifixion did not shake their messianic conviction. Indeed, as powerful as the resurrection experience was for them, it is doubtful that even this could have created that messianic conviction unless it had been etched into their minds beforehand.

Speaking personally, my own long-held belief is that the historical Jesus was the Christ, both in his own mind and eventually also in the minds of the disciples. Equally, however, this is also my conviction as a student of history. That he was the Christ is the hypothesis that makes best sense of all the evidence, both before and after the resurrection. There is no alternative explanation for the phenomenon of the postresurrection church worshiping the preresurrection Jesus. Recognition of the messiahship of Jesus of Nazareth is the point where personal faith and the logic of history meet.

Gospel

The creation of lists of Jesus' actions is an abstraction, an arid, irrelevant activity. As one runs one's eye down the list, whether Sanders's shorter list or one of the longer lists, one gets a sense of uninvolved detachment. Here is merely a figure in Jewish antiquity, no more engaging than Judas the Galilean, Simon bar Gioras, or Simon ben Kosiba.

25. See further Bauckham, "Messianism," 34-68, who contends that John reflects Jewish messianic expectations at the time of Jesus.

26. For argument for Jesus' messianic self-awareness based on the "I have come" sayings and Jesus' exposition of various psalms, see A. H. I. Lee, *From Messiah to the Preexistent Son,* WUNT 192 (Tübingen: Mohr Siebeck, 2005), 181-201.

By contrast, how different it is to read a passage from a gospel. It scarcely matters where, whether Jesus is debating with the Pharisees in Capernaum or standing by the bedside of Jairus's daughter. He meets us in the story. It is the divine genius of the gospel writer that he draws the readers *existentially* into the narrative, to involve us, so that we find ourselves making decisions about Jesus and therefore about ourselves.

Of course, we are reading history and biography of some kind, yet pericope by pericope the Jesus we meet is somehow addressing us, forcing us to reach conclusions about him and ourselves. The lists of activities, however, are lists and nothing more, leaving us at a distance as detached spectators. But the gospel, the divine kerygma, draws us into a drama that Christ himself is directing. In the gospel Christ himself meets us and requires the answer, "Who do you say I am?"

BIBLIOGRAPHY

Alexander, L. *The Preface to Luke's Gospel*. SNTSMS 78. Cambridge: Cambridge University Press, 1993.

Alexander, P. S. "Orality in Pharisaic-Rabbinic Judaism at the Turn of the Eras." In *Jesus and the Oral Gospel Tradition*, edited by H. Wansbrough, 159-84. Sheffield: JSOT, 1991.

Anderson, P. *The Christology of the Fourth Gospel: Its Unity and Disunity in the Light of John 6*. WUNT 2.78. Tübingen: Mohr, 1996.

Bammel, E. "Ex illa atque die consilium fecerunt." In *The Trial of Jesus*, edited by E. Bammel, 11-40. London: SCM, 1970.

Barnett, P. "Who Were the *Biastai?*" *RTR* 36, no. 3 (1977): 65-70.

———. "The Jewish Sign Prophets AD 40-70: Their Intention and Origin." *NTS* 27 (1980): 679-97.

———. "The Feeding of the Multitude in Mark 6/John 6." In *Gospel Perspectives*, vol. 6, edited by D. Wenham and C. Blomberg, 273-93. Sheffield: JSOT, 1986.

———. *Jesus and the Logic of History*. Leicester: Inter-Varsity, 1997.

———. *Jesus and the Rise of Early Christianity*. Downers Grove, Ill.: IVP, 1999.

———. *The Birth of Christianity*. Grand Rapids: Eerdmans, 2005.

———. *Paul: Missionary of Jesus*. Grand Rapids: Eerdmans, 2008.

Bauckham, R. "Nicodemus and the Gurion Family." *JTS* 47 (1996): 1-37.

———. "John for Readers of Mark." In *The Gospel for All Christians: Rethinking the Gospel Audiences*, edited by R. Bauckham, 147-71. Grand Rapids: Eerdmans, 1998.

———. *Jesus and the Eyewitnesses: The Gospels as Eyewitness Testimony*. Grand Rapids: Eerdmans, 2006.

Bell, H. I., and T. C. Skeat. *Fragments of an Unknown Gospel and Other Early Christian Papyri*. London: British Museum, 1935.

Beutler, J. *Judaism and the Jews in the Gospel of John*. StudBib 30. Rome: Editrice Pontificio Instituto Biblico, 2006.

Blomberg, C. L. *Interpreting the Parables*. Leicester: Apollos, 1990.

———. *The Historical Reliability of John's Gospel*. Leicester: Apollos, 2001.

———. "John and Jesus." In *The Face of New Testament Studies*, edited by S. McKnight and G. R. Osborne, 209-26. Grand Rapids: Baker Academic, 2004.

Bolt, P. G. "Mark's Gospel." In *The Face of New Testament Studies*, edited by S. McKnight and G. R. Osborne, 396-405. Grand Rapids: Baker Academic, 2004.

Bond, H. K. *Caiaphas in Context: Friend of Rome and Judge of Jesus*. Louisville: Westminster John Knox, 2004.

Borgen, P. *Logos Was the True Light and Other Essays on the Gospel of John*. Trondheim, Norway: Tapir Publishers, 1983.

Bruce, F. F. *Paul, Apostle of the Free Spirit*. Exeter: Paternoster, 1977.

———. "The Trial of Jesus in the Fourth Gospel." In *Gospel Perspectives: Studies in the History and the Tradition of the Four Gospels*, vol. 1, edited by R. T. France and D. Wenham, 7-20. Sheffield: JSOT Press, 1980.

Bultmann, R. *New Testament Theology*. London: SCM, 1952.

———. *Jesus and the Word*. London: Fontana, 1958.

Burney, C. F. *The Poetry of Our Lord*. Oxford: Oxford University Press, 1925.

Burridge, R. *What Are the Gospels?* Cambridge: Cambridge University Press, 1992.

Carson, D. A. *The Gospel according to John*. Grand Rapids: Eerdmans, 1991.

Casey, M. *Is John's Gospel True?* London and New York: Routledge, 1996.

Charlesworth, J. H. *Jesus within Judaism*. London: SPCK, 1988.

———, ed. *The Messiah*. Minneapolis: Fortress, 1992.

Charlesworth, J. H., and C. A. Evans. "Jesus in the Agrapha and Apocryphal Gospels." In *Studying the Historical Jesus: Evaluations of the State of Current Research*, edited by B. Chilton and C. A. Evans, 479-533. Leiden: Brill, 1994.

Collins, M. F. "The Hidden Vessels in Samaritan Traditions." *JSJ* 3 (1972): 97-116.

Comfort, P. W. *The Quest for the Original Texts of the New Testament*. Grand Rapids: Baker, 1992.

Conzelmann, H. *Jesus*. Philadelphia: Fortress, 1973.

Crossan, J. D. *The Historical Jesus: The Life of a Mediterranean Jewish Peasant*. Edinburgh: T. & T. Clark, 1991.

———. *The Birth of Christianity: Discovering What Happened in the Years Immediately after the Execution of Jesus*. San Francisco: Harper Collins, 1998.

Culpepper, R. A., and C. C. Black. *Exploring the Gospel of John.* Louisville: Westminster John Knox, 1989.

Daube, D. *The New Testament and Rabbinic Judaism.* London: Athlone Press, 1956.

Denaux, A. "The Q-Logion: Mt 11,27/Lk 10,22 and the Gospel of John." In *John and the Synoptics,* edited by A. Denaux. BETL 101. Leuven: Leuven University Press, 1992.

Dickson, J. *Mission-Commitment in Ancient Judaism and the Pauline Communities.* WUNT 159. Tübingen: Mohr Siebeck, 2003.

Dunn, J. D. G. "John and the Oral Gospel Tradition." In *Jesus and the Oral Gospel Tradition,* edited by H. Wansbrough, 351-79. JSNTSS 64. Sheffield: JSOT, 1991.

————. "Messianic Ideas and Their Influence on the Jesus of History." In *The Messiah,* edited by J. H. Charlesworth, 365-81. Minneapolis: Fortress, 1992.

————. *Jesus Remembered.* Grand Rapids: Eerdmans, 2003.

Eddy, P. R., and G. A. Boyd. *The Jesus Legend.* Grand Rapids: Baker, 2007.

Elliott, J. K., ed. *The Collected Biblical Writings of T. C. Skeat.* Leiden: Brill, 2004.

Ellis, E. E. *The Making of the New Testament Documents.* Leiden: Brill, 1999.

Ensor, P. W. *Jesus and His "Works": The Johannine Sayings in Historical Perspective.* WUNT 2.85. Tübingen: Mohr, 1996.

Evans, C. A. "Jesus in Non-Christian Sources." In *Studying the Historical Jesus: Evaluations of the State of Current Research,* edited by B. Chilton and C. A. Evans, 466-67. Leiden: Brill, 1994.

————. *Fabricating Jesus.* Downers Grove, Ill.: IVP, 2007.

Evans, C. A., and B. Chilton, eds. *Studying the Historical Jesus: Evaluations of the State of Current Research.* Leiden: Brill, 1994.

————. *Jesus in Context: Temple, Purity, and Restoration.* Leiden: Brill, 1997.

————. *Authenticating the Activities of Jesus.* Leiden: Brill, 1999.

Fitzmyer, J. A. *The Gospel according to Luke: Introduction, Translation, and Notes I-IX.* Garden City, N.Y.: Doubleday, 1981.

Fox, R. L. *Pagans and Christians.* New York: Knopf, 1989.

Freyne, S. *Galilee from Alexander the Great to Hadrian: A Study of Second Temple Judaism.* Wilmington, Del.: Glazier, 1980.

————. "Galilee and Judea." In *The Face of New Testament Studies,* edited by S. McKnight and G. R. Osborne, 22-35. Grand Rapids: Baker, 2004.

Fuller, R. H. *Interpreting the Miracles.* London: SCM, 1963.

Furnish, V. P. *II Corinthians.* New York: Doubleday, 1984.

Gardner-Smith, P. *Saint John and the Synoptic Gospels.* Cambridge: Cambridge University Press, 1938.

Gill, D. W. J., and C. Gempf. *The Book of Acts in Its Graeco-Roman Setting.* Grand Rapids: Eerdmans, 1994.

Goodman, M. *Rome and Jerusalem: The Clash of Civilizations.* London: Allen Lane, 2007.

Grobel, K. *The Gospel of Truth.* London: A. & C. Black, 1960.

Hanson, R. P. C. *Tradition in the Early Church.* London: SCM, 1962.

Harris, M. "References to Jesus in Early Classical Authors." In *Gospel Perspectives,* vol. 5, edited by D. Wenham, 343-68. Sheffield: JSOT, 1984.

Head, P. M. "On the Christology of the Gospel of Peter." *VC* 46, no. 3 (1992): 209-24.

Hemer, C. *The Letters to the Seven Churches of Asia in Their Local Setting.* Sheffield: JSOT Press, 1986.

Hengel, M. *The Charismatic Leader and His Followers.* Edinburgh: T. & T. Clark, 1981.

————. *Between Jesus and Paul.* London: SCM, 1983.

————. *The Johannine Question.* London: SCM, 1989.

————. *Studies in Early Christology.* Edinburgh: T. & T. Clark, 1995.

————. "Jesus, the Messiah of Israel: The Debate about the 'Messianic Mission' of Jesus." In *Authenticating the Activities of Jesus,* edited by B. Chilton and C. A. Evans, 323-49. Leiden: Brill, 1999.

————. *The Four Gospels and the One Gospel of Jesus Christ.* London: SCM, 2000.

Hill, C. E. "Papias of Hierapolis." *ExpT* 17, no. 8 (2006): 309-15.

Hoehner, H. W. *Herod Antipas: A Contemporary of Jesus Christ.* Grand Rapids: Zondervan, 1980.

Horbury, W. "The Messianic Associations of 'The Son of Man.'" *JTS,* n.s., 36 (1985): 34-55.

Horrell, D. G. "The Label *Christianos:* 1 Peter 4:16 and the Formation of Christian Identity." *JBL* 126, no. 2 (2007): 361-81.

Horsley, R. A. *Galilee.* Valley Forge, Pa.: Trinity, 1995.

Horsley, R. A., and J. S. Hanson. *Bandits, Prophets, and Messiahs.* Minneapolis: Winston, 1985.

Hurlbut, J. L. *Story of the Christian Church.* Grand Rapids: Zondervan, 1967.

Hurtado, L. *How on Earth Did Jesus Become a God? Historical Questions about Earliest Devotion to Jesus.* Grand Rapids: Eerdmans, 2005.

————. *The Earliest Christian Artifacts.* Grand Rapids: Eerdmans, 2006.

Janssen, L. F. "'Superstitio' and the Persecution of the Christians." *VC* 33 (1979): 131-59.

Jensen, M. H. "Herod Antipas in Galilee: Friend or Foe of the Historical Jesus?" *JSHJ* 5, no. 1 (2007): 7-32.

Jeremias, J. *New Testament Theology 1*. London: SCM, 1971.

Kähler, M. *The So-called Historical Jesus and the Historic Biblical Christ*. Chicago: Fortress, 1964.

Kelly, J. N. D. *Early Christian Creeds*. London: Longmans, 1963.

Kim, S. Y. *The Son of Man as the Son of God*. Grand Rapids: Eerdmans, 1985.

Koester, H. "Apocryphal and Canonical Gospels." *HTR* 73, no. 12 (1980): 105-30.

Lee, A. H. I. *From Messiah to the Preexistent Son*. WUNT 192. Tübingen: Mohr Siebeck, 2005. Pp. 181-201.

Lemcio, E. E. "The Intention of the Evangelist, Mark." *NTS* 32 (1986): 187-206.

Levine, L. I., ed. *The Galilee in Late Antiquity*. Jerusalem: Jewish Theological Seminary, 1992.

Llewelyn, S. R. *New Documents Illustrating Early Christianity*. Sydney: Macquarie University, 1994.

Mack, B. *A Myth of Innocence: Mark and Christian Origins*. Philadelphia: Fortress, 1988.

Mackay, I. D. *John's Relationship with Mark*. WUNT 182. Tübingen: Mohr Siebeck, 2004.

Manson, T. W. *The Sayings of Jesus*. London: SCM, 1961.

Martyn, J. L. *History and Theology in the Fourth Gospel*. Nashville: Abingdon, 1978.

Marxsen, W. *Mark the Evangelist: Studies in the Redaction History of the Gospel*. Nashville: Abingdon, 1969.

McArthur, H. K., and R. M. Johnston. *They Also Taught in Parables: Rabbinic Parables from the First Centuries of the Christian Era*. Grand Rapids: Academie Books, 1990.

McKnight, S., and G. R. Osborne, eds. *The Face of New Testament Studies*. Leicester: Apollos, 2004.

Meier, J. P. *A Marginal Jew: Rethinking the Historical Jesus*. Vol. 2. New York: Doubleday, 1994.

————. "The Historical Jesus and the Historical Samaritans." *Bib* 81, no. 2 (2000): 210-31.

Metzger, B. *The Early Versions of the New Testament: Their Origin, Transmission, and Limitations*. Oxford: Clarendon, 1977.

Meyer, B. F. *The Aims of Jesus*. London: SCM, 1979.

Meyers, E. M., and J. F. Strange. *Archeology, the Rabbis, and Early Christianity*. London: SCM, 1981.

Mitchell, M. M. "Patristic Counter-evidence to the Claim That the Gospels Were Written for All Christians." *NTS* 51, no. 1 (2005).

Montefiore, H. W. "Revolt in the Desert?" *NTS* 8 (1962): 135-41.

Morris, L. L. *Studies in the Fourth Gospel*. Exeter: Paternoster, 1969.

Moule, C. F. D. *The Phenomenon of the New Testament.* London: SCM, 1967.

Nineham, D. E., et al. *Historicity and Chronology in the New Testament.* London: SPCK, 1965.

Okure, T. *The Johannine Approach to Mission: A Contextual Study of John 4:1-42.* WUNT 2.31. Tübingen: Mohr, 1988.

Peel, M. L. *The Epistle to Rheginos.* London: SCM, 1969.

Perrin, N. *Rediscovering the Teaching of Jesus.* New York: Harper and Row, 1967.

Pines, S. *An Arabic Version of the Testimonium Flavianum and Its Implications.* Jerusalem: Israel Academy of Sciences and Humanities, 1971.

Plummer, A. *St. Luke.* ICC. Edinburgh: T. & T. Clark, 1901.

Porter, S. E. *Criteria for Authenticity in Historical Jesus Research: Previous Discussion and New Proposals.* Sheffield: Sheffield Academic, 2000.

Price, S. R. F. *Rituals and Power.* Cambridge: Cambridge University Press, 1984.

Reed, J. L. *Archeology of the Galilean Jesus: A Re-examination of Evidence.* Harrisburg, Pa.: Trinity, 2000.

Riesner, R. "Bethany Beyond the Jordan (John 1:28): Topography, Theology and History in the Fourth Gospel." *TynBul* 38 (1987): 29-63.

————. "Jesus as Preacher and Teacher." In *Oral Gospel Tradition*, edited by H. Wansbrough, 185-210. Sheffield: JSOT, 1991.

Robinson, J. A. T. "The New Look on the Fourth Gospel." In *Studia Evangelica*, vol. 1, edited by K. Aland et al. Berlin: Akademie-Verlag, 1959.

————. *Redating the New Testament.* London: SCM, 1976.

————. *The Priority of John.* London: SCM, 1985.

Rouseau, J. J., and R. Arav. *Jesus and His World.* Minneapolis: Fortress, 1995.

Sanders, E. P. *Jesus and Judaism.* London: SCM, 1985.

————. *The Historical Figure of Jesus.* London: Penguin Books, 1993.

Schweizer, E. *Jesus.* London: SCM, 1971.

Sherwin-White, A. N. *Roman Society and Roman Law in the New Testament.* Oxford: Clarendon, 1963.

Smalley, S. S. *John Evangelist and Interpreter.* Downers Grove, Ill.: IVP, 1998.

Smallwood, E. M. "High Priests and Politics in Roman Palestine." *JTS* 13 (1962): 14-34.

Stanton, G. N. *Jesus of Nazareth in New Testament Preaching.* SNTSMS 27. Cambridge: Cambridge University Press, 1974.

————. *The Gospels and Jesus.* Oxford: Oxford University Press, 1989.

Stuhlmacher, P. "The Messianic Son of Man: Jesus' Claims to Deity." In *The Historical Jesus in Recent Research*, edited by J. D. G. Dunn and S. McKnight, 336-44. Winona Lake, Ind.: Eisenbrauns, 2005.

Taylor, V. *The Four Gospels.* London: Epworth, 1960.

Telford, W. R. "Major Trends and Interpretive Issues in the Study of Jesus." In *Studying the Historical Jesus: Evaluations of the State of Current Research,* edited by B. Chilton and C. A. Evans, 33-74. Leiden: Brill, 1994.

Theissen, G. *The Gospels in Context.* Minneapolis: Fortress, 1991.

Theissen, G., and A. Merz. *The Historical Jesus: A Comprehensive Guide.* London: SCM, 1998.

Thiselton, A. C. *The First Epistle to the Corinthians.* NIGTC. Grand Rapids: Eerdmans, 2000.

Thomas, J. C. *Footwashing in John 13 and the Johannine Community.* JSNTSS 61. Sheffield: JSOT Press, 1991.

Tilborg, S. van. *Reading John in Ephesus.* Leiden: Brill, 1996.

Tuckett, C. "Thomas and the Synoptics." *NovT* 30, no. 7 (1988): 132-57.

Turner, C. H. "Markan Usage: Notes Critical and Exegetical, on the Second Gospel V; The Movements of Jesus and His Disciples and the Crowd." *JTS* 26 (1925): 225-40.

Vardaman, J., and E. Yamauchi, eds. *Chronos, Kairos, Christos.* Winona Lake, Ind.: Eisenbrauns, 1989.

Van Voorst, R. E. *Jesus Outside the New Testament.* Grand Rapids: Eerdmans, 2000.

Vermes, G. *Jesus the Jew.* Glasgow: Collins, 1973.

Walker, P. W. L. *Jesus and the Holy City.* Grand Rapids: Eerdmans, 1996.

Weeden, T. J. *Mark — Traditions in Conflict.* Philadelphia: Fortress, 1971.

Wenham, D. *Paul: Follower of Jesus or Founder of Christianity?* Grand Rapids: Eerdmans, 1995.

Wessels, G. F. "The Historical Christ and the Letters of Paul: Revisiting Bernard C. Lategan's Thesis." In *The New Testament Interpreted,* edited by C. Breytenbach et al., 43-46. Leiden: Brill, 2006.

Wilcox, M. "Jesus in the Light of His Jewish Environment." *ANRW* 2 (1982): 131-95.

Willitts, J. "Presuppositions and Procedures in the Study of the 'Historical Jesus'; or, Why I Decided Not to Be a 'Historical Jesus Scholar.'" *JSHJ* 3, no. 1 (2005): 61-108.

Wright, N. T. *The New Testament and the People of God.* London: SPCK, 1992.

———. *Jesus and the Victory of God.* Minneapolis: Fortress, 1996.

———. *The Resurrection of the Son of God.* London: SPCK, 2003.

INDEX OF MODERN AUTHORS

INDEX OF SUBJECTS

INDEX OF SCRIPTURE AND
OTHER ANCIENT LITERATURE